HOLISM
IN DEVELOPMENT

Holism
in Development

*An African Perspective
on Empowering Communities*

DEBORAH AJULU

06 05 04 03 02 01   5 4 3 2 1

MARC books are published by World Vision International, 800 West Chestnut Avenue, Monrovia, California 91016-3198, U.S.A.

ISBN 1-887983-15-5

Senior Editor: Rebecca Russell. Copy editor and typesetter: Joan Weber Laflamme. Cover design: Karen Newe. Cover photo: Simon Peter Esaku/World Vision.

This book is printed on acid-free, recycled paper.

Contents

Acknowledgments

I owe deep gratitude to many who gave ideas, patiently listened or read often not-so-well-expressed accounts that eventually merged together to form this study. A few who can be named include Robert Goudzwaard of Free University of Amsterdam, Holland; Dan Etherington of the Australian National University; Chris Sugden, Vinay Samuel and David Lim, all of the Oxford Centre for Mission Studies; David Cook of Green College, Oxford University; George Hobson of the European Division of the University of Maryland; Kwame Bediako of New College, Edinburgh University. Lastly, my greatest appreciation goes to Gwyn E. Jones, who even through ill-health gave his best.

Eight agency representatives gave generously of their time and resources to provide data for analysis in the production of this study: Brendan Gormley of Oxfam; Robert Dodd of Actionaid; Chris Batchelor of ACORD; Michael Walsby of APT Design and Development; David Hart of Tearfund; Jeff Thindwa of World Vision (UK); Joan E. Drury of Emmanuel International; and Leigh Thorsen of Y Care International.

Financial support sources, without which this study would not have been possible, came generously from the Hugh Pilkington Trust, Oxford, with special thanks to the executive director, Robin Shawyer; the Africa Educational Trust; TEAR Australia and executive director, Steve Bradbury; the INFEMIT; the Mustard Seed Foundation, USA; the Akrofi-Kristaller Memorial Centre for Research and Applied Theology; Family Welfare Association; and the BFWG Charitable Foundation.

Most important, spiritual and moral support undergirded the whole effort. Many thanks go to John and Hilary Maitland; Magdalene Meduoye; Colleen Samuel; my loving, patient and understanding children, Esther, Zac, Ruth, and children and relatives in Uganda; and other prayer partners. May the Lord be glorified.

Last but not least, I owe Victoria Hobson of the European Division of the University of Maryland my deep appreciation for the effort she put into editing and helping in other ways. Thanks also to Jenny Huxley of INFEMIT for doing some of the typing and printing.

Introduction

Problems of Development Theory and Practice, and Proposals for Solutions from a Biblical Perspective

The primary aim of this volume is to propose holistic empower ment from a biblical perspective as an alternative approach in the continuing search for effective means to combat poverty. The study outlines the challenges of persistent and ever-increasing poverty and expands traditional arguments for the persistence of poverty to include powerlessness. The approach is holistic for two basic reasons: First, people whom poverty affects must be treated as whole human beings with tripartite needs—spiritual, social and physical/material—all of which must be addressed. Second, communities must be treated as whole entities composed of the rich, the not-so-rich, the poor, leadership, and their structures and institutions.

This approach is based on a biblical perspective for two reasons. First, the biblical approach is not reductionist; rather, it is holistic and balanced. It can assist in redressing areas of concern especially where the spiritual side of human life had been ignored. Second, the biblical perspective offers ethical principles to guide development. An analysis of empowerment raises profound ethical questions: First, *what* principle sanctions empowerment? Second, *why* is empowerment important, or what is the reason for empowerment? Third, *how* is empowerment measured, or what is the ethical measuring criterion for empowerment? Fourth, *who* needs empowering?

I have used a case-study methodology to study eight British development agencies with rural development projects in East Africa (Kenya, Tanzania and Uganda)—four Christian and four non-Christian agencies. Powerlessness is recognized by all the agencies as a factor that underlies the persistence of poverty, and powerlessness affects not only the poor but also the rich and seemingly powerful and the state. Empowerment is interpreted by all these agencies as a people-enablement process and a means for tackling poverty at its roots. Ethical principles regarding empowerment play a vital role in each agency's development work; the Christian agencies apply ethical principles based on the Bible, and non-Christian agencies base their ethical principles on secular humanistic philosophy. The final conclusion is that holistic empowerment from a biblical perspective, as advocated in this study, is possible, although not simple or easy to achieve.

In the 1950s and 1960s Western growth and modernization models placed emphasis on mechanistic positivism and sought to solve the development problems of less developed countries through rationalistic approaches (Hettne 1990:5). Predominant was the view that development was transferable and could be administered in a top-down manner by governments through centrally planned and controlled programs and projects. Rapid economic growth would be ensured in this way. Economic growth came to be equated chiefly with "progress" and viewed as a linear process with successive stages through which all countries needed to pass in order to achieve developmental growth (Rostow 1960:3; Todaro 1977/89:63–65).

Initial results from the efforts of the 1950s and 1960s were impressive growth rates of per capita income, as well as improvements in several major social indicators, such as life expectancy and literacy (Griffin 1989:4–10; Todaro 1977/89:87). By the late 1960s and early 1970s it was expected that

> rapid gains in overall and per capita GNP growth would either "trickle down" to the masses in the form of jobs and other economic opportunities or create the necessary conditions for the wider distribution of the economic and social benefits of growth. Problems of poverty, unemployment, and income distribution were of secondary importance to "getting the growth job done." (Todaro 1977/89:87)

It became evident during this period, however, that income distribution within every less developed country was not only highly skewed but was becoming increasingly skewed even in countries where growth had been quite high. There was also widespread inequality in the distribution of other benefits of economic progress, such as access to health facilities and opportunities for education. K. Griffin points out that a number of cross-sectional studies of countries support arguments for the existence of growing inequality, especially in less developed countries where standards of living are also shown to be declining (Griffin 1989:16).

Worsening Poverty

The grim outcome of this inequality is persistently worsening poverty, especially in rural areas of less developed countries. This is explicitly accompanied by widening gaps between the rich and the poor among each nation's population as well as between countries. Add to this a high dependency of less developed countries on industrialized countries for foreign exchange in the form of export earnings, foreign aid, and foreign loans that have created heavy debt burdens. M. P. Todaro (1977/89:31) has provided some estimates that substantiate this scenario. To measure poverty, he drew on data from some 35 developing countries of Latin America, Asia and Africa, using 1988 population figures and 1975 poverty estimates from a study by Ahluwalia, Carter and Chenery (Chenery et al., 1974:8–9). He found that 35 percent of the population of less developed countries (1.37 billion people) in 1988 were estimated to be "attempting to survive at absolute poverty levels." Estimates for heavily populated low-income countries were much higher (for example, Bangladesh 60 percent, India 46 percent and Indonesia 62 percent). Todaro estimated "the staggering figure of 1.37 billion people who may be classified as suffering from absolute poverty in the late 1980s" (Todaro 1977/89:31). The International Fund for Agricultural Development (IFAD) estimates a similar figure, more than a billion total population living below the poverty line, of which about 939 million are in rural areas (IFAD 1992:xviii).

The gap between rich and poor is most commonly measured in terms of income. That gap exists in developed countries as well as in less developed countries. The gap is much wider, however, in less developed countries, where the richest 20 percent of the population commonly receives more than 60 percent of the national income, while the poorest 40 percent receives less than 20 percent of the national income. Among countries, approximately 81 percent of the world's income is consumed by relatively few developed countries, constituting only 23 percent of the world's population. The entire population in less developed countries, constituting 77 percent of the world's population, subsists on a meager 19 percent of total world income (Todaro 1977/89:28, 30). Additional figures expressing such economic disparities in world distribution of economic activities appeared in *Development Dialogue* (1994:53–54) as follows: The richest 20 percent of the world's population (most of whom live in developed countries) consume 82.7 percent of the gross national product (GNP), 81.2 percent of world trade, 94.6 percent of commercial lending, 80.6 percent of domestic savings, and 80.5 percent of domestic investment. This is compared with the poorest 20 percent of the world's population (mostly in less developed countries), who take in: 1.4 percent of the GNP, 1.0 percent of world trade, 0.2 percent of commercial lending, 1.0 percent of domestic savings, and 1.3 percent of domestic investment. One question that arises from this is simply how are poor countries to find the funds to develop?

In part, development budgets have been met through borrowing from developed countries. At first such borrowing was strongly encouraged by the West in the 1970s because of the massive stock of "petro-dollars" that the West had accumulated from oil price increases set by the Organization of Petroleum Exporting Countries (OPEC). But repayment of these loans soon became an impossible burden for debtor countries, so much so that as early as 1982 the largest of these debtor countries, Mexico, though itself an oil producer, declared a moratorium on its debt repayment. It was realized that "debt repayment and capital flight combined . . . create a net outflow of investment funds from poor to rich countries" (Friedmann 1992:4). The result was a worsening situation for debtor countries at a time when they could receive no further loans because they were no longer considered credit worthy.

Attempts by the World Bank and the International Monetary Fund (IMF) to assist debtor countries to remain credit worthy led to the institution of *structural adjustment programs*, embodying austerity measures for participating countries. Principal provisions included deregulation, the privatisation of government-owned enterprise, elimination of tariff barriers to overseas imports, measures to promote export production, devaluation of national currencies to cheapen exports, and "getting markets to work properly" by removing subsidies and establishing the "correct" set of prices that would permit efficient, long-run growth. (Friedmann 1992:5)

A number of debtor countries in Africa and elsewhere undertook to implement these austerity measures, with undesirable outcomes. The combined effect of the debt burden, the structural adjustment programs, and the desperate need for investment funding to promote production for exports "had disastrous consequences for both the poor and the environment" (Friedmann 1992:5). The aggravation of poverty led to a more serious search for ways to address poverty. The World Bank threw its weight behind this concern. The Bank's *World Development Report* devoted itself to world poverty (World Bank 1990). This in a sense put "poverty back on the development agenda" and declared a commitment to reducing poverty in the 1990s. In its *Annual Report* the World Bank stated "the fundamental objective of the World Bank remains sustainable poverty reduction" for fiscal year 1993 (World Bank 1993:37). This concern was reinforced by IFAD, which published in 1992 and 1993 *The State of World Rural Poverty*, providing the results of its studies in a number of developing countries on rural poverty, its causes and consequences.

The Nature of Poverty: The Case of East Africa

IFAD presented a significant treatment of world (particularly rural) poverty (IFAD:1992 and 1993), discussing types of poverty and factors underlying each, as well as processes that create and perpetuate rural poverty. IFAD asserted that rural poverty is a dominant feature of life in all the regions of the world, affecting about one billion people at the time (IFAD 1993:1).

Among the 110 developing countries it studied, IFAD argued that although urban poverty was also growing, rural poverty remained dominant, accounting for 80 percent of total poverty suffered in those countries. IFAD figures for proportions of rural populations whose income and consumption fell below nationally defined poverty lines were: for Asia 31 percent (46 percent if China and India were excluded); for Sub-Saharan Africa 60 percent; for Latin America and the Caribbean 61 percent; and for the Near East and North Africa 26 percent. Table I-1 below shows these figures for Kenya, Tanzania and Uganda for 1988.

	Total Population*	Rural Population		Rural Population Below Poverty	
		number*	% of total	number*	% of total
Kenya	23,077	18,000	78	9,903	55
Tanzania	25,426	19,930	78	11,958	60
Uganda	17,216	15,498	78	12,398	80

* in millions

Table I-1: Rural Population Below Poverty Line in East Africa (source: IFAD 1993:Table 6).

Poverty is manifested in so many ways, rendering its measurement and comparative analysis difficult. For many years poverty was treated merely as physical deprivation. Now it is recognized that poverty is more than physical deprivation; it also involves social and psychological aspects that prevent people from realizing their potential. This study argues a further aspect—the spiritual.

Six major indices are now applied to measure poverty, after acknowledging that by its very nature the poverty of the poor cannot be described by means of a single indicator. These indices are simply mentioned here: the Physical Quality of Life Index (PQLI) coined by Morris in 1979; the Human Development Index (HDI), UNDP 1990; the Integrated Poverty Index (IPI) which builds on Sen's pioneering contribution of 1976; the Basic Needs Index (BNI); the Food Security Index (FSI); and the Relative Welfare Index (RWI), which combines IPI, BNI and FSI (IFAD 1992:26f.).

Types of Poverty and Underlying Factors

IFAD identifies five main types of poverty: (1) interstitial poverty, or pockets of poverty surrounded by power, affluence and ownership of assets; (2) peripheral poverty, found in marginal areas; (3) overcrowding poverty; (4) sporadic poverty, which can be transitory but often ends up endemic; and (5) endemic poverty (IFAD 1992:28). These types of poverty are a consequence of underlying factors in varying combinations that must be addressed for the elimination of poverty. These factors, identified by IFAD (1992:29, 30) and closely parallel to those identified by Chambers (1983: chap. 5), are:

- *Material deprivation*, in terms of "inadequate food intake and poor nutritional status of food, poor health (physical stamina) and education, lack of clothing, housing, and consumer durables, fuel insecurity and absence of provision for survival in an emergency" (IFAD 1992:29). Material deprivation underlies almost all types of poverty, particularly interstitial, peripheral and overcrowding types of poverty.
- *Isolation*, both geographical location *and* socioeconomic and political marginalization of rural communities. Chambers defines isolation as "lack of education, remoteness, being out of contact" (Chambers 1983:113). The rural poor either live in remote areas "far from development and service institutions and so lack sufficient weight to influence political decisions"; or they lack transport and communication; or they suffer from illiteracy, which "cuts them off from access to information and interaction with the political process" (IFAD 1992:29). Most often, they lack all three.
- *Alienation* involves lack of identity and control, and refers to the alienation of the rural poor from growth processes such as new technology. Lack of education and limited access to training lead to a lack of marketable skills, which in turn leads to an inability to take advantage of new opportunities, creating a communication gap with the rest of the society.
- *Dependence and domination*, which undermine self-identity and confidence and in turn stifle self-reliance. IFAD states, "in a world of unequal social relations between landlord and tenant, employer

and employee, creditor and debtor, buyer and seller, patron and bonded labourer," the bargaining capacity of the rural poor is depressed (IFAD 1992:29). Chambers refers to this factor as "powerlessness" and maintains that it contributes to poverty in many ways, including exploitation by the powerful. He describes it as limiting or preventing "access to resources from the state, legal redress for abuses, and ability to dispute wage or interest rates," and as entailing weak negotiating power and feeble influence, especially on government to provide urgently needed services (Chambers 1983:113).

- *Lack of decision-making power and freedom of choice*, sometimes termed lack of participation. This occurs particularly in socioeconomic and political processes from which the rural poor are often excluded.
- *Lack of assets*, which often causes endemic poverty and may underlie all other forms of poverty. In most cases, as a result, the poor are forced to work at very low levels of productivity.
- *Vulnerability*, to both internal and social factors and external shocks. Vulnerability may arise through natural factors, changes in market forces and employment, demographic factors, marital and cultural factors, and war.
- *Insecurity*, often due to physical violence that entails loss of life as well as property. This is often a result of "low social status or physical strength" or of gender, religion, race, ethnicity or tribe.

Processes that Create and Perpetuate Rural Poverty

Rural poverty is a consequence of dynamic, inter-linked socioeconomic and political processes. These causal processes are identified by IFAD as policy-induced processes, dualism, population growth, resource management and environment, natural cycles and processes, the marginalization of women, cultural and ethnic factors, exploitative intermediation, internal political fragmentation and civil strife and international processes (IFAD 1993:9–18).

These processes vary in the intensity of their influence in different countries. On a scale of intensity varying from 0 to 5 (5 indicating highest intensity, implying that a process is significantly dominant in its impact), among 26 African countries studied by IFAD, domestic policy biases, population pressures, resource and environment degradation, international factors, and gender bias were identified as having significant influence on the magnitude and trends of rural poverty. "These are followed by exploitative intermediation, dualism, political conflicts and ethnic and cultural biases, in that order" (IFAD 1993:18).

In the East African countries of Kenya, Tanzania and Uganda, policy-induced processes or domestic policy biases scored 5 in all three countries. In Kenya, other processes that scored 5 included dualism, population pressure, poor natural resource base and degradation of the environment, and exploitative intermediation. In Uganda, other processes scoring 5 included population pressure, political conflicts and civil strife. International processes in all three nations scored a 4, along with natural cycles and disasters in Kenya and Tanzania, gender bias in Kenya and Uganda, and degradation of resources and environment in Tanzania. In short, these processes help create and perpetuate poverty in East Africa.

Solutions?

In most quarters, significant blame for worsening poverty has been placed on past development strategies and the manner in which they had been implemented (Lewis and Kallab 1986:6; Todaro 1977/89:42; Wignaraja 1984:7; Hettne 1990:5; Griffin 1989:25). Concern among development experts from the mid-1970s onward led to reconsideration of development theory and strategies in search of new possibilities. Problems identified as created by past strategies included, among others, overemphasis on the state as the main actor in development; top-down and trickle-down macro approaches that ignored the involvement of rural people, hence bypassing their real development problems; and application of modernity's Western mechanistic and technocratic efficiency models, through development projects, for achievement of quantitative economic growth and progress measured in terms of per capita gross national product, but overlooking important social factors and existing inequalities among people, among regions of the same country and among countries.

Economists and policy-makers thus sought what Todaro called the "dethronement of GNP" through direct attacks on (1) widespread absolute poverty, (2) increasingly inequitable income distributions, (3) rising unemployment and (4) dependency—as well as rejection of modernization's dominance in further development process. In Todaro's words, "In the 1970s economic development came to be redefined in terms of the reduction or elimination of poverty, inequality and unemployment within the context of a growing economy" (Todaro 1977/89:87). What followed was a trend of post-growth modernization paradigms designed to remedy past mistakes with the promise of "better" development.

Today, a corpus of literature bears testimony to this rethinking. These post-growth modernization doctrines tended to derive from neo-populist theories; to be more normative than positivist, generally treating development in terms of the way it should take place rather than the way it actually takes place; and to focus not so much on the form of development as on its content, with such themes as people-centeredness, empowerment, poverty focus, basic human needs, redistribution, holism, self-reliance and sustainability (Hettne 1990:152–53).

A number of current approaches have their roots in these doctrines, including alternative development, participation or participatory development, unified approach, counter development, people-centered development, human resource development, and sustainable development. Since the 1990s, *empowerment* has become a major issue (Friedmann 1992). One common element in all these approaches is that all conform to a humanist model of development that centers on people and also usually seeks harmony with the environment.

Empowerment as an Alternative Approach to Development

Considerable attention is being focused on empowerment in the continuing search for alternatives in approaches to rural development (Gran 1983; Berger and Neuhaus 1984; Alfonso 1986; Elliott 1987c; Werner 1988; Carmen 1990; Oakley 1991; Friedmann 1992). Of the literature cited here, only Friedmann gives an analytical framework of empowerment as an alternative, but other literature talks of it as a more or less realistic possibility. Like all previous approaches, empowerment is being considered after a process of rethinking triggered by disenchantment with mainstream models of development (especially modernity models), which have failed to alleviate mass poverty, and which have placed "emphasis on rapid cumulative growth, its urban bias, and the single-minded pursuit of industrialisation" (Friedmann 1992:vii). Korten and Carner have argued that the major failure of conventional development models—both capitalist and socialist—was that production needs outweighed people needs. Production-centered systems displayed values, systems and methods geared to the exploitation and manipulation (to the point of destruction) of natural resources to produce an ever-increasing flow of standardized goods and services and to creation of a mass consumer society to absorb them. The system created great bureaucracies (governmental and commercial) aiming to organize society into efficient production units and control people's lives in both public and private spheres, including people's access to sources of livelihood, and limited opportunities for creative individual initiative (Korten 1984:299). Todaro adds that these transferred Western values, attitudes, institutions and standards not only resulted in inappropriate styles and procedures for education and health, and for public bureaucratic and administrative structures, but they also resulted in the import of rich-country social and economic standards on the less developed countries' salary scales, of elite lifestyles, and of general attitudes toward private accumulation of wealth. This in turn led to a "brain drain" and bred corruption and economic plunder by a privileged minority. In short, this transfer process significantly contributed to the persistence of poverty or underdevelopment in less developed countries (Todaro 1977/89:42–43).

This rethinking has produced a new set of beliefs now held by many advocates of new alternatives, including empowerment. These beliefs are aptly outlined by Friedmann (1992:6–7). First, the state—which in most less developed countries is the same as the government (Midgley et al. 1986)—is part of the problem and should be bypassed by alternative approaches; it is unable to deliver development to the people, is over-centralized "bureaucratic, corrupt [lacks in good governance, accountability and transparency] and [is] unsympathetic to the needs of the poor. Often it is in the hands of military and civilian elites who treat it as their private domain" (Friedmann 1992:7; see also Midgley et al. 1986:8). This logically leads to a second belief: Since the state cannot be trusted, instead, concentration should be on people and their communities. The underlying assumption is, as Campero points out, that "the people can do no wrong and that communities are inherently *gemeinschaftlich*" (quoted in Friedmann 1992:6). That is to say, there is inherent goodness in people that allows members of communities to act together for mutual benefit. People are considered "moral and autonomous. People . . . possess ultimate wisdom about themselves. For many 'alternative' advocates, the voice of the people cannot conflict with itself, it speaks truly" (Friedmann 1992:7). It is therefore common sense to center on the people as chief actors in their own development.

A third belief also arises from the first, that "community action . . . is sufficient for the practice of an alternative development, and that political action is to be avoided." In other words, "given that the state is regarded as venal, politics is best avoided; it would only contaminate the purity of face-to-face encounters in the neighbourhood and village and thus (re)establish clientalistic relations that negate an authentic, people-centred development" (Friedmann 1992:6, 7). The point here is that avoidance of political action is tantamount to leaving the entire government apparatus out of the development process.

Like Friedmann, I cannot agree with these beliefs. But this study also differs from Friedmann in going further, including biblical principles in its critique of development assumptions. Regarding the state, my stance is that it is naive to bypass the state. The state is an indispensable actor in matters of development in developing countries for the very reason that the state in these countries not only "dominates political power relationships, [and] increasingly controls economic and social life" and resources, but dominates all aspects of the lives and affairs of its people (Midgley et. al. 1986:7, vii). The state is responsible for overall long-term national planning—for provision and maintenance of physical and social infrastructure and public and welfare services; for environmental, strategic and long-term planning; for security and other human rights; and for ensuring the smooth running of structures and institutions that make the whole nation a viable unit. To ignore the state in the light of this seems to me to be foolhardy.

Empowerment of people and their communities requires a strong state. Indeed, empowerment in the context of this study is treated in a wider context, calling for empowerment of the state apparatus to make it "more accountable to poor people and more responsive to their claims" (Friedmann 1992:7), especially for the dependent poor who need welfare services; and to call it to show justice in its dealings with the people. Similarly the Bible views the state as the authority responsible for securing justice in society, especially for the poor (cf. Hay 1989:81–84).

Having said that the state is central to the development process, it follows that political activity is to be seen as a concomitant to development activity. Friedmann contends that if social empowerment of the poor is advocated, their political empowerment must also be advocated. Unless people are empowered for political action, they remain perpetually defeated in other efforts they may try to make.

Regarding assumptions of the inherent goodness of people and the smooth working of their communities, Friedmann argues that no community is necessarily a pure *gemeinschaft*, even when its members participate in a moral economy based on reciprocity and trust. He notes the existence of inherent conflicts between rural and urban communities, and among groups based on, for example, religion, ethnicity, social class, caste, language or tribe, and gender difference. Some of these conflicts are understandable, given the limited resources these groups compete for (Friedmann 1992:6).

A holistic biblical position holds that no one is intrinsically good or capable of consistently doing good, because of the principle of human sin (Mark 10:18; Luke 18:19; Rom. 3:9–12, 23). The way to empowerment advocated in the Bible involves dealing with human sin as central to human greed and self-centeredness, the underlying cause of many problems under discussion here.

Most current approaches talk of pursuing people-centered development, but sometimes what is meant is not clear. If this term is interpreted to promote the furtherance of human self-centeredness, engendering the selfishness and greed that stifle wholesome development for individuals and community, then this approach may lead those who are empowered to become oppressors rather than stewards. Empowerment of people must lead to creation of a caring community characterized by neighborly love, stewardship and justice, all central to a biblical approach.

Empowerment in this context would require not only enabling individuals and groups of people to learn the art of conflict resolution, but also, and more important, to deal with human selfishness, greed and corruption, and to pursue building human character, which determines proper relationships among people. Just and caring communities and eventually nations can only result as people learn how to use their given resources for poverty alleviation and sustainable development, in essence requiring that two forms of empowerment be integrated: socio-political-economic and spiritual.

Approaches to the empowerment of rural people and their communities have tended to omit a moral perspective from their framework. Explicit clarity regarding what is meant by *moral* is often lacking in those approaches that do include it in their frameworks. A biblical view of morality refers to judgment of the goodness or badness of human action, behavior, or character, as well as the discernment of good and bad according to God's moral laws. Sin, a human disposition, is a violation of God's moral laws. Appropriate empowerment will be that which encompasses both moral/spiritual and material/physical aspects of human needs. This study proposes, as a hypothesis, that an empowerment approach with a moral framework is more likely (than an approach without one) to contribute significantly to alleviation of poverty and to sustained development. (More detailed discussion of this concept can be found in chapter 8.)

Concepts Related to Empowerment

Empowerment necessarily presupposes not only power that brings about empowerment, but also powerlessness, which gives the reason for empowerment. Power in this study (as defined in chapter 6) is a resource, capacity, or means for empowerment. On the one hand, powerlessness means lack of power, and therefore power is needed to empower the powerless. On the other hand, misuse of power produces powerlessness, a serious factor underlying the persistence of poverty (chapter 7); hence the need to instigate proper use and/or distribution of power.

It is not always possible to draw a clear line of demarcation between the rich and the poor. Presented everywhere is a wide range of distribution in income, or capital, or wealth, or property. However, for purposes of analysis, the two poles may be said to be that of "the poor," who are the victims of powerlessness, and of "the rich" and seemingly powerful, who also show a form of powerlessness, being helpless to eliminate the poverty that they contribute to.

Empowerment must dually address the causes of powerlessness as well as the instigation and building of enabling conditions and mediating structures and institutions that empower both the poor and the rich. This is the path to overcoming the poverty suffered by the poor, so that all are enabled to engage in sustained development.

Ethics in Holistic Empowerment

Because economics is concerned with real people, ethical questions are often encountered in development work (Crocker 1991:457). Yet modern economics is "self-consciously 'non-ethical' in character" (Sen 1987:2). Sen considers how economics first developed historically as an offshoot of ethics. Aristotle recognized that ethical deliberations are consequential to actual human behavior and, says Sen, considered the end of social achievement to be attaining "the good for man," adding that it was more notable to attain the end for a nation or city-state than for a single man. Sen argues that "this 'ethics-related view of social achievement' cannot stop the evaluation short at some arbitrary point like satisfying 'efficiency.' The assessment has to be more fully ethical, and take a broader view of 'the good'" (Sen 1987:4).

A second origin of economics to which Sen refers "is characterised by being concerned with primarily logistic issues rather than with ultimate ends and such questions as what may foster 'the good of man' or 'how should one live?' The ends are treated as given. What matters is to engineer the best way to meet them; and human behavior is viewed as determined by motives that are easy to characterize" (Sen 1987:4).

As time has progressed, economics and its applications have increasingly adopted this engineering approach, with the result that modern economics has become distanced from ethics. Sen, while not writing off the achievements of a nonethical approach, claims this has resulted in the impoverishment of modern economics. He sees an urgent need to pay "greater and more explicit attention to the ethical considerations that shape human behaviour and judgment" (Sen 1987:9) and to promote explicit application of ethics in development.

Evidence of the Need for Ethics in Development

All the agencies represented in interviews for this study (see Part III) responded that ethics was of paramount importance in their operations. Crocker (1991) describes a proliferation of activity in the area of development ethics. He mentions first the seminars and joint research activity by more than 100 Asian scholars in 1979–80 that led to the production in 1983 of *Ethical Dilemmas of Development in Asia*, edited by G. Gunatilleke, N. Tiruchelvam and R. Coomaraswamy, members of the Marga Institute, the Sri Lanka Centre for Development Studies. Latin-American philosophers and social theorists addressed ethical issues in conferences such as the 1974 Third National Conference of Philoso-phy in Costa Rica and in important publications (Bunge 1980; Ramirez 1986, 1988; Camacho 1985). In Oceania, the Seventeenth Waigani Semi-nar at the University of Papua, New Guinea, in September 1986. was devoted to the ethics of development. This was followed by publication of many papers, and discussions continue." In the Western world Crocker attributes pioneering efforts on this topic to Goulet, who since the early 1960s has been an important contributor of research. Other writers Crocker refers to include Berger, Wilber, Vogeler and De Souza, Weisband, O'Neill, Segal, Dower, Engel, Steidlmeier, and Sen and Nussbaum. Crocker describes the establishment of the International Development Ethics Association (IDEA) in 1984, which sponsors con-ferences and seminars (Crocker 1991:458–61).

But what is development ethics, and why is it needed?

Development ethics has been defined as "the normative or ethical assessment of the ends and means of Third World and global develop-ment" (Crocker 1991:457). Goulet, in more interpretive definitions, considers that

> genuine ethics may be defined as a kind of *praxis* which generates critical reflection on the value content and meaning of one's so-cial action. Unlike mere extrinsic treatment of means, ethical *praxis* conditions choices and priorities by assigning relative value alle-giances to essential needs, basic power relationships, and criteria for determining tolerable levels of human suffering in promoting social change. (Goulet 1983:620)

He writes:

> The term "ethics" is employed to mean those conditions of knowl-edge and will men require in order to exercise a genuine choice of ends or of means. Some of these conditions are manifestly cogni-tive—men must know certain things. Others are structural: men must not be fully determined by the social forces which impinge on them. All are deeply subjective, since they are grounded on

diverse levels of self-awareness. Freedom, of course, cannot be treated in a vacuum; it is always freedom for something. Were it otherwise, there would be no "oughtness" and no ethics in freedom itself. (Goulet 1985:332)

These definitions emphasize a rejection of the maxim that the end justifies the means. Ethics involves evaluating both the end and the choices of means. Goulet argues that ethics can operate as "a means of the means," meaning that "development ethics must define concrete instruments which support the legitimate struggles of oppressed groups." He adds that it would be

> Futile to glorify human dignity unless one builds structures which advance human dignity and remove obstacles to it. . . . Ethics can . . . play its normative role in development strategising by entering inside the constraints and contexts of key development decisions and actions. Ethics has a twin mission: to identify the values which ought to be promoted, and to collaborate with . . . societal actors who can safeguard these values while simultaneously transforming institutions and behavior in ways which keep human and cultural costs within tolerable bounds. (Goulet 1983:620)

For Goulet, development ethics "teaches men by making them critically aware of the moral content of their choices." Second, "it coerces them to the extent that it commands good, and forbids bad, action." Third, "it gives exploiters a bad conscience and the exploited victims rational grounds for revolting against their lot." And fourth, "it builds institutions inasmuch as norms must be embodied visibly in rights, duties, and laws" (Goulet 1985:332).

In answer to the question, What is development?, Dower says it "is a process of social change that can be influenced by human action and ought to take place."

Despite the fact that development has sometimes been "used in a value-neutral way to designate such things as economic growth or modernization," development ethics is still essential (Crocker 1991:467). In a general normative sense, development means "beneficial alterations," that is, social changes that people can and should influence. In a more determinant normative sense, development "is that particular kind of change advocated as . . . 'the object of moral commitment'" (Crocker 1991:467).

We need moral reflection on society's basic goals because such things as economic growth and modernization may be morally problematic and in need of replacement, modification, or supplementation with more adequate concepts of "fullness of being." We need critical and explicit reflection on the ends as well as the means of development, on the *what* as well as the *how*. Given that the non-normative sense of development can be easily confused with the normative senses, it is often best to speak of "authentic" or "good" development as the theoretical and practical goal of development ethics. (Crocker 1991:467)

Crocker supports Sen's appeal to all development theorists to "engage in explicit moral dialogue in which moral values and ethical principles are articulated, defended, and applied" (Crocker 1991:467). He also believes that development ethics should go beyond the theoreticians to include all those who affect and are affected by development—practitioners, policy-makers, donors, politicians, activists, governments and citizens, urban dwellers and rural dwellers, people in the North and South, and in the West and East (Crocker 1991:473–74).

Relativism and Absolutism in Development Ethics

Examples from rural development illustrate some of the weaknesses and strengths of relativism and absolutism. In one case government health experts decided that for malaria eradication, all village swamps and bushes had to be sprayed with DDT to kill off mosquitoes. Among those villages were two communities with swamps where farm-fishing contributed to income. The government experts did not consult the communities before spraying. The results, of course, were that mosquitoes were killed, but so were the two communities' fish and their livelihood. In this case, what would have been the moral course of action? The government in this country holds "absolute" authority. The government was not morally right to use its absolute authority to apply to all communities, disregarding the unique differences exhibited by each community. Relativism, which requires dealing with each community according to its values and goals, would have been the right moral course of action.

In a second example, absolutism scores an advantage. A developing African country's local NGOs involved in rural development were encouraging local participation, sustainability and self-reliant sufficiency. Rural industries were also being established and encouraged to supply agricultural hand tools such as hoes and pangas. Some outside donors arrived at the scene to help the local NGOs improve agricultural production. They decided to do this by providing the projects with agricultural hand tools. These hand tools were supplied free or at highly subsidized prices, which meant the locally produced hand tools were more expensive. Agricultural production improved, but the community participants in these projects were no longer buying the locally produced hand tools. What happened to the sustainability and self-reliant sufficiency aimed at by the local NGOs? What happened to the rural industries set up for this purpose? The local industries were, of course, killed off, thus destroying the market for agricultural produce that would have been purchased by local industry workers. And farmers could not easily get replacement tools, thus choking off further agricultural growth that may have occurred. Relativism, applied here, resulted in executing whatever plans seemed good for the situation. An operative absolute applying in this situation might have prevented the outside agency from undermining "bigger picture" aims.

Theoretical Application of Ethical Principles

To demonstrate the seriousness of their intentions, members of the International Development Ethics Association (IDEA) produced a declaration of ethical principles proposed to guide the search for ethics-related alternatives to inadequate strategies of modernization. This declaration (cited in Crocker 1991:475–76 n. 45) in Merida, Mexico, during the Second International Conference on Ethics and Development in July 1989 proposed:

1. To intensify the search for and study of an alternative for social transformation, supported by at least the following ethical principles:
   a. Absolute respect for dignity of the human person, regardless of gender, ethnic group, social class, religion, age or nationality.
   b. The necessity of peace based on a practice of justice that gives to the great majorities access to goods and eliminates misery.
   c. Affirmation of freedom, understood as self-determination, self-management, and participation of peoples in local, national and international decision processes.

d. Responsible use of nature and respect for biological cycles and the equilibrium of ecosystems—especially those of tropical forests—in solidarity with future generations.

e. Recognition of exploited peoples—their cultural traditions, their thoughts, their interests and their needs—as subjects rather than objects of development.

2. To strengthen IDEA's efforts to maintain an international, intercultural and interdisciplinary dialogue bringing together intellectuals, grassroots organizations, and decision-making groups to construct an ethic applicable to different "development" alternatives.

Although neglect of ethics is not the only cause of problems with economic development, inclusion of ethics is undoubtedly a significant step in the right direction.

A Biblical Perspective on Empowerment

Certain questions arise from any analysis of empowerment: What is the purpose? What is the moral standard of measure? Who needs empowerment? The Bible offers, as a foundational principle of empowerment, the assertion that human beings are highly valued by their Creator but that this value has been distorted and needs to be restored. True empowerment does this. The Bible asserts that God elevated human beings to a special position among creation, as bearers of the image of God (Gen. 1:27; Pss. 8:5,6; 139:13,14). After the Fall, God in his love for humanity provided redemption for human beings through the death and resurrection of his only Son, the God-become-man Jesus (John 3:16; Rom. 5:8; 2 Cor. 5:21; 1 Pet. 2:24). Thus creation and redemption provide an ultimate identity and dignity applying to every person and to communities in relation to God, to one another and to nature. These assertions offer a far-reaching basis for empowerment. (Chapter 2 treats human dignity and identity at greater depth.)

The biblical perspective on the purpose of empowerment is, in brief, that fallen human beings may—through good relationships with their Creator, each other and the rest of creation—become responsible stewards, accountable to God for their use of material possessions, wealth and all given resources. The Bible teaches that human beings are not only made in the image of God, but also created for fellowship with God and one another, and stewardship of creation (Gen. 1:28; 2:15, 24f.; 3:8f.; 4:9; Mic. 6:8). Empowered human beings will be able to utilize and share resources equitably within harmonious relationships with their Creator, with each other and with nature (environment) for the enhancement of human life. (Stewardship is discussed in detail in chapter 3.)

The second question concerns a moral standard of measure for empowerment. The Bible talks of justice based on the immutable character of God. Because of the Fall, human systems are likely to be flawed, rendering justice difficult to achieve. Establishment of justice in community and institution of just community structures should be a true mark of an empowered community. (Detailed discussion of justice is presented in chapter 4.)

The final question asks, Who needs empowerment? Empowerment in this study applies to the whole society or the whole community—both "the poor" and "the rich" and those in the middle. The poor need empowering because they are powerless, but the rich also need to be empowered. The powerful who, through misuse of power, not only create powerlessness by oppression and injustice but also amass wealth, possessions and the world's resources are impoverished by corruption, bribery and selfish greed, and may feel powerless in the face of this moral poverty. The Bible acknowledges the existence of poverty in all its forms and treats it with utmost seriousness. The Bible also recognizes that much poverty is caused by oppression and injustice instigated by those who are rich and powerful. The biblical call for empowerment seeks to affect not only the poor, but also those among the rich who are oppressors and unjust, whom the Bible addresses in its empowerment of community and society.

PART I

A BIBLICAL PERSPECTIVE ON EMPOWERMENT

1

A Biblical Social Ethic for Holistic Empowerment in Development

Christianity, the majority religion in the world, views the Bible as the authoritative revealed Word of God for all human beings. By its nature, the Bible is not an economic (or development) textbook; however, it contains, among others, principles of God's mandate for human well-being, human development and human care for the environment.

However, the capabilities of other (non-Christian) development theorists and scientists should not be underestimated, "despite possible distortions . . . or awful interpretations of the meaning of economic life" (Goudzwaard 1980:5). Goudzwaard elaborates by arguing that in the Gospels there is one law for all creation that provides a norm for all human beings, both Christians and non-Christians, since they all share the same world. In such "a world all scientists are confronted with the same normativity" whether they recognize one origin of the world or not. And "because of this common normativity for all creation, truthful insights may be found in the writings of even the most atheist scientist" (Goudzwaard 1980:5).

Goudzwaard states that in economic science, which governs development, in which Christians involve themselves as in other areas of life, there should be openness to communication; there should not be an expectation of disagreement with all statements of secular thinkers. He emphasizes that "real confrontation can only take place on the basis of communication." Christian economists therefore

should not go out into an intellectual desert. . . . They must stand
in the present-day economic reality and economic theory, testing
everything in that forum and trying to preserve what is good. In
addition, Christians should not try to hide the presuppositions of
their theoretic efforts, especially not if they differ from those which
currently prevail. These presuppositions must be made clear . . .
in a crucial way, opening themselves to an evaluation by and com-
municating with the general scientific community. (Goudzwaard,
1980:5)

The Bible offers pragmatic guidelines for working toward setting free
the positive and constructive aspects of human nature, while constraining negative and harmful tendencies of the fallen nature inherent and
manifest in human behavior and operative in human structures
(Chewning 1989:7–8). Concern for the spiritual aspect of life; concern
for accountability in social ethics; and concern for a balanced view of
humanity each lend support for exploring a biblical perspective on development.

Reductionist Economics

Fundamental disagreement exists between holistic and reductionist
theories of economics. The original root of *economics—oikonomia—*refers to stewardship of household and community. The term derives from
oikos, meaning "household," and *nomos*, which means "law" or "rule."
Hence *oikonomia* means "management of the household so as to increase
its use value to all members of the household over the long run" (Daly
and Cobb 1990:138). Another definition might be "a stewardly activity,
a care for one's patrimony" (Goudzwaard 1980:28). From these definitions the scope of *oikonomia* expansively includes the larger community,
the land, shared values, resources, institutions, language and history.
This is the sense in which the Bible uses the term *economics;* "the New
Testament 'steward' is a servant in charge of both the property and affairs of his master" (Thompson 1960:ix). In biblical term "stewardship
refers to man's condition under God. God is the ultimate Owner of all
creation; man is the responsible servant who, for a few brief years, is trusted
with a commission to handle rightly the property and affairs of the Divine master" (Thompson 1960:ix-x). A more reductionist interpretation

of *economics* is currently adopted by most development approaches, especially as economics has become the dominant discipline in the development process.

Chrematistike is the term referring to "the branch of political economy relating to the manipulation of property and wealth so as to maximise short-term monetary exchange value to the owner" (Daly and Cobb 1990:138)—or, more simply, "the use of money or the making of profits" (Goudzwaard 1980:28). Current interpretation and usage of *economics* is certainly closer to *chrematistike* than to *oikonomia*. In application as well as definition, the whole process of development has also tended to reductionism, ignoring other disciplines in its measurement of results, insofar as it reduces the needs of human beings to those measured only in quantitative (economic) terms (Chambers 1988:3).

The Bible asserts that God, the Creator, owns the earth and all things in it and has entrusted to human beings the care and preservation of the rest of creation. Such a stewardship role presupposes that the dynamics and capabilities of its execution are possessed by all human beings. Further, the Bible views wholeness or "fullness" of human life as constituted by both physical/material and moral/spiritual dimensions (Gen. 2:7). This implies that in development situations human needs are more than economic.

Concern for the Spiritual Aspect of Life

Maslow's widely accepted analysis of the hierarchy of human needs (which has undergone some revision since) gives material needs basic priority over spiritual needs. This classic distinction between the material and the spiritual has been closely adhered to through overemphasis on meeting basic material and physical needs in development activities at the expense of spiritual ones (Lutz and Lux 1988:9–13; Maslow 1954:149–80). The discipline of economics generally requires quantification or measurability of all variables and indicators in analysis. This requirement precludes spiritual aspects, which by nature are difficult to quantify. Scientific inquiry claiming to be "amoral" or "value-free" by definition implies exclusion of moral or spiritual values. But is any science nonideological? Economic development, in its assumptions and interpretations, has itself developed under the influence of a modern scientific worldview that polarizes rational objective reality from personal subjective faith and values. However, this is a distinctly Western worldview. Society should be viewed as involving processes that grapple with the tension between objective givens and subjective meanings.

In Maslow's analysis of human needs, spiritual needs are categorized as "self-actualization." Lutz and Lux say these needs are "for creative development, and are the paramount needs in the life of a mature and healthy adult" (Lutz and Lux 1988:12). They quote the research discussed by Maslow (1954:chap. 11) and Rogers, indicating that desirable self-actualization tends, among other things,

> to be creative and spontaneous rather than impulsive and self-centred. They are non-power-seeking; they tend to recognize the worth and value of others; their attitudes are highly democratic rather than authoritarian; they prefer decentralised organization structures; and they prefer cooperative rather than competitive relationships with others. (Lutz and Lux 1988:13)

This research indicates spiritual needs are of crucial importance in the development and empowerment of human beings who seek to grow into fulfilled "actualized adults." It is good news that the Maslow analysis revision (1968) acknowledged that human needs cannot be viewed in a static step-by-step manner "in which the basic needs are gratified, one by one, before the next higher one emerges into consciousness" with self-actualization placed at "some far-off distant goal at the end of a long series of steps" (Lutz and Lux 1988:15). Rather, all needs are a present possibility all the time. The development process thus must consider both material and spiritual needs, since both are vital to holistic human development.

Concern for a Social Ethic for Development

Development is a process that concerns itself with human beings. Concerted efforts in secular circles to establish ethical principles to guide development (Crocker 1991; Goulet 1985 and 1983) have generally lacked a religious element.

Religion in general makes a distinctive contribution to development in a number of ways. Niebuhr argues that while "a secular moral act resolves the conflicts of interest and passion, revealed in any immediate situation, by whatever counsel" and normally heeds the counsel of moderation—"in nothing too much"—

> a religious morality is constrained by its sense of a dimension of depth to trace every force with which it deals to some ultimate origin and to relate every purpose to some ultimate end. It is concerned not only with immediate values and disvalues, but the problem of good and evil, not only with immediate objectives, but with ultimate hopes. It is troubled by the question of the primal "whence" and the final "wherefore." (Niebuhr 1956/60:15)

The concern of religion over the question of whence and wherefore, Niebuhr contends, occurs because religion is concerned with human life and existence as a unity and coherence of meaning. Every human being, according to Niebuhr, is religious, since it is impossible to live at all without presupposing a meaningful existence on some level.

Religion also contributes to identifying the tension between "what is" and "what ought to be." In this, religion dictates that moral acts seek to establish what ought to be, and constrain its followers by obligation to aspire for the ideal. The religion of the Bible teaches that the ideal has been realized in history by the God-become-man Jesus, who empowers his followers with his Spirit to attain the same ideal as they imitate him. This ethic is founded not so much on "moral rules which are to be obeyed without question at all times" but on a character and a lifestyle to emulate and imitate (Cook 1992:16; Yoder 1972:chap. 7).

Human beings everywhere accept some form of authority to which they appeal as a reference point, both to explain actions and to give the final word. How does religion determine what ought to be? What is the source of its authority? Christians believe that the Bible says something authoritative to all human beings, particularly on ethical issues (Cook 1988:45).

This, of course, is not to excuse Christianity's supposed adherents for justifying injustice—witness the Holocaust, the Rwanda genocide, the Inquisition, and so on. In contrast, the Bible itself depicts the Creator of humanity as deeply concerned with justice for and defense of the poor and the weak (1 Sam. 2:8; cf. Pss. 113:7; 140:12; Jer. 9:23, 24) and the creation of loving and caring human communities (Deut. 15:4–11;

Mott 1982:viii; Kirk 1979:205). In other words, biblical ethics involves commitment to the moral demands of God.

In the Old Testament, God in his concern about right behavior and attitudes in every area of life, gave a set of laws through which he revealed how he wanted human beings to live. These laws are foundational to the legal, moral and religious codes of nearly every culture through the ages and across the world. Laws concerning stealing, truth-telling, the sacredness of life, sexual behavior, and possessions and property are found in almost every culture and represent "God's universal, absolute laws for all human life," establishing necessary conditions for the preservation and continued existence of human life and society. Without them, society and human life disintegrate (Cook 1992:14).

In the New Testament, Jesus, as he lives out his life of service on earth, is a sort of "visual aid" revealing God's ethic. Jesus comes both to transcend and to fulfill the Old Testament (Matt. 5:17 and 38f.). As God incarnate, Jesus is said to be God's Word made flesh (John 1:14). By this authority, whenever Jesus spoke or acted, it was God speaking directly to human beings, and acting for humanity to witness and judge for themselves. "Jesus is the ethics of God in flesh-and-blood terms . . . a human life which all human beings are to emulate and imitate" (Cook 1992:15–16). Imitation is a very important concept in the application of Jesus' ethics, transcending both the pharisaic "Do what I say, but don't do what I do," and the Golden Rule, "Do unto others as you would have them do to you" (Mark 12:28f.; Matt. 22:40; citing Lev. 19:18). Instead, he taught "you also should do as I have done to you" (John 13:15, 34; 15:12).

Jesus' ethic entails introduction of structural changes involving imitation of his life and teaching. For example, he introduces a change to the Golden Rule; in his life, servanthood replaces dominion (Matt. 20:25–28; John 13:4–17); forgiveness must be exercised (Yoder 1972:134), as God in Jesus has forgiven (Luke 23:34; Matt. 6: 12, 14f.; 18:32f.; Luke 11:4; Eph. 4:32; Col. 3:13), for forgiveness absorbs hostility (Yoder 1972:134); love must govern everything, love of God and love of neighbor, in fulfillment of God's law (Matt. 22:37–39; Mark 12:30–31; Rom. 13:9–10). Niebuhr sees love as central in Jesus' ethic but observes that "love may be the motive of social action but justice must be the instrument of love in a world in which self-interest is bound to defy the canons of love on every level" (Niebuhr 1956/60:9). In other words, in Jesus' ethic, love and justice operate together.

Concern for a Balanced View of Humanity

Adherents of the "expert-model" of development tend to see people, especially the poor, as responsible for their poverty and believe that they should be left to it. A more optimistic view, held especially by the "bottom-up" school of development, sees people, in particular the poor, as inherently capable and good: "Local communities . . . are considered moral and autonomous. People are said to possess ultimate wisdom about their own lives. . . . The voice of the people cannot be in conflict with itself; it speaks truly" (Friedmann 1992:7). This school forgets the distortion of sin in human beings. There is rarely a balance between these two views of humanity. The Bible adopts a realistic view of life that sees all people as valuable before God, who created them all in his image.

In the beginning all creation was considered very good (Gen. 1:31a). There were good relations between the creation and God the Creator, and among the creatures themselves. Then there was the Fall (Gen. 3), which spoiled the "good" creation and distorted its relationships. As a result, God's mandates for the welfare of his creatures were no longer adequately followed, leading to the poverty and powerlessness experienced by a large proportion of each generation. As a result of the Fall, the earth itself became unproductive; droughts, floods and earthquakes occurred; and human beings became selfish, greedy, corrupt and spiritually blind—and increased in wickedness. But still God provided some basic guides or principles for human beings to remedy the situation—spiritually, by redemption through faith in Jesus' death, and also socially, economically and politically by obedience to God's laws for socioeconomic and political ordering of life (Matt. 20:28; Mark 10:45; Titus 2:14; Chewning 1989:7, 8; Hay 1989:chap. 2).

2

Human Dignity and Identity

Rural development in the past, and still to a degree, has been concerned with issues relating to infrastructure and thereby the potential for production (in agriculture, rural industries, crafts and commerce) and the provision of social services (health, education, and so forth). Emphasis has been on production and service skills and provision of physical facilities, in line with Maslow's hierarchy of human needs, which ranks material/physical needs ahead of other human needs of a social and moral/spiritual nature. Such approaches have neglected human dignity and identity, which Maslow categorizes under social needs (Lutz and Lux 1988:10).

But dignity and identity are inseparable human attributes that contribute to the makeup of the personality of an individual. A healthy personality displays balanced dignity and identity, which implies balanced self-image or self-evaluation. Given that human development has something to do with people's development, one of the primary goals of development should be to see individuals acquiring balanced human dignity and identity. "Person" (or "people") in development should not be reduced to a number or some abstract entity. Neglect of human dignity and identity in development activities must be seen as a serious omission to be redressed, because wrong self-evaluation "can be crippling in its consequences" (McGrath and McGrath 1992:ix). An erroneous self-image, whether too low or too high, results from lack of an appropriate measure of human dignity and identity, and it is destructive for the individual and society at large. Adequate development of human dignity and identity is the foundation for other human growth.

The poverty of the rural poor is undergirded by powerlessness among both the poor and the rich. Powerlessness, particularly among the poor, is characterized not only by a lack of physical and social infrastructure, as well as social services, but also by a lack of human fulfillment and balanced understanding of self, dignity and identity among individuals and people groups.

This powerlessness of the self results from (relative and absolute) deprivation and conditioned inertia, as well as lack of socioeconomic and political power to control one's own affairs and one's community-development process. A corollary following from this is that alleviation of poverty among rural people consists primarily in their empowerment. Such empowerment applies human dignity and identity as the building blocks or foundation in empowering people. Every person should be recognized as possessing dignity and an identity that must be respected. This empowerment process must involve the building up of dignity and confidence among individuals and groups—not only among the poor, who are downtrodden, but also among the rich who often think too highly of themselves (or perhaps think too lowly of themselves and find their identity in consumerism and material acquisition). It is vital that people not remain in bondage to false perceptions of themselves, either too low or too high.

Preoccupation with self-awareness and self-discovery is a phenomenon largely of the twentieth century (McGrath and McGrath 1992:24). In recent years this has led to an upsurge of interest in human dignity and identity, commonly reduced to "self-esteem." McGrath and McGrath cite increasing concern in contemporary Western culture among both "secular and Christian counselling to liberate individuals from an unjustified negative evaluation of themselves" (McGrath and McGrath 1992:ix). The poor often have a negative self-image, feeling they can contribute nothing to the situation. This keenly affects development. Partly due to the upsurge of interest in self-esteem, it is important to note that in identifying human dignity and identity as foundational principles for empowerment, focus here is grounded not in secular humanism but rather in each person's very being as an image-bearer of God.

In Western culture, positive self-esteem is viewed as crucial for mental health and a well-adjusted personality, "a complex idea involving a judgment concerning personal acceptability and worthiness to be loved, along with associated emotions" (McGrath and McGrath 1992:xi). A post-Freudian ego psychologist, Bandura, "views self-efficacy—a belief in the self as competent to control the environment—as critical for good mental health. According to his theory, many mental health problems result when people view themselves as passive victims of environmental events and forces" (cited in McGrath and McGrath 1992:21). In a nutshell, the humanist position reduces the whole notion of human dignity and identity to individual self-esteem. This position does not provide a solid basis for the origin of the notion of human dignity and identity. McGrath and McGrath contend that the Western emphasis "to promote positive self-esteem often seems to rest upon highly questionable theological foundations." Such central Christian themes as the reality of sin and the demand for humility "seem to have been abandoned or compromised. The price paid for positive self-esteem is often a dilution or distortion of the gospel" (McGrath and McGrath 1992:x). Even in Christian circles two strongly opposing views surface. One urges individuals to have a strong positive view of themselves. The other urges exactly the opposite, for individuals to have a strongly negative view of themselves.

Human Dignity and Identity in the Bible

A biblical view of human dignity and identity both complements and contradicts humanist or secular views. The Bible relates the concepts of dignity and identity, to a large extent, to the doctrine of *Imago Dei* (human beings made in the image of God) in the Old Testament and to Jesus Christ as the second Adam and his redemptive work on the cross in the New Testament. Humanity being created in the image and likeness of God (Gen. 1:26, 27) confers dignity to humanity; and, in the aftermath of the Fall, Jesus' death on the cross allows people "to find their true human worth and [identity] in the context of the call of God to give their allegiance to him" (Sugden 1991:59; also Deut. 7:7–8; 1 Cor. 1:26; Eph. 2:12–19; 1 Pet. 2:10).

Christian anthropology defines humanity as the creation of God, redeemed by Christ and destined for eternal life through Christ's resurrection. To remove this perspective is necessarily to ground human identity in human valuation.

Imago Dei as the Basis of Dignity and Identity

Imago Dei refers to the creation of humanity in God's image and likeness (Gen. 1:27). Emphasis is placed on the event or action of creation, according to Westermann. "It is not a declaration about man, but about the creation of man," an "action of God who decides to create man in his image." The purpose is primarily relational (Westermann 1974:56). Barth adds that this purpose is founded on divine love:

> God wills and posits the creature neither out of caprice nor necessity, but because he has loved it from eternity, because he wills to demonstrate his love for it and because he wills not to limit his glory by its existence and being, but to reveal and manifest it in his own co-existence with it. . . . Because God loves the creature, its creation and continuance and preservation point beyond themselves to an exercise and fulfilment of his love . . . to which creation in all its glory looks and moves and of which creation is the presupposition. (Barth 1958:95)

God's love is exercised and fulfilled within a covenant relationship, initiated by God himself. "In virtue of its being and nature the creature is destined, prepared and equipped to be a partner of this covenant." God does not have to do with the "subject" of another lord, nor does God have to do with a person who is a lord in his own right "but with his own property, with the work of his own will and achievement" (Barth 1958:96).

The biblical account of the purposeful act of God in love to create humanity differs vastly from other cosmogonies, such as those of the Ancient Near East, for instance, in which man is created to be the servant of the gods, to relieve them of their toil. Clines provides a sample of Mesopotamian creation narratives from the Atrahasis Epic: Create a human to bear the yoke; Let him bear the yoke, the task of Enlil; Let man carry the load of the gods (Clines 1968:99). Here man is condemned to an eternal yoke of slavery by the gods who are supposed to have created him. The biblical narrative in Genesis (1:26–27), complemented in the Psalms (8:5–8), links man's status to kingship and dominion (Clines 1968:95). The doctrine of the image of God in Genesis "affirms the dignity and worth of man and all [humanity]—not just kings or lords [or the elite]—to the highest status conceivable short of divination" (Clines 1968:53). Humanity's dignity is founded on his being a creature, for "God by creating man in his own image has given man his human dignity," according to Westermann. The essence of *Imago Dei* is the notion of a divine-human relationship, with a human destination of communion with God, his *telos*.

God, as Creator, is presented by the Bible as a personal God. Creation by a personal God is the basis of "personhood" for humanity. Hobson quotes Boethius's definition of a human being as a *person:* "the individual substance of 'a rational nature,'" having "weight and dignity in himself as a specific historical individual being who is rational" (in Hobson 1989:54). The concept of *Imago Dei*, conferring identity and dignity to humanity, is fundamentally relational and not qualitative, as perceived in some philosophies.

According to priestly writings, *Imago Dei*—as revealed in the Genesis passages and developed in the history of Israel as a people and in the history of the church—speaks of all human beings as "persons with inviolable dignity and free self-consciousness, individually unique beings in relation to other unique beings like themselves" (Hobson 1989:71). If God created human beings as special creatures, in special relation with God, and placed a high value on human persons (Gen. 9:6), then this can never be established on rational or empirical grounds. The human person as a creature is called to recognize and accept with humility and reverence the weakness, insufficiency, dependence and finiteness of its creaturely nature. Thus, it also accepts that its rights, meaning, goal, purpose and dignity lie only in the Creator, who turned to it with purposeful love. Meanwhile, the creature's relatedness to fellow creatures within the Creator's covenant is expressed within mutual love. Such mutual love seeks "neither to use the other nor to be engulfed in the other, [rather] it upholds and evokes the singularity, uniqueness and ineffability of the other" (Hall 1986:150). The creatures stand alongside each other in their relationship on an equal footing—"not above but with, not below but with." In other words, "neither a position of superiority nor one of servitude, neither oppressed nor oppressor" (Hall, 1986:156). In love, the other person becomes truly "Thou," enabling me to become "I."

The ontology of the tradition of Jerusalem suggests very distinct ethical guidelines for human relatedness at every level. It insists on equality of worth while recognizing diversity of gifts and offices. It denies every form of servitude while commanding each freely to serve the other. It provides the ontic basis for reciprocity of being between persons by holding in tension communal solidarity with respect for individuality. (Hall 1986:157)

The Second Adam—
Incarnation, Redemption and Re-creation

In the New Testament, Jesus is depicted as God's second "creation" of the perfect human being after the Fall. The first Adam sinned and introduced death, and through him all die; the second Adam, Jesus, brings life, and through him all may live (1 Cor. 15:22, 45–49). Through incarnation, Jesus comes to earth as the perfect image of God in human flesh; through redemption, the fallen creation is re-created to conform to that image, as the new creation (2 Cor. 5:17), which is to inherit God's kingdom. The Fall marred and distorted the image of God in which humanity originally had been created. This resulted also in the distortion of relationships between human beings and their Creator, among human beings themselves, and between human beings and the rest of creation. Because of this spoiled image, human dignity and identity have become denigrated.

The society into which Jesus was born was an epitome of human society everywhere. The New Testament thus portrays Jesus attacking and challenging aspects of the social structure of his day that undermined human dignity and identity in others. Jesus questioned the status differentials of his society. At the time of Jesus, status constituted a very powerful element by which people were controlled. Conceptually, status is based not on what people are but on the value the culture places on various individuals and groups of people. For example, in Jesus' society, Pharisees used the term *sinner* in a technical sense to describe people who were marginalized and excluded from normal Jewish life. Such people included tax-collectors, prostitutes, drunkards and lepers. Other categories of people identified and discriminated against in Jewish society were the sick, women, children, Samaritans and Gentiles (Mott 1984:13). Jesus crossed status boundaries to give a new identity to those who were discriminated against and marginalized. Those labeled sinners by the existing status system, he called rather "the lost" (Luke 15; 19:1–10).

The redefinition is significant. They are not sinners to be hated and driven away. They are lost needing to be found and rejoiced over [and with]. "Lost" implies a different status; there is something to be found and recovered. (Mott 1984:13)

Jesus elevated the status of women (John 4; 8:3–11; Mark 14:3–9); he welcomed children (Mark 9:37; Matt. 18:3; 19:14); he healed the sick and lepers (Matt. 4:5; Luke 17:12–14); and he accepted Samaritans and Canaanites (John 4; Matt. 15:21–28).

Jesus' purpose for coming to earth was primarily to inaugurate the kingdom of God (Mark 1:15), with its moral demands, and to die for the redemption of those who would become members of that kingdom. He was, in effect, introducing a concept of empowerment. He said he had come in the anointing of God's Spirit

to bring good news to the poor. He has sent me to proclaim release to the captives and recovery of sight to the blind, to let the oppressed go free, to proclaim the year of the LORD's favor." (Luke 4:18, 19)

Jesus gave those who expressed faith in him a new identity as children of God born into God's kingdom, and thus as people of God. Not only in his life but even more in his death Jesus sought to restore the marred image, and hence the identity and dignity, of humanity. Redemption and re-creation were made possible for all who would believe in him.

Paul, too, emphasized as the basis of human identity this salvation in Christ, "by grace" rather than "works" (see Eph. 2:8, 9; Rom. 3:21–31). For Paul, human worth "is in part defined by the ability of everyone to contribute their gift to the good of the whole" (Sugden 1991:61; see also 1 Cor. 12:12–31). The New Testament, therefore, provides an understanding of empowerment in which every individual has a God-given dignity and identity based on his or her createdness in the image of God that is re-created in Jesus, the second Adam.

What Is a Person?

When the value of a human being as discussed above is not upheld or is drastically eroded, and when equality among human beings is undermined, individual human life will not be appreciated for itself, but only insofar as that individual can serve some cause or notion estimated for some reason to be of greater and more lasting importance (Hobson 1989:71).

> [The nature of man] is not [properly] understood if he is viewed merely as the most highly developed of the animals . . . nor is it [well] perceived if he is seen as an infinitesimal being dwarfed by the enormous magnitude of the universe. (Clines 1968:53)

Any attempt to judge the worth of an individual person outside of the biblical view seems bound to define and view the human person qualitatively according to varying philosophical criteria, rather than as a substance or entity having intrinsic value.

Some classical philosophers interpreted *person* not in terms of an individual entity but in terms of a universal concept—such as a member of a race or a state or a corporation—that was believed to be enduring, as opposed to an individual whose existence was considered ephemeral. These philosophers failed to conceptualize fully the unity of body, soul and mind in an individual human being. A dualistic conceptualization views the body as material and mortal, and therefore of no real value; and the soul (for Plato) and the mind (for Aristotle) as imperishable and eternal and detachable from the body and the rest of the material world, which presumably perish. For these philosophers the soul and mind, being eternal, were fundamentally incompatible with the material, perishing body.

In addition, Hellenistic culture and religion, which spawned these philosophies, were suspicious of matter.

> The material world, including the human body, was regarded as inferior; it was the locus of temptation, of evil, of danger, and therefore it was fundamentally "unreal." . . . The function of religion in Hellenistic civilization, as well as most philosophy, was [considered] to lift persons out of their bondage to the flesh and put them into proximity to the transcendent, supramundane realm of pure spirit. Salvation in the typical religions and philosophies of this civilization meant salvation "from" the world. (Hall 1990:56)

In other instances a person's worth is determined on the basis of his or her contribution to society, evaluated according to varying criteria.

The biblical account, to the contrary, reveals God in Jesus Christ conferring value to a whole person—both material and rational. In other words, the Christian God values the body. The biblical creation narrative in Genesis 2 depicts God "personally fashioning the human body, and blowing breath into its mouth to 'get it going'" (Hall 1990:56). This account posits that the material world, as well as the human body and its functions, are good. According to Genesis, "God saw everything that he had made, and indeed, it was very good." (1:31). At the same time, the Bible provides an understanding of the body as eternal, as well, based on the bodily resurrection of Christ.

> The value conferred to the human body by the resurrection of Jesus Christ . . . was rooted by the early Christian thinkers in the doctrine of Creation and in particular in the worth of man as made in the image of God. (Hobson 1989:41)

Therefore the whole person is to be given value, not simply fragmentary aspects.

This holistic view of humanity has important ramifications for rural development and empowerment. The important point here is that one's true value cannot be located in oneself—as if this value were a quality or possession of one's own nature—but can be found only in relation to God. Value resides in one's personhood, that is, in being a creature made in the image of a personal God.

So, while secular views are not personal and are based on various qualitative philosophical criteria, a biblical view is one of the few worldviews that ground human dignity and identity absolutely in personhood, regardless of human qualities, status, class, or any other differentials entered into the definition; the *Imago Dei* concept makes a statement about human worth as well as about the meaning of human existence. All humanity, accordingly, possesses inviolable dignity. This holistic biblical view establishes a basis for empowerment for all human beings, not merely for some special groups or individuals. Such a view of human dignity and identity supplies an absolute foundational principle for an empowerment process that aims at human fulfillment for all. This is vital within rural development.

3

Stewardship

Stewardship, in biblical usage, refers to the use and allocation of resources required for empowerment. The twin concepts of divine ownership and divine gifting of the earth's resources including land, call for careful use and equitable distribution of such resources. God, the Creator, owns the earth and all its resources, but has entrusted their keeping, with accountability, to human beings (Wright 1983:68; Goudzwaard 1980:15–16).

The concept of stewardship in Genesis is traceable to the creation event, in which Adam and Eve are described as created in the image of God. Interpretation of the term *image* has been historically influenced by the dominant theology and anthropology of the age (Barth 1958:192ff.; Clines 1968:54ff.). For our discussion, a number of scholars follow the understanding accorded to the term by ancient religious traditions. In the ancient Babylonian and Egyptian religions in Mesopotamia and Egypt respectively, Hehn (1915) pointed out, the king was described as an image of a god, and as such was the representative or viceroy of the god (Westermann 1984:151). Later scholars based their interpretation of the Genesis text on Hehn's explanation. Westermann quotes two such studies: First, von Rad writes: "As earthly rulers . . . erect images of themselves in the provinces as signs of their presence, so too has God put human beings on earth in his image and likeness as a sign of his majesty." Second, Jacob and van der Bussche state: "God created the person as his representative, his vizier who in some way is like the master. The person becomes God's attorney and administrates his goods" (in Westermann 1984:152). In both cases the image of God in the Genesis text is comparable to "what Egypt and Mesopotamia say about the king as the image of God. A person as the image of God corresponds to the king as the image of God; both are God's viceroy and representative" (Westermann 1984:152).

Similarly,

> The term *[image]* referred to the statue in the temple, or the king on the throne, who represented an invisible god who lived on the mountain. The king was the substitute for the god and account-able to him for the way he rules. The "image" was the regent, or agent or overseer of God. He was responsible for God's territory in that area. He was the tenant of his property, responsible to him for its management. This concept of management on behalf of another comes across clearly in Genesis 1:27–28, the verses which describe man and woman being made in the image of God. (Samuel n.d.:6)

The concept of the image of God in this context is about humanity's role as God's steward of creation, which God declared "very good" (Gen. 1:31). Also implicit in the idea of the *Imago Dei* is the sense that human beings should demonstrate the attributes of God, summarized as "creativity, purpose and discernment of values" (Hay 1989:18). Hobson takes this further, that human beings, made in the image of God, have a God-given power to create, though not from nothing. They can order, act, speak and name (Gen. 2:19); they cannot make life where none was, but they can nourish life; they can be fruitful and multiply. They can have dominion by filling the earth and subduing it, although, because of the obligation to care for creation, this dominion and subduing cannot mean domination, plunder, or exploitation. Human beings can accomplish these obligations "not in [themselves] autonomously . . . but in relation to Original and Prototype, God, from whom [humanity] has the power [to do these things] as a gift" (Hobson 1989:75–76).

Thus stewardship demands the maintenance of relationships in which people can act in the image of God. In other words, stewardship is inextricably bound to the image of God in which humanity is made.

Biblical Stewardship

The creation narrative in Genesis (1:26–30) presents humanity created as part of and yet distinct from the rest of creation. Humanity's distinctiveness is marked by being made in the image of God, and by inferred capacity to enter into a relationship with God and to act as God's steward for the rest of creation. In this stewardship role humanity is given dominion over God's creation, not to dominate and exploit, but to respect creation, to care for it, to preserve it, and to use it wisely to sustain and nurture life. In literal terms, humanity is charged with an agricultural responsibility. The first humans are placed in a garden to work or till, to care for this garden with its flora (Gen. 2:15) and to name the animals of the fauna (Gen. 2:19–20). This requirement assumes respect for each animal and plant for what it is and entails some "intellectual effort and scientific endeavour as man seeks to understand and differentiate the various elements of creation" (Hay 1989:19). Humanity's stewardship, as set out in the Bible right from the beginning, is to be exercised within a right relationship with God and God's good creation, even in spite of the Fall and the flood.

This concept of stewardship is found in both the Old Testament and the New Testament. Old Testament usage tends toward the technical or literal sense, describing an actual office or vocation in society. New Testament usage is more figurative or metaphorical.

> The Steward in the literature of the Old Testament is a servant but not an ordinary servant who simply takes orders and does the bidding of others. . . . He is a rather superior servant, a sort of supervisor or foreman who must make decisions, give orders and take charge. . . . The Steward is one who has been given the responsibility for the management and service of something belonging to another, and his office presupposes a particular kind of trust on the part of the owner or master [who is usually a king or ruler]. (Hall 1990:32)

Stewardship in the Old Testament underlies requirements regarding the use of resources, especially of land. Land is a dominant theme of the Old Testament, in particular in the Pentateuch and early historical books.

These books enshrine God's covenant promises to give land to the patriarchs. In fulfillment of these promises, as well as the redemption story of Exodus, the quest for land is central.

> The land was [also] part of the pattern of redemption, because the social shape of Israel was intimately bound up with the economic issues of the division, tenure and use of the land. (Wright 1983:50)

For ancient Israel land was a physical source of fertility and life, a place for gathering the hopes of the covenant people, and a vibrant theological symbol. In the context of the history of the Jewish people, land meant a future both secure and without anxiety. The viability of each family unit was based on ownership of a piece of land given to it as inheritance (1 Kings 21:1–3). Above all, land meant satiation (Deut. 8:7–10). Security and well-being were no longer dependent on a grudging taskmaster, but constituted the generous gifts of the bounteous God, who gives rain, growth and food or "water and manna" (Brueggemann 1977:47–53).

More important, land was a trust whose ultimate owner was God (Lev. 25:23). This twin perspective of divine largesse and divine ownership of land implied both rights and responsibilities for Israel, which were undergirded by the strong moral commitments like those given in Deuteronomy (7:7f.; 8:17f.; and 9:5) and by maintenance of the relationship with Israel's God. This relationship required dependence on God's faithfulness and reliability and called for strict observance of economic justice, which the prophets enforced, while God's ownership of the land implied responsibility to God, to one's family and to one's neighbor (Wright 1983:51–59).

Stewardship in the Old Testament also defined the role of the king or ruler with regard to handling of resources, especially land, vis-à-vis his subjects. As steward, the Israelite kings were not to control the land, as was the case with the Canaanite kings (Wright 1983:58) but to manage the land entrusted to them but never possessed by them. Rulers were to manage the land properly and enhance it for the sake of the people of God under their rule and to whom they were bound by common loyalties and memories. Use and distribution of the land had to be ordered by moral principles. God's stipulations for a king in Deuteronomy (17:14–20) included the proviso that he be one of the children of Israel, a brother with knowledge, memories and experience of the history of the children of Israel. Furthermore, God set limits on the king's behavior (Deut. 17:16–17); namely, the king must not multiply for himself horses, wives, or silver and gold. Such actions explicitly went against God's mandate for the king and his people, who covenanted to be totally reliant on God, source of their kingdom's authority and ultimate ownership. Multiplication of horses for armaments would represent an effort on the part of the king to become self-reliant. Multiplication of wives would suggest self-indulgence or a desire to make political alliances. And multiplication of silver and gold would be an attempt to enhance the king's own splendor.

Along with these prohibitions, the king was instructed to read and live by the Torah, to which he was to be subject. The Torah was a fundamental affirmation that Israel's resources were founded in Yahweh's graciousness. Keeping of the Torah would keep Israel in the land; neglect of the Torah would lead to loss of their land. Land was explicitly not for one's own security, but rather for providing for brother and sister. The king was continually warned against the temptation to regard land as a possession, handled apart from its spiritual significance. In fact, 1 Samuel 8:11–17 records a solemn warning to the children of Israel—who rejected God as their king—regarding the character of the earthly king who would rule over them. This earthly kingship would result in a distortion of stewardship. Such a king would be a confiscator; would reduce Israel to slavery; would lead Israel away from Yahweh; and would violate use of the land, keeping and enhancing it for his sole benefit. In short, the nature of an earthly king would be to covet and exploit, a warning fulfilled in King Saul, David and Solomon, and in the kings after them (Brueggemann 1977:10).

In addition to the stewardly role of the king the Old Testament offers many other examples of stewardship: Genesis 43 and 44, in which the steward is the person accountable to Joseph; 1 Chronicles 27 and 28, in which stewards are those responsible for various properties and aspects of King David's kingdom; and Daniel 1:11, 16, in which the steward takes charge over the Hebrew prisoners of King Nebuchadnezzar.

Generally, Old Testament usage of the term *stewardship* has to do with "management of domestic affairs, the rule or realm of a person in authority, or the dominion of a monarch. In this sense, stewardship is the responsibility of authority and management committed to an officer or king" (Scheef 1960:18).

In the New Testament Gospels, figurative use of the idea of steward-ship can be found in a number of passages, such as Matthew 20:8; Luke 8:3; 12:42ff.; 16:1–4; and John 2:8. In these references the steward is a servant-manager of something or someone not belonging to himself. The master is not an earthly king or lord, like Pharaoh or King David, but implicitly God in Christ. Followers of Christ during Christ's earthly absence are charged with responsibility for Christ's household. As stew-ards of his household, his followers are accountable for those who dwell in his land. These passages record Jesus' teaching about stewards, refer-ring to some as faithful, caring and wise, to others as dishonest, unpro-ductive and even cruel. Jesus addressed many of his teachings on stewardship to leaders of the Jews, urging these leaders to exercise proper stewardship for the welfare of God's people.

The term *steward* in the New Testament is from the Greek rendering *oikonomos*, deriving from *oikos*, meaning "house," and *nomos* meaning "one who plans, administers or puts in order." A steward thus looked after the needs of the household and of all its members. *Household*, as used biblically, conveys that the entire world is God's household or family. Stewardship, therefore, implies the ordering of life in the world and creation, not merely in relation to money, budgeting, finances, or the ordering of affairs of only one family unit.

Both Old Testament and New Testament imply that an important and superior position is accorded the steward, a position in which the steward identifies closely with the master. However, both Old Testa-ment and the New Testament usages also bring out a second, aspect of stewardship, clearly expressed in Isaiah 22:25–21 and Luke 12:42–48: the obligation of a steward to understand and constantly remember that he does not retain ultimate ownership or authority over what he man-ages, because all belongs to God alone. Though superior, the steward is still a servant who is "strictly accountable to [the] master and will be deprived of [that position] unless he upholds in his actions and attitudes the character and true wishes of this other one [God] whom he is al-lowed and commanded to represent" (Hall 1990:34). If the steward for-gets this and begins to assume he is autonomous and at liberty to behave as he pleases, as though unambiguously in charge and hence not ac-countable, this steward shall be most severely punished.

These two passages in Isaiah 22:15–21 and Luke 12:42–48 empha-size the unavoidable responsibility of those who have much to take care of those who have little or nothing. In other words, what from one standpoint is the superior authority of a steward is from another his greater responsibility. Luke's passage sums it up:

> From everyone to whom much has been given, much will be required; and from the one to whom much has been entrusted, even more will be demanded. (Luke 12:48b)

In the context of election theology, this implies the choosing of a few on whom responsibility is placed on the behalf of many, never for their own sake. Stewards of God's universal grace are to care for all the families of the earth. Because what any individual is given is for a wider company, much is given to God's intended stewards and in turn much is required of them. Individual talents are a means to something greater, not an end in themselves (Hall 1990:36). There may be a temptation here to compare and confuse this principle of election with the elite principle from which capitalist growth theory derives its trickle-down concept of development. The elite principle is undergirded by privilege, status, or class apart from any serious obligation or institutable law requiring that the needs of others outside the privileged group be met. This elite principle, more often than not, tends to lead the few to accumulate more and more material wealth, with the "trickle" tending to flow back to them rather than down to the poor, who become even poorer in the process.

In Christian theology, *election* refers to something quite different, undergirded with stewardly responsibility and accountability, set against severe judgment and punishment upon failure to fulfill the expected role. Old Testament accounts set a stage on which the steward is not only equipped with resources to expedite the stewardly role but is also handed principles defining conditions within which the role is best performed. The Old Testament provides economic laws directing the "haves" to provide for the "have nots"—such as the gleaning laws that forbade people to consume all they had produced; and the laws governing land rights, including the Sabbath year and the Jubilee year, which provided a protected land-tenure system based on equitable and widespread distribution of land and preventing unjust accumulation of ownership by a few wealthy (as would be the case under the elite principle). These laws were instituted to govern society so as to effect a just and responsible lifestyle for the people of God. The laws were a constant reminder to God's people that their human fulfillment was inextricably bound up in their relationship not only with God but with the God-given land and natural resources they stewarded. That relationship was to be ordered by the Torah's moral principles of justice, equality and equity in order for those resources to yield their true bounty and for man to experience true humanity (Samuel and Sugden 1982:42). In other words, the purpose of Old Testament law was that God's people were to demonstrate their love for God by "a just lifestyle through their use of land, their work, their legal system, social relationships and political institutions." These arrangements would make possible a true and dig-nified humanity for individuals, and would enable the community to foster a lifestyle that enriched human life for all (Samuel and Sugden 1982:51).

The New Testament tends to elevate stewardship even further. In 1 Corinthians 4:1–2 people are called to be servants of Christ and stew-ards of God's mysteries, the gospel itself, which God gives to the whole family of humanity. Here Paul applies the concept of stewardship ex-plicitly to himself as an apostle and implicitly to the church at large. Paul's message is that people exist not to serve themselves but as ser-vants of God's mysteries, to serve the interests of those God has at heart.

In Ephesians 2:19—3:11, stewards are regarded not as hired hands or outsiders of the household, but as partners and members of God's household, in which they participate in different responsibilities. Par-ticipation allows stewards to share the bounteous grace of God with others and to bring them in turn into God's household. This passage refers specifically to stewardship of grace rather than stewardship of material things, but stewardship continues to center on the idea of entrustedness for the purpose of sharing.

An eschatological aspect of stewardship is also apparent in Luke and implicit in the Isaiah passages quoted above. The Jerusalem tradition that influenced much in the Epistles was deeply conscious of an immi-nent end. 1 Peter 4:7–11 expresses the stewardship theme in apocalyp-tic terms: such an awareness of the nearness of the end ought to reinforce good stewardship of the varied gifts of God's grace for the ultimate glory of the master, God, who comes to demand an account from each of his stewards. This teaching attempted to reduce or eliminate the temp-tation for individuals to isolate themselves and their talents pridefully, and sought to create a fuller recognition of the human transience all humanity faces, and thus the need for human creaturely solidarity and compassion, as God intended (Hall 1990:39).

Like the Old Testament and the Gospels, the Epistles also sound a warning note regarding proper exercise of stewardship. In 1 Corinthians 3:21–23, for example, stewards of God's mysteries "ought not to make names for themselves or form parties around this or that great one" (Hall 1990:36). In other words, the Epistles forbid factionalism and impose limitations to avoid misuse of the privileged position of steward of God's blessings for self-aggrandizement.

Distortion of Stewardship

The Bible recognizes that the introduction of sin into the human realm curtailed human ability to be true stewards of God.

> In pride the human creature reaches beyond the limits of its creaturehood. It grasps at equality with God. . . . Pride is born of the deep dissatisfaction of the creature with the limits of its creaturehood, its lack of permanency, wisdom and power. Pride is behind the Babel search for mastery.
>
> Sloth on the other hand, describes the state of indifference to our fallen condition. It means adapting oneself to less than righteous, less than just, less than peaceful, less than human circumstances. If pride implies reaching too high, sloth means sinking too low, settling for something less than real humanity. If pride means forgetting that one is human and therefore "capable of failing," . . . sloth means adjusting to failure and being fatalized by one's condition. (Hall 1990:93; see also Hall 1990:91–94 and Niebuhr 1941:198–216)

As a result of sin, relationships of humanity with God, with others and with the rest of creation are distorted. The image of God in man, although not destroyed, is marred. Human beings are alienated from God and hide from God (Gen. 3:8). Once communion with God is broken, humanity becomes incapable of leading a life pleasing to God and is no longer fully capable of being God's faithful steward.

Human relationships become grievously disordered with, for example, men dominating women (Gen. 3:16). Self-regarding shame becomes pervasive, as symbolized by clothing (Gen. 3:21). And murder erupts (Gen. 4), such that "violence and exercise of brute strength are now significant in human society," thus naturalizing the tendency for one man to dominate and exploit another (Hay 1989:22).

Consequences of a perverted relationship with God include the cursing of the ground (Gen. 3:17–19; 4:12), so the ground does not yield and work becomes toil. Human beings begin to kill animals for food and ruthlessly to exploit natural resources (Hay 1989:21).

> Shared access to and responsible stewardship of earth's resources, *land and resources*, have become the greatest single cause of strife and warfare between man. Some resources are hoarded by a few and denied to others. Some are squandered, polluted or abused. Possession of resources, instead of being used as an opportunity for mutual sharing, as an unmerited gift, has become a matter of conquest and seizure, a tool of oppression, greed and power. (Wright 1983:71)

Wright goes on to describe the corruption of *work*, which becomes toilsome, frustrating and a necessity for survival (Wright 1983:71). The quest for "*economic growth* becomes pathologically obsessive"—to the point of idolatry (Goudzwaard 1984; Wright 1983:72). And *the end product* of economic processes is manipulated unjustly.

> Claims of ownership are privatized and regarded as absolute, in the absence of any sense of transcendent responsibility for others. Grossly unfair trading arrangements prevent the poor of the world from enjoying even the fruit of the resources they have got. (Wright 1983:73)

Proverbs 13:23 states that "the field of the poor may yield much food, but it is swept away through injustice." Distortion of stewardship has meant the distortion of human economic life, which stands in need of redemption.

Remedy for Distorted Stewardship

In the Bible, recognition and awareness of the consequences of sin are not enough. Yet the narrative provides a remedy. The gospel of Jesus Christ is the means of God's grace, by which humanity is enabled to overcome sin and these consequences that prevent humanity from exercising true stewardship. The Bible presents Jesus as the model steward of God, who defines and demonstrates the applicability of the stewardship God expects. Jesus is a just and faithful steward. Unlike the unjust steward in Luke 16, he desires nothing for himself. He is totally obedient to the Father, whom he represents and who is pleased with him. He is a real representative and true image of the Father who sent him. He is concerned with the lost whom the Father sent him to save, and he lays down his life for them rather than save his own life. He who is from God and belongs to God is the initiator and enabler of Christian stewardship.

Those who respond to the demands of the gospel by faith are thus "graciously brought into a stewardship of God's grace that has already been enacted by God's chief steward" (Hall 1990:44). To enable his people to carry out this stewardship, God gives them his Holy Spirit, who empowers them. The Bible presents the Holy Spirit as the dynamic Empowerer by whom fallen, helpless human beings are enabled to rediscover their relationships with their Creator God, with each other, and with the rest of creation. They are re-created into the true image of God and also equipped with resources—spiritual, mental, physical and material (all of which are defined as God's varied gifts of grace)—for the execution of stewardship. This empowerment hinges on the principle of grace: "You received without payment; give without payment" (Matt. 10:8). In their stewardly role God's people are to share the good news of their own empowerment—the gospel—among others still helpless and powerless. Those who are empowered become Jesus' stewards as participants in God's varied grace. Like Jesus, their lives are to be governed by the ethics of the kingdom of God, which impinges on all human presumption in relation to both material realities determining lifestyles and intangible realities include authority and the wielding of power. Stewardly qualities such as humility, servanthood, lack of pretension and ostentation, and parental behavior toward those for whom one bears responsibility—the poor, the helpless and the powerless.

Implications of Stewardship

A normative implication linked to accountability in the use of resources is that God owns the earth and all its resources, which he entrusts to all humanity. Those who possess resources must regard them as entrusted to them by the real owner, God, who will require an account of them. God intends such resources to be used and shared for the good of all; therefore, access to and use of those resources are meant to be made available to all. This shared right sets moral limits to both the right of private ownership as advanced by the capitalist notion of property and ownership, as well as the right of state ownership advocated by communist concepts of resource ownership. On the one hand, ownership does not entail an absolute individual right of disposal but rather a responsibility for administration and just distribution. "The right of all to use is prior to the right of any to own" (Wright 1983:69). On the other hand, corporate ownership in the Bible is in the context of corporate responsibility, which does not rule out individual ownership. The condemnation of King Ahab for taking Naboth's field (1 Kings 22) is a good example. Biblically, private ownership with responsibility is right, good and necessary to the identity, security and fruitfulness that accrue from such ownership within certain bounds and under certain corporate constraints.

Second, in the sharing of produce, the needs of all set moral limitations on the right to consume or enjoy the end products of economic processes utilizing God-given resources. Responsibility to God for what is done with what is produced does not differ from responsibility for what God gives directly. There is no mandate in the Creation account for private use, nor for hoarding or consuming at the expense of others. The Creation principle of stewardship, implying mutual responsibility for the good of the whole human community, opposes ultimate privacy in property ownership and consumption. In fact, the rich are obliged to help the poor who cannot provide for themselves.

Third, in terms of the responsibility of work, human beings have a right and an obligation to work, as a Creation provision rather than a result of the Fall. Work is part of the image of God, whom the Bible presents as a worker (Gen. 2:3). Work, Hay maintains, "remains essential to human dignity and integral to man's nature" (Hay 1989:74). Deliberate or voluntary idleness is condemned (2 Thess. 3:6–13). So is deprivation or denial of work to someone else, which is tantamount to an offense against that person's humanity and the image of God in that person, and hence is sin. Human beings are to apply their God-given talents and resources to work and contribute fruitfully to the common good of whole communities. Biblically, work is interpreted in its widest possible meaning, rather than in reductionist terms limiting its significance to paid employment (Wright 1983:68–70; Hay 1989:72–76; *Oxford Declaration* 1990: nos. 13–26). Human beings are to work as God's "stewards in the faithful management of the world recognising that they are responsible to God for what they do with the world" and its resources (*Oxford Declaration* 1990: no. 2). Stewardship is thus concerned with the preservation of the nonhuman creation (Goudzwaard 1980:28–29), as well as with aspects of God's economy that ensure God-given resources are utilized in a manner meeting the needs of all beings, especially the poor.

Stewardship is absolutely essential for the empowerment of the rural poor. Lack of resources is a primary factor contributing to the powerlessness of the poor. In rural development, land is the basic resource for and of all people. Land is central to individuals' productive resourcefulness as well to their secure living. The vital importance of land to life in general and to rural life in particular can never be overemphasized. Brueggemann argues that land is a central theme of biblical faith. The Bible treats land in two senses: first, in a literal sense as the actual earthly turf where people can be safe and secure, where meaning and well-being are enjoyed without coercion; and second, in a metaphorical sense to express the wholeness of joy and well-being characterized by social coherence and personal ease in prosperity, security and freedom. This dual interpretation affirms that land is never simply physical ground, but is always physical ground freighted with social meaning derived from historical experience. Excessive spiritualization strips away at recognition that the "yearning for land is always a serious historical enterprise concerned with historical power, belonging [and destiny]" (Brueggemann 1977:2).

Landlessness is a scourge endemic to much rural poverty. When people are poor and landless, they are hounded by a pervasive sense of being lost, displaced and homeless. The poor, like most of humanity, yearn to belong somewhere, to have a home, to be in a safe place where they can be secure to pursue fulfilling modes of living. Brueggemann identifies loss of place and the yearning for a place at two levels: the sociological displacement level, and the psychological dislocation level. Sociological displacement is responsible for the world's numerous refugees, the homeless displaced people, and the urban migrants from rural areas who become highly mobile and rootless. Psychological dislocation results in increasing numbers of persons becoming disoriented and characterized by what Berger calls the "homeless mind," expressed as restlessness among youth, forgottenness among the elderly, and power-lessness among the poor, all in the face of urban "progress" (Bruegge-mann 1977:1). Stewardship involves taking care not of things but of people, who need land to live on and to fulfill basic needs from.

The whole concept of stewardship in the Bible is based upon use and distribution of land and other resources, especially with regard to the poor.

Contemporary Implications of Stewardship

Hall (1990) identifies a criticism of biblical interpretation of stew-ardship, observing that the New Testament does not develop fully the community and institutional dimensions of stewardship, elements of which are basic to the process of empowerment for rural communities. He points out that the New Testament does not expand on how the concept can be applied to the Christian community's daily life in soci-ety, or how it conditions dealings of Christians with institutions includ-ing government, political, social and economic structures, or how the concept leads to an ethic of social responsibility—or what it means for human relations with the extrahuman world. However, the early church was not in a position of social, political or economic power. Its role was mainly religious. Its followers were a minority and often subjected to persecution. Biblical metaphors, however, took for granted the church's intended influence on society as the light and salt of the world, leaven in the lump, or a city on a hill. The writers of the New Testament looked to the future for a fuller working out of the implications of the gospel message. The expectation of an imminent end preoccupied the minds of some of these Christian thinkers and writers. Hall argues that this expectation led them to "concentrate almost exclusively on the spiritual and internal ecclesiastical implications of stewardship" (Hall 1990:46).

Despite this criticism, the metaphor of stewardship is still appli-cable in present contexts. Land laws, especially the Jubilee in the Old Testament, embodied practical concern for the family, which was the small-est unit in Israel's kinship social structure and is still so today in rural communities. It was this focus of identity, status, responsibility and se-curity for the individual Israelite that the Jubilee aimed to protect.

The material and worldly meaning of stewardship as a serious voca-tion is increasingly being recognized by both the church and the secular community. The result is that many biblical scholars are among the contemporary writers on the need for stewardly responsibility of humanity for the world and its resources today. Many of these writings critique the quest for unlimited progress or growth that is pursued in the name of world development and yet results in "uneconomic growth that impoverishes rather than enriches," with its attendant "wild facts," such as the hole in the ozone layer, the carbon dioxide-induced greenhouse effect causing global warming, and deforestation, pollution, contamination and radiation poisoning (Daly and Cobb 1990:1). These looming threats hang over the whole global economy, while increasing poverty in the poorest nations sinks the powerless into "deeper poverty, hunger, debt, dependency, environmental degradation and contamination, loss of control over the arms race and the bureaucratization of states" (Goudzwaard 1984:12; Daly and Cobb 1990:1–2).

Application of the stewardship concept to humanity as a whole is one of many ways in which the Bible defines humanity's posture vis-à-vis the Creator and other creatures. The commandment the Creator gives to love God and neighbor does not exclude non-Christians. Although the New Testament describes and prescribes appropriate life for God's stewards, directed especially to believers of the gospel, the stewardship concept is the Creator's mandate for all humanity. Hall argues that God's object in calling a few as a witnessing people, in the midst of the world, is not to create a higher race—an elite—but, through such a community, to keep before humanity the identity and vocation that the Creator intends for all human creation. The Creator's call to respond to the gospel is given to all human beings with no exceptions, and God's intention is that every human being should respond (1 Tim. 2:3–4). Stewardship is therefore a general human calling, not a call only for Christ's followers. The whole human species is intended by God to act as his stewards within the creaturely sphere.

Stewardship in the biblical sense refers to something one *is* and not just to something one *does*. It describes the very being, the very life of those who covenant with God to be co-creators and co-workers in the plan God has for humanity. Deeds of stewardship, therefore, arise out of being a steward (Hall 1990:129).

The natural order works on the principles of diversity, interdependence and decentralization. Maintenance replaces the notion of [exploitative] progress; stewardship replaces ownership [especially the ultimacy of private ownership]; and nurturing replaces [manipulative] engineering. Biological limits to both production and consumption, are acknowledged, the principle of balanced distribution is accepted, and the wholeness becomes the essential guideline for measuring all relationships and phenomena. (Rifkin, cited in Hall 1990:239)

In the Bible true stewardship is the backbone of true human dignity and identity; it leads to true justice and equity, which together lead toward elimination of poverty. These are the biblically based ethical principles by which holistic empowerment can be effectively achieved.

4

Justice and Equity

Political, economic and social relationships, arrangements, structures and institutions often foster and perpetuate the powerlessness of the poor. Justice calls for, among other essentials, just treatment of the poor, requiring that their position and opportunities be improved in a way that empowers all to participate.

Biblical Justice

In the Bible the terms *righteousness* and *justice* are used interchangeably. These two words share one root in Greek, *deik*, from which stems other words, including:

- *Dikaiosyne:* righteousness, uprightness; righteousness or righteous conduct that makes a human being acceptable to God. It denotes God's righteousness in discerning good and evil, and preserving the good and punishing the evil among men. In Wisdom writing, knowledge of God constitutes righteousness.

- *Dikaios:* upright, just, righteous. It denotes the upright person who trusts in God and keeps the law, as distinct from sinners. When applied to God, it denotes his attitude in discriminating between the upright and the sinner.

- *Dikaioo:* to justify, or to do justice to, vindicate, treat as just, ac-
  quit, pronounce or treat as righteous, make or set free, etc. (Brown
  and Seebass 1978:352–58; Rooy 1980:2; Beisner 1992:5).

In Hebrew the words *righteousness* and *justice* originate from two roots.
The first is *tsdq*, translated "righteousness."

> The root meaning is probably "straight": something which is fixed
> and fully what it should be and so matches a "norm." It is used
> literally of actual objects when they are, or do, what they are sup-
> posed to [e.g., accurate weights and measures, Lev. 19:36; Deut.
> 25:15; straight paths, Ps. 23:3]. So it comes to mean . . . "right-
> eousness" in a very wide sense. (Wright 1983:134)

The second Hebrew root, related to *justice*, is *spt*:

> It can mean: to act as a law giver; to act as a judge by arbitrating
> between parties in a dispute; to pronounce judgment, declaring
> guilty and innocent respectively; to execute judgment in carrying
> out the legal consequences of such a verdict. (Wright 1983:134)

Also:

> The whole process of litigation, or its end result of verdict and its
> execution; it can mean a legal ordinance, usually case law, based
> on past precedents (Ex. 21—23 . . .); it can also be used in a more
> personal sense as one's legal right, the cause or case one is bring-
> ing as a plaintiff . . . what needs to be done in a given situation if
> people and circumstances are to be restored. (Wright 1983:134)

Justice and righteousness in the Bible are attributes of God, and his
throne is established on these attributes (Isa. 5:16; Ps. 89:14.). "God
reveals what he is by what he does. His righteousness is known to us
because he rules the world in righteousness and justice. Whatever God
does is, by definition, righteous" (Wright 1983:136; Pss. 9:16; 11:7; 96:13;
98:2, 9; and Gen. 18:25.). God's concern for justice in the world as its
sovereign creator (Mott 1992:6; Ps. 99:1–4) is presented in the Bible as
rooted in his intrinsic nature and character. Justice in the Bible is thus
not "a mere idea, norm or moral good. It is a trait of the most high God

himself" (van der Walt 1980:112). God's righteousness and justice, and other closely related attributes, including holiness *(qodesh)*, steadfast love *(hesed)*, truth *(emeth)*, and faithfulness *(emunah)*, are transcendent; they qualify God's essential "otherness" from humanity. These intrinsic attributes of God's character pervade all God's qualities and acts. God in his very nature is both the ultimate standard of righteousness and justice and the one who ultimately decides and executes what is right and just (Isa. 5:16).

The biblical conception of justice refers "not so much to a state of affairs . . . but to an activity—the activity of putting right a disordered or disproportioned state of [human] affairs" (Hay 1989:79). One of the consequences of such a disordered state of human affairs is injustice, condemning large sections of society to poverty through oppression, marginalization and perversion of the law, all of which lead to and/or stem from powerlessness.

The *Oxford Declaration on Christian Faith and Economics*, produced by a group of international evangelical economists and theologians in 1990, states that in some biblical passages there is a common link of powerlessness among groups of the poor—widows, orphans, resident aliens, wage earners and slaves—who suffer, among other things, social conflict and social wrong. "The justice called forth [in the Bible includes the aim] to restore these groups to the provision God intends for them" (no. 38). In other words, biblical justice is mandatory for the entire human society, which must act to bring justice to those suffering injustice in all aspects of human life.

> One essential characteristic of Biblical justice is the meeting of basic needs . . . not just for life but for life in society. . . . Justice requires special attention to the weak members of the community because of their greater vulnerability. . . . Justice is so fundamental that it characterises the personal virtues and personal relationships of individuals as they faithfully follow God's standards. . . . Justice requires conditions such that each person is able to participate in society in a way compatible with human dignity. Absolute poverty, where people lack even minimal food and housing, basic education, health care and employment, denies people the basic economic resources necessary for just participation in community. Corrective action with and on behalf of the poor is a necessary act of justice. This entails responsibilities for individuals, families,

churches, and governments. . . . Justice may also require socio-political actions that enable the poor to help themselves and be the subjects of their own development and the development of their communities. (*Oxford Declaration*, nos. 38–41)

Justice is vital for the moral and civil functioning of any human society. It is vital to personal virtues and human relationships; for human dignity, personal confidence and capacity to participate in social life; for compassion necessary to intervene in preventing or alleviating extreme suffering of others; and for the empowerment of the poor to change their situation and become contributing members of the community. Justice, as an ideal for all human society and a goal for nations and communities to work toward, compensates for the reality of human fallenness.

Communitarian and compensatory or remedial justice involves "doing what is required to make it possible for everybody to belong in the community." "People should get no more nor less than they deserve. Good must be rewarded, and evil must be punished" (Wogaman 1990:20). But here Wogaman fails to capture the point of the *Oxford Declaration*, that justice is empowering. Making "possible for everybody to belong in community" can be achieved while still attaining all the inequalities that deny empowerment to the poor. Although the Bible does indeed speak of rewarding good and punishing evil, biblical justice is not measured strictly according to what individuals "deserve," especially as called forth for the poor. Measuring justice as individuals deserve necessarily involves an in-built bias against the poor, who may find themselves deserving nothing.

Mott, in turn, describes biblical justice as "the correction of the situation in which the strong have exploitive power over the weak. In deliverance the people are returned to the situation of life which God intends for them. Justice is a restoration to community." He views this justice as a community empowering concept—the community takes responsibility to make its weaker members "strong again, restoring them to participate in community" (Mott 1992:8; also Lev. 25:35–36). Mott further views God's justice as "the model of justice oriented to the needy" (Mott 1992:6; Pss. 35:10; 146:9). What Mott says makes considerable sense in light of the fact that the justice required in the Bible recognizes that the poor have been wronged; hence justice needs to be oriented to them as the ones in need of compensatory justice.

Justice and Love—Opposed or Compatible?

Separation of justice and *agape*, Hughes argues, is impossible since both are attributes of the one God. It is inconceivable to think that "God has to choose between being just . . . or [loving]: if He chooses to be just, He must be unloving; if He chooses to be [loving] He must be unjust" (Hughes 1983:50). Joseph Fletcher also claims that "Love and Justice are the same, for Justice is Love distributed [and] nothing else" (quoted in Outka 1972:85). Indeed, Jesus' teaching expresses the way in which law and *agape* can be held together. Jesus maintains that fulfillment of the Law is expressed by loving him and the Father. In Matthew 22:35–40 Jesus summarizes the Old Testament Decalogue of Exodus 20 and asserts that love for God and neighbor fulfills the whole Law. Paul, in Romans 13:8–10 and Galatians 5:13–14, also takes up the summary of the second part of the Law relating to loving one's neighbor: "therefore love is the fulfilling of the law" (Rom. 13:10b).

Love, then, is the dynamic principle in fulfillment of the Law. "The true observance of the Law engages the very heart of man's being. External conformity must spring from the innermost source of love" (Hughes 1983:49).

Justice divorced from love deteriorates into a mere calculation of interests and finally into a cynical balancing of power against power. Without love societies lack the push and pull from their members to move them to greater approximations of justice. Love forces a recognition of the other's needs. Love judges abuses of justice. Love lends passion to justice. Finally, in so far as love is already victorious over sin, it is a powerful force preparing the ground for justice by making us open to the needs and interests of others. Justice, in short, is love worked out in arenas where the needs of each individual are impossible to know. (Stivers 1984:118)

Both justice and love need to be applied to the powerless, to those who need to be empowered as well as those who wield oppressive power and perpetuate injustice. For justice to be rightly applied, it must occur within the context of *agape* love—divine unconditional love that necessarily leads to neighborly love.

Social justice in the Bible is based on the idea of neighborly love predicated on the doctrine of creation and redemption (all human beings are creatures made in God's image; all, then, are in principle redeemed by Christ and destined for fellowship with God). Neighborly love is concerned with and disposed to promote the welfare of people in general, as a group or groups, directly or indirectly. This is what social justice is about. The aim of social justice based on a system of laws is to secure order and to create a framework in which people may live with dignity in community and carry out their purposes. Without neighborly love—as a biblical concept—we cannot determine adequately what is just. Natural law is not enough, because its basis in reason cannot ensure it against human sin and prejudice, and class or other special interest. Human use of reason is partially vitiated by sin. The key to justice lies in its *purpose*. This purpose, as revealed in Jesus, is the common good of all, and the ultimate good of all beings created in God. We cannot fully understand this purpose without reference to the revelation of that purpose through God's covenant with Israel and then supremely through the redemption of all human beings by Christ.

Biblical justice is actually an enactment of the character of God. Application of justice in the Bible is explicitly described in Jeremiah 31:31–34, which Jesus enacts by the shedding of his blood on the cross.

Application in Israel

Israel, as the Bible's case study of God's righteousness and justice in application, demonstrates the way justice is to be applied. In the Exodus account of the enslaved (wronged) nation of Israel, God demonstrates his justice as deliverance.

> In the midst of oppression God takes sides and brings the oppressed to security and well-being. . . . [People are delivered] from political and economic oppressors (Judg. 5:11), from slavery (1 Sam. 12:7; Mic. 6:5), and from captivity (Isa. 41:1–11 . . . Jer. 51:10). Providing for the needy means setting them back on their feet, giving [them] a home, leading to prosperity, restoration, ending oppression (Ps. 68:5–10; 10:15–18). Justice removes oppression, it does not merely help the victims of oppression to cope within it. (Mott 1992:7)

Israel's existence was founded on God's righteousness and justice. Therefore, God expected Israel to demonstrate imitative justice. "Having been put 'right,' . . . they were to maintain righteousness. Having experienced justice, they were to 'do justice'" (Wright 1983:142). Israel was to model to other nations the application of God's justice, especially as an expression of gratitude for deliverance by God from the oppression and injustice they had suffered (cf. Samuel and Sugden 1991b:172). Specific social structures and arrangements were to ensure just economic and social relationships required by the just character of their God, embodied in the covenant given to them in Deuteronomy 10:12–22.

The Law and the Prophets provided God's charter for the ordering of society. God gave the Law, in particular the Decalogue, to preserve the rights and freedoms gained in the Exodus. Israel had to translate these into responsibility toward God and one another, so that the people could live in wholeness, total welfare, and a state of soundness and harmony, that is, in the *shalom* that God originally desired for humanity. The Law, especially the Deuteronomic Law, was addressed to, and gave regulations and put limits on, those in authority, including kings, whose responsibility it was to administer justice (Deut. 16:18–20; 17:14–20; also Prov. 31:8–9). Many times those in authority violated God's law.

> They took care of themselves and not the sheep, they failed to take care of the weak, the sick, the hurt and the lost. They ate the best grass and trampled what they could not eat. They muddied the waters they could not drink. So God raised up prophets . . . to recover and make relevant the law's emphasis on justice which the kings had forgotten. (Samuel and Sugden 1991b:174)

When rulers and leaders failed in their accountability to the people, God raised the prophets to challenge them to fulfill their duties. The prophetic message was therefore an outcry of God's disgust at Israel's rulers' failure to observe the Law and their apostasy in leading people away from their God. The prophets linked this failure to the failure of Israel to "know" their God (Isa. 1:3ff.; Hos. 4:1ff.), resulting in gross social injustice and great wickedness. The ideal for Israel was to know God, as expressed through the practice of justice (Jer. 22:13–19; Job 29:12–17). The Jeremiah passage inveighs against the king of Israel who exploits his subjects by inordinate personal demands at the cost of great oppression to everyone else.

> To know God is not to engage in private piety or subscribe to certain orthodox statements or worship correctly on the Sabbath. "To know God is to do justice." Conversely, the sign of not knowing God is to do injustice. The one who does injustice . . . is, in effect, an atheist, denying God by the quality of life that puts having a beautiful palace above concern for persons. (Brown 1978:91)

Social injustice is therefore always bound up with religious apostasy. The prophets' denunciation of injustice and idolatry was contingent on the fact that injustice is a direct denial of God's character of justice— justice that he yearned to see expressed among his people. The prophets condemned conspicuous accumulation of wealth by the rich and their affluent lifestyle (Isa. 5:8; 58:4–7; Mic. 2:1–2; Amos 6:4–7). The prophets also condemned oppression of the poor, including the weak and vulnerable widows and orphans, the dispossessed and the victimized (Isa. 3:14–15; 10:1–2; Jer. 22: Amos 8:4–14; 2 Sam. 12; 1 Kings 22). What the Bible calls for, through the prophetic message in particular, is clearly revealed to have a deep-seated and fundamental bias in favor of the poor. Jeremiah succinctly refers to Josiah, one of the "good" kings of Israel: "Did not [he] eat and drink and do justice and righteousness? Then it was well with him. He judged the cause of the poor and needy; then it was well. Is not this to know me? says the LORD." (Jer. 22:15b-16).

This biblical bias toward the poor is often misinterpreted to mean that God has a favorable bias toward the poor per se, that is, that it is virtuous to be poor, and therefore God loves the poor more and gives them more than their just claims. This, however, is not the case. God gives special attention to the poor because they are the wronged victims of chronic injustice, which God detests and demands to have redressed. The content of prophetic messages against oppression and injustice in the Bible confirms that much of the poverty in Old Testament times is attributable to injustice and oppression. Such injustice and oppression make people powerless. God gives the poor priority because "their wretchedness requires greater attention if equal regard called forth by equal merit of all persons in the community is to be achieved" (Mott 1992:6). God's justice demands that those who cannot by themselves secure their own rights be vindicated. Concern for the basic needs of all calls for equal provision of basic rights, which in turn requires unequal response to unequal needs; justice must be partial in order to be impartial.

Justice Fulfilled in Jesus

In Isaiah 11 there is talk of the future establishment of God's perfect *shalom* as the climax of the enactment of God's perfect justice. The prophets talked of God establishing a new covenant of forgiveness through a new king. According to the New Testament, although the ultimate fulfillment of this prophecy with regard to the establishment of God's true and perfect justice is still in the future, the new king has already come in Jesus. Jesus enacts the new covenant of forgiveness in continuation of the Old Testament concern for the poor (Isa. 61:1–2), which he applies to himself (in Luke 4:18–19, 21). The passage in Jeremiah (31:31–34) about the new covenant, viewed then as a future hope, becomes a present reality in Jesus: "God can 'now' be known" (Brown 1978:92).

Jesus came at a time when Jewish society was characterized by social oppression sanctioned and reinforced by religion. Legalistic interpretation of the Law by the Pharisees, teachers of the Law, resulted in oppression, harsh treatment and discrimination against certain groups of people, such as the sick, who were thought to be receiving their just reward for their sins; Gentiles and lepers who were hated as unclean; Samaritans and tax-collectors who were regarded as national enemies; and women, who were treated as inferior to men. Jesus sought to include all the people in these groups into the new people of God, to demonstrate the ethics of God's kingdom. Jesus went beyond justice as it was construed by his society, which demanded that wrong be denounced and the guilty punished without mercy. Jesus' ministry sought to incorporate all the outcasts into society and empowered them to participate in a new community. He reached out across barriers of social and religious scruple and tradition and extended forgiveness and fellowship in the name of Israel's God, to create justice through proper relationships between people. He called for repentance from distorted relationships by open challenges to injustice. He challenged lack of compassion in the name of religion: by healing on the Sabbath (Luke 6:1–11); and by his involvement and commitment to the outcasts and the hated, such as lepers (Luke 5:13), women (Luke 7:36–50), Samaritans

(Luke 10:30–37), tax-collectors (Luke 19:1–10) (Samuel and Sugden 1991b:177).

Throughout his teaching, Jesus was preoccupied with outlining the requirements for the new people of God. He was not abolishing the old Law; rather, he was fulfilling the Law. His Sermon on the Mount succinctly summarized his teaching. Among those requirements, God's people "were to demonstrate that they were free from greed, hate, resentment, lust, dishonesty, and the will to dominate and manipulate others. Jesus taught them to share their goods, to forgo retaliation, to help anyone in need whose path they crossed and to be at all times servants" (Samuel and Sugden 1991b:177). Brown adds, "Jesus is not offering mere information about cosmic reality, but empowerment to 'do justice', for that is what it means to 'know God' under the terms of the 'new covenant' which his death ushers in" (1978:92). Jesus' ministry was thus empowerment. He empowered not only outcasts, by restoring them into society in a way that enabled them to become full participants, but also oppressors by challenging them to turn to God—a change empowering them to do justice and create a just society.

Justice in the Epistles

The Epistles express the practical application of Jesus' ministry. Jesus' death and resurrection make possible the reconciliation of human beings to God and to each other. The central message of the Epistles is that salvation from distorted relationships to God and to one another is possible only by God's grace through faith in Christ's death. Paul observed the oppressiveness of wrong relationships between Jews and Gentiles, men and women, free and slaves. Paul went on to show how God established justice and demonstrated that all are equal heirs in the sight of God, for Jesus died for all. Justice thus implies establishing right relationships among people and removal of all barriers of status and class distinctions (Gal. 3:28). The church's role is to effect reconciliation with God and among people (2 Cor. 5:17–18). Proper relationships between people ensure justice for all. In fact, the early church founded a whole new system of distribution which encouraged giving and receiving according to ability and need. Resources were shared and freely given for the good of the body, rather than for individual advantage (Acts 4:32–35; 2 Cor. 8:1–5; Jeune 1987:222).

Does this mean that God's justice is directed to and must be exercised by only the church and Jews? No, because God as the Creator of all people gives his guiding principles to all people, without distinction. God's justice is universal to all his creation.

Universality of God's Justice

Is God concerned for justice to non-Jewish nations or the unchurched? The answer to this is that God's justice concerns all nations and all peoples on the earth. The Bible affirms God to be the Sovereign Lord over all nations and peoples as the creator. God "has not only made the universe but he has revealed many of its guiding principles. All men can have some knowledge, however distorted, of these, and all men are accountable to their Maker for the way in which they have sought to obey them" (Nixon 1978:114–15). God, the Moral Governor of the world, has provided guiding principles for the ordering of life in every society.

It would be reasonable to expect the existence of some generally shared morality that establishes common agreement on what is right and wrong for social cohesion (see Mitchell 1967:20). But human nature, distorted by the Fall, introduces such differences in human need (to which moral law or justice must respond) that this general truth, that some shared morality is essential to the existence of society, finds different conceptual expressions that tend to conflict in practice. This has resulted in the existence of a number of different theories of justice. Wogaman (1990), referring to six theories of justice dealt with by Lebacqz, identifies two categories into which these six theories fall: those grounded primarily on philosophy (Mill, Rawls, or Rozick); and those grounded on theology (such as theories put forth by the U.S. National Conference of Catholic Bishops, Niebuhr, or Miranda). Of the philosophers who developed highly influential theories of justice—namely Plato, Aristotle, the Stoics, Hobbes, Rousseau, Hegel and Marx—none depended on Christian theological views. But Wogaman observes that when Christians articulate a rational structure of justice theory, they must inevitably make use of reflections exploring actual causal relationships in the workings of human society in a secular context, which no theory can ignore. "The Patristic writings, for example," he writes, "appear to make substantial use of Plato and Stoicism. St Thomas Aquinas was very dependent upon Aristotle. Many Liberation theologians use Marx.

Neo-conservative theologians and ethicists are heavily indebted to Locke and Adam Smith" (Wogaman 1990:18). Dodd corroborates this: "Petrine and Pauline valuation of the *communis* sensus hominum" was a possible derivation from Stoicism. He also describes Jesus' Sermon on the Mount in Matthew 5:44–48 as resembling "what may be called a Stoic commonplace" (Dodd 1946:162–63). This evidence affirms biblical teaching that God's justice according to the doctrine of natural law can in principle be "known quite apart from grace despite the darkening of man's intellectual capacities by the Fall" (Schrey et al. 1955:119).

> There is an undeniable affinity between the law of the covenant in the Old Testament and the other forms of ancient oriental law, as also between the apostolic injunctions in the New Testament and Stoic morals. In both cases the relationship . . . shows a certain overlap in content, and therefore we may say that the Bible bears witness to a certain degree of knowledge about God's will which is not directly derived from his covenant with Israel. (Schrey et al. 1955:120)

The point is that this revelation has an all-embracing character that corresponds to the all-embracing and all-sovereign being of God, the Creator and Preserver of all. Reasoned human knowledge, in particular that which comes to expression in legal and juridical systems, "has a relationship to God's revelation which the authors of the Wisdom literature tried to express" (Schrey et al. 1955:132–33).

Philosophy by itself provides no solid basis as the ultimate reality for making judgment. In contrast, the Bible presents a concept of justice based on the character of an immutable and infinite God, fount of all wisdom and understanding.

> Justice is rooted in the very being of God . . . justice divorced from love deteriorates into a mere calculation of interests and finally into a cynical balancing of power against power. (Stivers 1984:117–18)

The problematic connection of law with the quest for power, which is the way of the world without God, is forcibly demonstrated in the biblical account of the condemnation of Jesus (Schrey et al. 1955:123).

In the Old Testament, the covenant God made with Noah (Gen. 9:1–17) was between God and all creation. "The writer . . . was quite deliberate in emphasizing, all through, the universality of [this] covenant—all mankind, every living creature, the earth itself are party to it" (Dodd 1946:164). In Genesis 22:18 God promises to bless all nations through Abraham. Thereafter, God promises to use Israel as a nation to be a light or model of his purposes and laws to other nations. God's laws to Israel as a society were an indication of his concern for justice for the whole of his creation. In fact, the prophetic message of God's judgment for failure to keep the law was directed to other nations as well (Amos 1—2:3; Ezek. 27, 28), indicating those nations must have known such laws. A number of other Old Testament passages address people and nations outside of Israel as the people of God; for example, the Book of Job; Jeremiah 8:7; Isaiah 1:3.

> The Wisdom literature bears witness to the fact that there were general principles about moral ordering of things which could be cast in the form of maxims applying to all men. The categories of law are not normally used, but the idea of universal principles underlying conduct is easily extended to a concept of duty extending to all. (Nixon 1987:115)

In the New Testament Gospels, Jesus' own ministry, although primarily directed to Jews, was concerned to include all people in his teaching. In his pronouncements he expected these truths to be discernible by all, if only they were willing to discern them. In Jesus' own life he submitted to the valid laws and judicial practice of both Jews and Romans.

In Acts and the Epistles, Paul first (in Acts 17:22–31) declares that God is sovereign over all nations and has issued a universal call to repentance in the face of coming world judgment: "He has fixed a day on which he will have the world judged in righteousness" (Acts 17:31). In Romans, Paul reiterates the universality of God's law in discussing Gentiles: "For what can be known about God is plain to them, because God has shown it to them" (Rom. 1:19). Gentiles, therefore, rightly fall under God's judgment. They are "without excuse" in idolatrous perversion of God's law (Rom. 1:18–32; cf. Wisd. 12:23—13:9). Romans 2:14–15 affirms that those without the Law still show its effects through their consciences and reasoning. Paul's argument is thus that both Jews and Gentiles are responsible to God. "God has revealed to them certain basic facts about his own nature and the sort of moral response that he requires in men" (Nixon 1978:118).

> The Bible . . . does not measure the laws of the nations by reference to some 'natural law' which is a constitutive element in human life external to the revelation of God. The law known among the nations is the law which is grounded in the claim of God which is his Word, that is to say, in the universal confrontation of all men by the self-revealing God. (Schrey et al. 1955:135)

In the Bible God establishes justice for all his creation calling for good relationships between human beings and God, among human beings themselves, and between human beings and creation. Moral philosophers in their notions of justice are not entirely without God's law. But human philosophy is affected by the Fall and fails to align fully with God's revelation for justice, according to the Bible. God's direct revelation is neither totally contrary nor totally opposed to natural conceptions of justice, because the Redeemer and Creator asserts that creation works best when his universal laws of justice are carried out.

In summary, justice in the Bible is not an abstract concept of some standard. It is rooted in the character of God and is an activity of God in restoring human affairs rendered disordered and disproportionate by the Fall. God's justice requires equality, that is, equal treatment for everybody; there are no second-rate beings. Human responsibility requires accepting each other as equals and reflecting God's character of justice.

In application, biblical justice is shown in Jesus to be empowering, whereby people are treated with equity and fairness. This is the measure of effective holistic empowerment that communities should aim for. Those who are marginalized and excluded from resources and power are to be emancipated and given access to such resources and power, both of which belong ultimately to God. Jesus requires the justified to engage in imitative justice learned from his example and teaching.

> Because the Christian pays respect to the law in Christ, he will follow Jesus in his denunciation of mistaken notions of just dealing. He will be ready to criticize any legal attitude which neglects the weightier matters of the law, judgment, mercy and faithfulness,

by pettifogging insistence on the trivialities (Matt. 23.23). . . . He will challenge self-gratification . . . (Luke 17.10). He will find means to rebuke the wiliness, and the inhuman self-righteousness . . . (John 8.1–11). He will know the mind of the early church, which found no room for discrimination between races, classes or sexes (Gal. 3.28). (Schrey et al. 1955:125)

5

Combating Poverty
in the Bible

*P*oor and *rich* are correlative terms in that a causal relationship can exist between them; that is, one person may be rich because another is poor, or the poverty of one person may be the riches of another. In fact, in the Bible these terms tend to occur together as opposites. Though both poverty and riches may sometimes result from unrelated causes, in many cases the two appear directly and causally linked. Conrad Boerma maintains that "poverty and riches are not independent phenomena. One person is poor because another is rich. Poverty is not a state of deprivation which has come about by chance; it is a result of the richness of the rich" (Boerma 1979:3). Indeed, often the poverty of the poor is a direct result of the indifference, negligence, or oppressive and exploitative activities of the rich, whether at a personal level, institutional and structural levels, or the international level.

Both the poor and the rich are caught in institutions, structures and systems that foster and perpetuate poverty. Both need to be liberated, and the factors that hold them from making positive contributions toward the fight against poverty need to be eliminated through empowerment. There is need for a conscious awareness "of the way in which the relationship between rich and poor affects the development of the society in which they live," as well as to "see the intrinsic structural connection between poverty and riches" (Boerma 1979:3).

Poverty as a Scandal in the Bible

Poverty is a scourge to human life. The Bible condemns poverty as a scandalous condition and demands justice for the poor. Julio De Santa Ana, in discussing the responsibility of the rich, makes the categorical statement that poverty "is not agreeable in the sight of God, He wants an end to it" (De Santa Ana 1977:19). Jesus' gospel is a protest against the scandal of poverty and a call to eradicate it from human life. He announces the Good News of the kingdom to the poor, who are suffering from deprivation as victims of hunger and oppression.

> "Poverty is not a virtue but an evil" which constitutes a challenge to the justice of the Lord who is the King of creation. [The blessedness or] the privilege of the poor lies neither in their material circumstances nor in their spiritual disposition, but in the way in which God conceives the exercise of his Kingdom: "Blessed are the poor," not because they are better than others, or better prepared to receive the Kingdom which is to come, but because God seeks to make his Kingdom a tangible manifestation of his justice and love for the poor, the suffering and those who live in misery. (De Santa Ana 1977:17)

The idealization of poverty as a virtue in the Bible should not be understood as a *mystique* of nonpossession. Joseph Fletcher argues that the virtuous poverty referred to in the Bible is not penury or pennilessness, but rather having modest possessions.

> The Gospels do not distinguish the Haves from the Have-Nots but the Have-Too-Muches from the Have-Enoughs. The poverty they idealize means only a lack of luxuries, while destitution would be a lack of necessities. Jesus was of the poor, the modest, the minimum-income *am haaretz*. But Jesus was not one of the beggars. His people lived modestly but not desperately. (Fletcher 1960:211)

The ethical issue related to the possession of material goods is this: a built-in danger exists that people will idolize their possessions. Fletcher aptly observes, "Sometimes wealth corrupts its owners, and sometimes poverty produces piety! . . . Sometimes wealth is used by saintly people, and sometimes poverty produces aggression and greed" (Fletcher 1960:212). Poverty can be dehumanizing and can lead to distorted human behavior, stifling virtuous morals and tying individuals to vices, criminal behavior, juvenile delinquency, aggressive greed, apathy, fatalism, negative self-esteem and dependency. All these work against development, thus gnawing at the human fiber of life. This is a further reason for nontolerance of poverty in the sense of destitution.

Biblical Descriptions of the Poor

The Bible has a rich vocabulary for describing the poor and their situation. "The poor are mentioned about 245 times with six main terms which are almost always rendered in modern translations by 'poor'" (quoted in De Santa Ana 1977:10 n.i). Other scholars agree that there are between five and seven Hebrew root words from which derive terms that occur more than 200 times in the Bible to describe the poor and poverty. These are *penes, ani* or *anaw, dal, ras, ebyon, misken,* and *ptochos* (see also, e.g., Stott 1984:216; Perkins 1982:34; DNTT 1976:820–29; Boerma 1979:7–9).

Penes is a respectable poor person who is industrious; *ptochos* is a marginal poor person who does nothing beyond holding out his or her hand. In this sense *penes* is the relatively poor but enterprising person who can be helped to become self-reliant; and *ptochos* is the absolutely poor and dependent person for whom welfare services would be required. The other Hebrew terms, together with these two, define the poor in the Old Testament as the downtrodden, humiliated, oppressed, the crouching beggars with hands stretched out for justice, the weak and helpless, the destitute, the needy, the dependent, those forcibly subjected by a powerful oppressor, the socially low, and also the widows, the fatherless and strangers. In the New Testament the poor include manual workers who struggle to survive on a day-to-day basis; the destitute; those reduced to meekness; those brought low; the weak; the tired and overburdened; lepers; and very often the common people *(ochlos)*. *Ochlos* includes tax-collectors, the sick, sinners and all outcasts—those with no address or homestead or the dispossessed who could be manipulated.

Such a rich vocabulary demonstrates that the concept of poverty in the Bible carries "a wide variety of meanings and nuances" (Boerma 1979:23). It also implies the weight that the Bible attaches to this concept and the thoroughness with which it is treated, along with its causes and its consequences.

Biblical Interpretation of *Poor*

In both the Old Testament and the New Testament *poor* describes both the specific case of the poor in spirit and the more general case of the socioeconomically poor.

The Poor in Spirit

In Isaiah 66:2 the Lord says, "But this is the one to whom I will look, to the humble and contrite in spirit [*ani uneceh ruah*], who trembles at my word." In this sense Moses is described as the poorest *(anaw)* of men (Num. 12:3), poverty *(anawah)* should be desired (Zeph. 2:3), and the messianic king is declared poor *(ani)* (Zech. 9:9) (Jones and Conn 1978:219). According to Stott, the poor in spirit are those spiritually meek and dependent on God. "Since God succours the destitute and defends the powerless, these truths inevitably affect their attitude to him. They look to him for mercy. Oppressed by men and helpless to liberate themselves, they put their trust in God. It is in this way that 'the poor' came to be synonymous with 'the pious', and their social condition became a symbol of their spiritual dependence" (Stott 1984:219). The Bible describes "a people humble and lowly [who] seek refuge in the name of the LORD" (Zeph. 3:12; see also 2:3), and "the humble and contrite in spirit who trembles at my word" (Isa. 66:2; 49:13). In the psalms expressions of the dependence of the poor upon God come into sharp focus, and so too do God's promises to come and help the poor (e.g., Pss. 25:16; 34:1–6, 15–18; 37:5, 7, 11; 40:1; 86:1–14, 14–17; 149:4).

The poor in spirit are aware of their need for God's pardon. They are sinners who nevertheless keep the Lord's covenant and wait on him (Ps. 25:8–10, 21). They are the righteous who are blessed by the Lord and who wait for him and keep his ways (Ps. 37:9, 22, 29, 34). In the New Testament they are the upright and devout who watched and waited for the restoration of Israel and the liberation of Jerusalem, like Simeon and Anna (in Luke 2:25–38) (Escobar 1982:103). "Their faithfulness to the Lord means waiting for his coming in 'humility and poverty'" (De Santa Ana 1977:7).

Spiritual poverty is thus an attitudinal condition. It is as possible for the materially rich to be "poor in spirit" as it is for the materially poor to not be "poor in spirit." In other words, "spiritual poverty" is not to be equated with indifference to material things of the world but rather refers to a voluntary and loving submission to the will of God.

The Socioeconomic Poor

There have been attempts to interpret all biblical terms regarding the poor to refer chiefly to spiritual poverty. This overspiritualization, even to the extent of making destitution look desirable, arises from interpreting in isolation Jesus' teaching of the first beatitude in Matthew 5:3. "Blessed are the poor in spirit, for theirs is the kingdom of heaven" seemingly portrays poverty as a spiritual condition unrelated to social and political phenomena. But closer scrutiny of Jesus' teaching in the context of the whole New Testament discloses something different—that the poor of whom Jesus spoke were not primarily the poor in spirit. In the Lukan tradition, for example, the poor are those who are "really poor . . . really hungry . . . who really weep and are persecuted. The poor are oppressed, [harassed and helpless like sheep without a shepherd], afflicted and cannot defend themselves against the powerful" (Jones and Conn 1978:216).

Stott's analysis of the poor in the Bible identifies three conditions of poverty: the humble poor (or the poor in spirit already mentioned), the indigent poor and the oppressed poor. The latter two groups, the socioeconomic poor, are those deprived of the basic necessities of life and the powerless victims of human injustice, or the socio-politically marginalized poor, who also suffer from structural poverty (Stott 1984: 216).

Biblical teaching asserts God's concern for the literally poor as well as their centrality in Jesus' mission (as prophesied by Isa. 61:1, 2) and confirmed by Jesus as he focused his ministry on the poor and identified with them in his life and death. Additionally, Scripture recognizes two levels of socioeconomic poverty, in which some of the poor are industrious and need only some assistance to become self-sustaining, and some are dependent and need welfare assistance. Both could be assisted by empowered institutions and structures and community organizations in public and private sectors and in civil society.

Poverty in Ancient Israel

The children of Israel start as oppressed slaves in Egypt suffering severe economic oppression, from which God frees them. When the children of Israel were wandering nomads in the wilderness, there appear to have been few class distinctions among them, though they had leaders. They all ate the same manna from heaven, and it was recorded that "he who gathered much did not have too much, and he who gathered little did not have too little. Each one gathered as much as he needed" (Exod. 16:18; 2 Cor. 8:15). This suggests a socioeconomic balance of consumption. This is still said to be the case with most nomadic communities (Von Waldow 1970:186).

When Israel ceased its wandering and settled as a farming nation, archeological evidence shows there was uniformity in the manner of constructing houses, implying similar standards of living throughout the community. "Excavations in Israelite towns bear witness to this equality in standards of living. At Tirsh . . . houses of the 10th century B.C. are all of the same size and arrangement. Each represents the dwelling of a family which lived in the same way as its neighbours" (De Vaux 1968:72f.). However, as time progressed, economic development inevitably led to differentiation. People with means began to acquire land and private possessions, and "poverty emerged as a social problem. Social tensions increased . . . [with] the development of the army and the monarchy along the lines parallel to the patterns among neighbouring peoples. Different social groups came into being with conflicting interests" (Boerma 1979:23). Israel's kings committed all the exploitative and oppressive acts Samuel had warned the children of Israel about (1 Sam. 8:10–18). "Slowly but surely, poverty ceased to be a purely material circumstance and was seen as a sign of inferiority. It was experienced as exploitation. To an increasing degree, the poor man became the victim of oppression" (Boerma 1979:23).

Other Causes of Material Poverty

The Bible writers provided a variety of other causes of poverty, including sometimes interpreting poverty as the fault of the poor person. "Under Herod, the Pharisees parted company more and more with the mass of the population. It is better to suffer than to be poor, one of them wrote. The poor man was compared with the leper, the blind, the childless, even with the dead. Poverty is a curse" (Boerma 1979:25). In other words, poverty was seen as punishment from God, as in the case of a transgressor of the law (Deut. 28:15–46; Lev. 26:14–26) or an evildoer (Isa. 3:16–24; 14:1; 5:9–10). Thus, material poverty in the Bible could result from either self-imposed or externally imposed factors.

Self-Imposed Poverty

In Scripture, self-caused factors resulting from humanity's own sinfulness and rebellion against God's law could include laziness or sloth (Prov. 6:6–11; 10:5; 19:15, 24; 20:13; 21:17, 25, 26; 22:13; 24:30–34; 26:13); greed, gluttony or extravagance and drunkenness (Prov. 21:17; 23:21; Jer. 6:12, 13); foolishness (Hos. 4:6; Ps. 106:13–15; Prov. 10:14–16; 11:14; 13:18); idleness (Prov. 14:23; Eccles. 10:18; 1 Thess. 5:14), worthless pursuits or pleasure-seeking (Prov. 12:11; 21:17; 23:20, 21; 28:19); or shortsightedness (Prov. 21:5; Matt. 7:24–27; Luke 14:28–30). These sorts of cases are also recorded in the Wisdom literature of other peoples and reflect observations on the human experience still relevant today (Beisner 1988:195; De Santa Ana 1977:1).

Externally Imposed Poverty

Externally imposed poverty in Scripture is "an involuntary social evil to be abolished not tolerated," and the poor—particularly widows, orphans and aliens—are "people to be succoured not blamed. They are regarded not as sinners but as the sinned-against" (Stott 1984:217).

External factors due to the corruption of the earth include such acts of nature as floods, droughts, famines, earthquakes and epidemics; there are also those due to human action or neglect. Poverty due to human neglect is condemned just as much as that resulting from direct action.

Individual acts of negligence and/or directly willed actions of oppression and exploitation of other individuals or groups are described in various ways: the wicked mock the poor (Prov. 17:5); the greedy hate their neighbors and oppress the neighbor for money (Prov. 14:20, 21; 22:16). Beisner observes that in some cases, especially in terms of negligence, poverty results from violation of clear provisions of God's law, for example, laws requiring generosity to the poor (Deut. 14:19; 15:7ff.; Lev. 25:35ff.; 26:12; Ps. 111:1–9; Prov. 14:20ff.; Job 31:16ff.; Ezek. 16:49);

those requiring the keeping of pledges made to the poor (Exod. 22:25ff.; Lev. 25:36f.; Deut. 24:10f.); and those demanding prompt payments of wages, or concerned with gleanings and share of harvest (Exod. 23:10f.; Lev. 19:9; 25; Deut. 14:28ff.; 16:9ff.; 24:14ff.; 26:12ff.). In other cases poverty results from violation of justice, either in acts "of civil rulers" who refuse to defend the rights of the poor in courts of justice (Job 24:1–12; Isa. 1:21, 23; Amos 5:10, 12, 13) or who violate justice them-selves (Isa. 10:1, 2; Prov. 28:15, 16) (Beisner 1988:196).

Scripture says God cares when people do not care about the poor, or when they oppress and exploit others. The people of Israel were given a stern warning by God regarding how to care for the poor as they were entering the Promised Land (Deut. 15:7–11). Further warnings (e.g., Deut. 16:19, 20 and also the Wisdom literature) cited future rewards or damnation directly related to the way individuals treated the poor. The manner in which Israel treated the poor reflected its allegiance to and treatment of the Lord, their God (Prov. 14:31; 19:17; 3:27f.; 11:24, 25; see also Luke 16:19–31).

The prophets declare in very strong language the manner of direct acts of oppression that the poor suffered. In Amos, the rich are depicted as those "who *trample* the head of the poor into the dust of the earth, and push the afflicted out of the way" (2:7); and the rich "*trample* on the poor and take from them levies of grain" (5:11). The rich build their lifestyle on oppression of the poor (6:1–7). Rich women—the prophet calls them "cows"—"oppress the poor," "*crush* the needy" and incite their husbands to more oppression of the poor to sustain their con-spicuous consumption (4:1). Furthermore, the rich subvert justice by bribing judges so that the poor are denied justice in courts (5:10–15) (Sider 1977:56). Upon all these individual acts of oppression divine judg-ment was pronounced by the prophets. Affluence built on oppression was to end with exile (Amos 6:7). To the rich women the pronounce-ment is this: "The LORD God has sworn by his holiness: The time is surely coming upon you, when they shall take you away with hooks, even the last of you with fishhooks. Through breaches in the wall you shall leave" (Amos 4:2–3). The rich are warned thus: "You have built houses of hewn stone, but you shall not live in them; you have planted pleasant vineyards, but you shall not drink their wine" (Amos 5:11).

Scripture condemns personal acts of oppression. But human action also leads to structural and institutionalized social, economic, political and legal forms of oppression that result in systemic or structural poverty that the poor are unable to change. Structural poverty also results from institutional arrangements that either completely neglect issues concerning the poor or function in ways that directly contribute to increased poverty. Such structural poverty is also loathed by God and condemned in Scripture. In Amos 2:6–7 the prophet condemns the selling of "the needy for a pair of sandals." This act is interpreted by biblical scholars as legalized oppression (Sider 1977:121). Isaiah (in 10:1–4) also speaks in more categorical terms against legislators devising unjust laws. The prophet strongly voices God's displeasure with rulers who use their official position to pass unjust laws and thereby bring about unfair but legal decisions. God detests institutionalized evil and wants justice to be maintained in the courts (Deut. 16:19, 20; Isa. 1:16, 17; Amos 5:15). Amos says, "let justice roll down like waters, and righteousness like an ever-flowing stream" (5:24). The legal system must flow without corruption, free of anything that "allows the wealthy to buy their way out of trouble but gives the poor long prison terms" (Sider 1977:122–23).

In Psalm 94 the psalmist refers to a corrupt government,

> Can wicked rulers be allied with you,
>   those who contrive mischief by statute?
> They band together against the life of the righteous,
>   and condemn the innocent to death. . . .
> He will repay them for their iniquity
>   and wipe them out for their wickedness;
>   the LORD our God will wipe them out.
>   —Psalm 94:20-21, 23

Corrupt governments create suffering among the poor by decree or statute, an abomination before God, who wills justice. God's people are therefore warned "to avoid alliances (Psalm 94:20) with wicked governmental establishments that frame mischief by statute" (Sider 1977:123).

The account of King Ahab (in 1 Kings 21) killing Naboth and taking his land is a story about a wicked ruler and unjust social institutions that God destroyed. God does not tolerate evil economic structures, oppressive social structures, wicked rulers and unjust legal systems that create and foster poverty and destroy human lives. Again and again God allowed Israel and Judah to be attacked or exiled and destroyed precisely for their economic oppressiveness, social injustice and idolatry. "The eyes of the Lord God are upon the sinful kingdom, and I will destroy it from the face of the earth" (Amos 9:8). This word was fulfilled, in the case of Israel, one generation after Amos, when the northern kingdom of Israel was completely wiped out.

Wealth in the Bible

Accumulated wealth in the Bible is denoted by two Greek words, *ploutos*, meaning "riches," and *thesauros*, meaning "treasure." In the Bible, "material wealth can also be personified as a demonic power, Mammon *(mamonas)*" (DNTT 1976:829). Riches, *ploutos*, occurs 234 times in the Bible (165 in the OT and 69 in the NT) and is defined as "abundance of earthly possessions of every kind," or "possession of goods, super-abundance of something" (DNTT 1976:840). *Plousios* means "rich" or "a rich person." "To be rich is to have an existence which is full of good things, where there are no shortages. As a result it can be called happy and blessed" (Boerma 1979:9).

Old Testament View of Wealth

In the Old Testament wealth is generally considered a sign of God's blessing. This was particularly true during the nomadic and semi-nomadic periods in Israel's history.

> There are no social differentiations in this kind of community. . . .
> In such a society private property is never used to oppress the neighbour, or, as is the case in a capitalist society, as a means to come to more property. Instead it is used generously to entertain guests and to help the poor. (Von Waldow 1970:186)

In the Pentateuch one tangible sign of Yahweh's blessing on the patriarchs was their wealth, consisting mainly of flocks and herds, children and slaves (Gen. 13:2; 30:43). Such wealth was not regarded as a private possession; it usually belonged to the family or tribe, and everyone within the tribe benefited from the prosperity of the tribe. "If one man is rich, all the members of the tribe are rich" (Boerma 1979:11). Accumulation of wealth came by way of war plunder, presents, or skill, all as a sign of God's blessing. Deuteronomy emphasizes the close connection between human actions and divine response. God's favor is shown when Israel lives and acts according to God's ordinances; God blesses Israel "in all the work you undertake" (Deut. 14:29; see also 7:13; 15:10, 18; 23:21; 24:19; 30:16). In Deuteronomy 28:1–14 wealth is a reward for obeying "the LORD your God" and "diligently observing all his commandments." During this period in Israel's history, "riches are a consequence of observing God's law" (Boerma 1979:11).

In the Wisdom literature, too, wealth is a sign of God's favor. "Where God blesses he gives numerous descendants (Pss. 112:2; 128:3f.; Job 42:13), landed property (Ps. 37:22), abundant livestock (Job 1:10; 42:12), and wealth (Ps. 112:1–3; Prov. 10:22)" (Wittenberg 1978:141).

After Israel settled in Canaan and acquired property, each family within a tribe had a share, as promised by Yahweh. Soon growth in commerce and trade led to social and economic development, bringing in their wake social differentiation. Little by little there emerged "a small upper class of the rich and influential, who . . . destroyed the people of God by injustice and violence and so brought deserved judgment on the whole people" (DNTT 1976:841).

The institution of monarchy had an added effect on socioeconomic development and resultant social differentiation. The monarchy expanded, developing new cities and royal courts and setting up mercenaries for military campaigns, which created extensive needs for crown land. 1 Samuel 8:10ff. speaks of the "ways of the king" who would "take the best of your fields and vineyards and olive orchards."

The result "was characterized by a sharp class division between the small group of wealthy landowners and the bulk of the impoverished country population" (Wittenberg 1978:145). This sharp class division led directly to the extremely critical evaluation of earthly wealth by the pre-exilic prophets. Amos, Isaiah and Micah in particular directed violent attacks at their affluent contemporaries.

> They deprecated the accumulation of wealth which is demonstrated first and foremost in expensive buildings. The well-to-do had summer and winter houses (Amos 3:15) built out of hewn stones (Amos 5:11), a building technique introduced in Israel first by Solomon, and later by Ahab in his extensive building projects in Samaria, and finally copied by the upper strata of society. The exterior of their houses was decorated with ivory (Amos 3:15) and surrounded by beautiful gardens (Isa. 1:29–31), and within they were furnished with luxurious furniture such as ivory beds

and couches (Amos 3:12; 6:4), all signs of the affluent standard of living. This is evidenced also by the quality of food which the wealthy consumed. Only the best types of meat were used (Amos 6:4), and expensive wine bowls were used for drinking (Amos 6:6; cf. also Isa. 5:11). Dress (Isa. 3:16–24) and entertainment (Isa. 5:11–12; Amos 6:4) were also characterized by luxury. (Wittenberg 1978:141–42)

The prophets' condemnation of affluence was not a criticism of wealth and enjoyment of wealth per se, but grew out of their recognition of the close link between luxury and oppression. "The condemnation of luxury is a correlate to the prophetic condemnation of social injustices, and both have to be considered together" (Wittenberg 1978:142). The message of the prophets is clear (Amos 4:1), and the link between wealth and oppression is also clear (Amos 3:9f.).

New Testament View of Wealth

In the New Testament the Pentateuch view of worldly wealth as a sign of God's favor no longer applies. Like the pre-exilic prophets, writers of the New Testament tend to view wealth with suspicion. The gospel is an "attack on the accumulation of wealth by the rich" (De Santa Ana 1977:17). For Jesus, wealth is a gift from God, and it is wrong to claim ownership and possession of what belongs to God. However, Jesus did not reject the rich. Rather he challenged them to follow the path of justice. To those who placed their hopes in wealth, Jesus' message was hard to take (see the rich ruler referred to in Luke 18:18–25); sometimes Jesus portrayed the rich as fools, as in Luke 16:13–21. His message stressed the idea that wealth leading to self-reliance and failure to acknowledge dependence on God leads to condemnation before God. Wealth easily leads to idolatry when human beings are tempted to place their trust in it and to worship abundance rather than to trust and worship God. Acceptable wealth is that which a person enjoys with trust in the providence and loving care of God, maintaining priorities and seeking "first the kingdom of God and his righteousness," so that "all these things will be given to you as well" (Matt. 6:33; cf. Luke 12:31). What Jesus says is that no one can serve two masters; no one can serve God and wealth (Luke 16:13; see also, Luke 12:22–34; Matt. 6:25–34; Luke 16:19–31).

In the Epistles, James 5:1–6 stresses that "appropriation of wealth necessarily implies some form of injustice" (De Santa Ana 1977:18). John (in 1 John 3:17) emphasizes the incompatibility between accumulation of worldly wealth and the practice of brotherly love. Paul (in 1 Tim. 6:17–19) warns those who are rich in this world's goods not to accumulate and store up wealth but to put their wealth at the disposal of the needy. In other words, the rich are exhorted that the "basic purpose of wealth is to help those who live in misery" (De Santa Ana 1977:18).

De Santa Ana argues that the "existence of poverty announces [the ruin of the rich], for they seem to place more trust in the abundance of material possessions than in God. The rich man adores money—Mammon—and his attitude is one of true idolatry which the living God cannot accept" (De Santa Ana 1977:19).

Dangers of Wealth

Dangers posed by wealth include preventing people from faithfully listening to and obeying God's Word, thus causing them to forget God; hindering people from entering God's kingdom; rendering people insensitive to the ultimate Day of Judgment, when Christ returns; subjecting people to powerful temptations; offering false security; and promoting greed, covetousness and selfishness, which lie at the root of worsening inequality.

Idolatry of wealth arises from the error of equating *being* with *having*, and *identity* and *worth* with possessions. People see the security given by possessions as their god, and they cling to possessions for their identity and worth (Johnson 1981:80). Both the Old and New Testaments warn that accumulation of possessions will lead to forgetting God as the giver to be reverenced, that wealth chokes out people's faith in God (Deut. 6:10–12; 8:13, 14). Proverbs 30:9 offers a prayer to avoid falling into the trap into which Jeshurun (Deut. 32:15) and the man in Psalm 52:7 have stumbled.

The Gospels (Matt. 13:22; Mark. 4:19; and Luke. 8:14) point out that riches and the pleasures of life can choke the growth of faith among those who initially listened to God's Word. The story of the rich man and his five brothers (Luke 16:19–31) is an example of people so enmeshed in their affluence that they were unable to listen to Scripture (the Law and the Prophets) and be saved. The story of the rich fool (in Luke 12:13–21, especially v. 21) is an example of those who store up treasures on earth for themselves, but who do not become rich in the sight of God. Matthew 6:21 adds that where a person's treasure is, that is where his or her heart will be also.

The rich and self-righteous may be so fascinated by their earthly riches and possessions that they are unable to see beyond, to realize their need for God; instead, they regard their lives and property as their own, thereby violating God's lordship and their own role as responsible stewards of God-given wealth (Nurnberger 1978:155; Pilgrim 1981:112). "As the response to God is the most fundamental of all responses," people should acknowledge that life comes from God, that their "identity and worth are established, not by what [they] can seize, but by what has been given to [them] in grace" (Johnson 1981:80). No one should define himself or herself by possessions or any other idol.

God's Kingdom

Passages in the Gospels (Matt. 19:23; Mark 10:24; Luke 18:24) speak of wealth as an insurmountable barrier to entry into God's kingdom. Jesus uses hyperbole—that it is easier for a camel to pass through the eye of a needle than for a rich person to enter God's kingdom. The point is the incompatibility between abundance of riches and faithful discipleship (Pilgrim 1981:120). The parable of the great banquet (Matt. 22:1–10; Luke 14:15–24) shows how earthly concerns make people unconcerned about the invitation to the kingdom.

Impending eschatological reversal—in which comfortable conditions of the rich give way to harshness, while those of the poor who are struggling in hardship now become easy—is particularly well expressed by the woes to the rich (Luke 6:24–26), preceded by the blessings of the poor (Luke 6:20–23). Judgment, in the form of woes, is pronounced upon the rich, those who are "filled" and highly esteemed by others. These people enjoy privileged social and economic status. In Luke, no specific charges are raised, such as gluttony, dissipation, or oppression. Nonetheless, the life of the rich stands under divine judgment, and on the Day of Judgment, the rich will be brought low while the poor are exalted.

James 5:1–6 explicitly warns the rich about the exploitative and oppressive way they have treated the poor. They are urged "to weep and wail for the miseries that are coming to you."

Powerful Temptations

Wrong attitudes that people hold toward riches lead them into temptations of many kinds. Luke 16:14–15 speaks of some attitudes associated with people who love money: they justify themselves before others and they set themselves up before others. Jeremiah 5:28 cites negligent attitudes. And Paul says,

> But those who want to be rich fall into temptation and are trapped by many senseless and harmful desires that plunge people into ruin and destruction. For the love of money is a root of all kinds of evil, and in their eagerness to be rich some have wandered away from the faith and pierced themselves with many pains. (1 Tim. 6:9–10)

Luke 21:34 further warns those who are rich against the temptations of dissipation, drunkenness, and the anxieties of life that could weigh down their hearts and keep them from being ready for the unknown end.

The basic pitfall for the rich is that they tend to look for security in their possessions. The story of the rich fool (Luke 12:16–21) expresses this, just after Jesus has said that "one's life does not consist in the abundance of possessions" (Luke 12:15b). Yet the rich fool still falsely assumes that human life may be measured and secured by the amount of his or her possessions. (Other verses bearing on this point include Job 20:28; 31:24, 25, 28; Ps. 49:10; Prov. 11:28; 18:11; 27:24; Jer. 17:11; 1 Tim. 6:7, 17).

Greed, covetousness, selfishness and pride often lead to worse inequality by widening the gap between the rich and the poor. Old Testament writings point out that "it is not enough to keep from oppression and injustice; covenant with God demands we deliver the oppressed . . . ; it is a sin to turn away one's face from the needy . . . We are, rather to turn our ear to the cry of the poor . . . ; if we do not, God will punish us" (Johnson 1981:99).

In the New Testament, Luke 12:15 warns against all kinds of greed, and Paul (I Timothy 6:17) warns the rich not to be arrogant, since all they possess is given by God, not only for their enjoyment but also for generous deeds and sharing with those who lack. Doing this will ensure them a secure future life. In Psalm 62:10 the rich are told not to trust in increasing riches; and the writer of Ecclesiastes (5:10) warns of the lack of satisfaction and hence meaninglessness in the pursuit of wealth. Luke's story of the rich man and poor Lazarus (16:19–31) is in essence a warning to the rich who exploit the poor and live in selfish luxury, unmindful of beggars dying at their doorsteps. All these warnings are intended to cause the rich to look for and find true riches in a life of trust in God and in radical sharing with the poor.

Walter Pilgrim, commenting on the story of the rich man and Lazarus, maintained that the repentance required of the rich man and his five brothers is "an ethical and religious reversal of their lives in which the vast discrepancy between their wealth and the poor is removed and the principles of justice and mercy are accepted and practised" (1981:118). In other words, this is not a blind condemnation of wealth. Rather, the Bible calls for recognition and enactment of the moral and ethical obligation of the rich toward the poor: to act justly and generously, and to institute just relationships and community structures that further equity and the rights of the poor.

> If we recognize that we and all that we have are gifts from God, we will respond to his covenant with justice and care for our fellow humans. If we refuse to acknowledge this dependence on God, we will make an idol of possessions and do evil to our fellow humans in order to gain ascendancy over them.
>
> The way people use possessions articulates their response to God. If they respond by idolatry, then the movement is toward self-aggrandizement, oppression, and injustice; if by faith, the movement is toward appropriate sharing of possessions according to their needs. The command to love the Lord with all the heart is given content by the command to love one's neighbor as oneself. (Johnson 1981:100)

Combating Poverty in the Bible

Wealth is a gift from God; otherwise God would not have given the ability to create wealth. Poverty in the Bible, as already discussed, is neither glorified nor ignored but treated with utmost seriousness. The God of justice, righteousness and grace desires justice for all creation; hence, God is against oppression, exploitation, slavery, alienation and suffering of any kind. The Bible regards poverty as an evil, a constant and painful fact, whose consequences are the establishment of relationships of dependence and oppression which lead to the false elevation of the powerful (false because it is not in accord with the true will of God) and to the humiliation of the helpless. In this perspective, poverty and misery are seen as abnormal. (De Santa Ana 1977:2)

The Bible does not offer a blueprint for fighting poverty, but its pages describe ways in which God takes sides with the poor and champions their cause in order to eliminate poverty. The Bible addresses root causes of poverty but also deals with the symptoms. One attempt to offer a biblical alternative to reduce poverty is suggested by Boerma:

- Opposition to poverty through socio-economic and political structures.
- Opposition to poverty through the community as the people of God. (This demand for solidarity in its general sense implies that the rich should be expected to be involved, underscoring not only the importance of organizing the poor to fight their poverty but also challenging the rich to contribute to that fight.)
- Opposition to poverty through the self-confidence of the person. (Boerma 1979:30)

Structural Measures

Structural solutions toward alleviation of poverty must not only take account of needs but also restore just conditions by addressing fundamental systemic and structural causes of poverty.

The Exodus was a momentous display of God's power to free the oppressed slave nation of Israel. God acted to end this socioeconomic and political oppression and gave freedom to the slaves (Sider 1977:54), who were to establish new and just structures for their society.

The Torah, the Law given to Israel, which forms the Pentateuch, concerns itself with human existence, personal freedom, and equity in ownership of property and means of production. It embodies legislation about the poor. The Torah gives what Gustavo Gutiérrez calls "positive and concrete measures to prevent poverty from becoming established among the people of God" (1974:360). For example, detailed legislation is enacted regarding impartial justice in the courts, in particular for the poor and powerless (Exod. 23:6, 8; Lev. 19:15; 25; Deut. 15 esp. v. 15; 24:17; 27:19) and regarding accumulation of wealth and consequent exploitation. This legislation applied to all, including the rulers and the king (Deut. 17:14–20). Thus in Israel care for the poor constituted some measure of good governance. Laws governing land were radical, promulgated in such a way that not only was the stability of the family unit—which depended on possession of land—guaranteed, but also the way land was used ensured adequate provision for the poor—the alien, the widow and the orphan. What remained in the fields after the harvest and the gathering of olives and grapes was not to be collected but left for the alien, the orphan and the widow to gather (Deut. 24:19–21; Lev. 19:9–10). Fields were not to be harvested to the very edge; that was left for the poor and aliens (Lev. 23:22). Every seven years the fields were to lie fallow, "so that the poor of your people may eat" (Exod. 23:11; Lev. 25:2–7). And every fiftieth year, any fields and houses separated from their owners, either through debt or sale, were to be returned (Lev. 25:10ff.).

Other legislation concerned release from debt (Deut. 15:1–18) and slavery (Exod. 21:2; Deut. 15:12–15); the forbidding of interest on loans (Exod. 22:25); respect for human dignity in all (Exod. 22:22–24;27); and establishment of the Jubilee year, concretely instituted to return the community to a position of equity, especially in respect to ownership of assets and means of production. The keeping of these laws was buttressed by the knowledge that Yahweh himself was behind them and cared for the poor; hence "the people's attitude to him [their Creator and Lord] would be reflected in their attitudes to them [the poor]" (Stott 1984:217: see Prov. 17:5; 19:17).

The prophets of the Old Testament also attacked structural causes of poverty. Their attacks intensified as wealth and power became more and more concentrated in a few hands because of increasing corruption and the growth of trade and commerce in cities, leaving the countryside in increasing poverty.

The prophets saw in the poor an oppressed socioeconomic group whom Yahweh, the judge of Israel, protects. They inveighed against every form of oppression by which people were made and kept poor. They condemned traders for dishonest business, for exploiting their customers and for selling the righteous into slavery (Amos 2:6, 7; 8:4–6; Hos. 12:7; Mic. 6:10f.; Isa. 3:14f.; Jer. 5:27f.; 6:12); for exacting exorbitant interest and imposing oppressive lending conditions on the poor;

they railed against non-payment of wages and deceit, selfishness, violence and manipulation of justice on the part of the rich (Isa. 1:23; 5:23; 10:1, 2; Jer. 22:13–17; Ezek. 34:18, 19; Amos 5:7; Mic. 3:9–11); they spoke out against corrupt gains and seizure of property (Isa. 5:8; Ezek. 22:29; Mic. 2:1, 2; Hab. 2:6; 1 Kings 21) (Jones 1978:221; Boerma 1979:37). The prophets also confronted kings and leaders, and challenged their evil ways (1 Sam. 13; 15; 2 Sam. 12; 1 Kings 21; Matt. 14:4).

The prophets' message was a constant reminder to Israel that as the people of the covenant, their obedience and worship of God—expressed in the first four commandments of the Decalogue—must come first. The people's knowledge of God was inextricably bound up in the way they treated the poor. To know God was to do good to the poor (Jer. 22:16). "Anyone who oppresses and robs the poor oppresses and robs God" (Boerma 1979:43). The prophets continued to proclaim that the God of the covenant is also the sovereign Creator and owner of the earth and all its resources. The land is the Lord's, given to Israel to be equitably shared through good stewardship, so that there are no poor among God's people (Deut. 15:4; Lev. 25:23f.; Ezek. 36:5). "To regard property as a possession to be made use of without taking other people's rights into account is to ignore the biblical conviction that man is simply a steward of the goods of the earth" (Boerma 1979:43).

The prophets, as God's spokesmen, saw poverty not simply as a destiny or chance inferiority or a result of laziness or pleasure seeking, but rather as injustice, the flouting of God's law by the rich and powerful through acts of exploitation, and oppression, through the use of violence and the practice of injustice.

> The strong and powerful use considerable resources . . . not to further relationships within which men are placed by God, but in support of their own ends. In this way they violate God's law and his ordinances. They tear apart what is to be a unity. They create disaster. Thus poverty is injustice perpetuated by violence. (Boerma 1979:43)

The solution the prophets seek is not simply to "ask the rich to allow some of their wealth to trickle down" to the poor "as happens in the [secular] debate over development" (Boerma 1979:41). Rather, speaking for God, they call for radical and fundamental changes to restore God's justice and righteousness in the land (Amos 5:24).

The Wisdom books are also as explicit in demanding justice for the helpless (Ps. 82:3, 4; Prov. 22:22, 23; 29:7, 14; 31:8, 9; Job 29:11–17).

In the New Testament Jesus introduced the gospel as good news to the poor. It involved the proclamation of liberty to captives, recovery of sight to the blind, freedom for the oppressed and inauguration of God's kingdom of righteousness and justice. In his teaching Jesus was constantly challenging excesses of injustice by the establishment of his time, and denouncing the false teachings by which the Pharisees, the teachers of the Law and rulers loaded unbearable burdens onto the poor. Jesus' death and resurrection dealt not only with the inward personal burden of individual sin but also condemned to destruction all kinds of external oppressive powers of this world. Paul describes this in Colossians 2:15 as Christ disarming "the principalities and powers and [making] a public example of them, triumphing over them" (Costas 1982:84).

The gospel is good news because it introduces a completely new moral ethic needed to achieve and maintain the quality of life to be found in the new kingdom of God. This is not a patching of the old with the new; rather it is a pouring of new wine into new wineskins, by which all things are made new (Matt. 9:16, 17; 2 Cor. 5:17). Receipt of the gospel implies commitment to total transformation of the corrupted world, with all its corrupted systems, into a place where the fullness of life God intended becomes possible. The process must start in the present, although perfect consummation of freedom from all oppression and poverty is still in the future.

Community or Social Measures

Poverty in the Bible "is not just a matter of politics; it is just as much an attack on the unity of the people of God. It is intolerable for the community that one person's status should be totally different from that of another" (Boerma 1979:66). Such disparities render it difficult to talk of one another as brother and sister.

The concept of community in the Bible is central to all God's dealings with people. He chose Israel as a society through whom he would work out his purposes for the rest of his world's people to emulate. The kingdom of God that Jesus brings is focused on the community. The individual is treated within the environment of a community. The Law given in the Old Testament, especially the Decalogue, is addressed to the individual, but in such a way that the individual's application of the law is within the community, whose moral and spiritual health is the real aim (Wright 1983:35). Whenever Jesus encountered a person, he bade that person return to his or her own community. God and the Holy Spirit give different abilities and gifts to individuals chiefly for the building up of a community or "for the common good" (1 Cor. 12:7).

In the biblical fight against poverty, the life of the community is particularly important because some causes of poverty, due to corruption of the earth, are beyond the human realm. "There were droughts, floods and other natural disasters. There were sickness and death, bringing in their wake widows and orphans who had to get by with no means of support" (Boerma 1979:67). The biblical remedy for such caprices of fate was requiring that the community take responsibility and "care for the victims, accepting them and compensating them for what the forces of nature have destroyed." After all, Israel as a society was "a covenant community of God and man, an antidote against the vicissitudes of fate. Social life [was] in any case characterized above all by a strong sense of solidarity; the sense of being one people, even the people of God, strengthens this solidarity" (Boerma 1979:67).

> On the negative side, people are not to steal, or cheat, "do injustice," or oppress others. Positively, the covenant demands that the poor and needy be helped by restoring them to their land, by leaving a corner of the field for gleaning, by lending without interest, by storing up third-year tithes in town for the poor, and by almsgiving. (Johnson 1981:100)

There seems to be very little evidence that these mandates were carried out to the letter. The Law and the prophets speak vehemently against members of the Israelite community who had prospered at the expense of fellow members in the land that had been promised and given to them as a gift.

> There will, however, be no one in need among you, because the Lord is sure to bless you in the land that the Lord your God is giving you as a possession to occupy, if only you will obey the Lord your God by diligently observing this entire commandment that I command you today. . . . I therefore command you, "Open your hand to the poor and needy neighbor in your land." (Deut. 15:4-5, 11)

Despite this explicit command, poverty was still found, indicating that Israel had ceased obeying God's commands, and thus, according to some writers, had ceased being God's people. God's harsh judgment on oppressive acts against the poor, the needy and the alien thus comes—as clearly expressed in Ezekiel 22:29–31.

The Bible views mutual community concern for the poor as a rule, not an exception. Israel's strength and power, even among other nations, was founded on its solidarity, expressed through brotherly spirit and mutual service. The Law reminded them that they had been slaves and God had set them free, giving them a prosperous land "flowing with milk and honey." As beneficiaries of God's bounty, then, they were to regard possessions and property as things to be shared justly among all the members of the community:

> One man's prosperity is closely connected with that of others. You cannot be rich by yourself. To accept poverty and injustice for larger or smaller groups, or for individuals within the community, would be to regress into the slavery in Egypt. The Exodus and its subsequent ratification in the giving of the Law on Sinai brings liberation because in these events God gives all his people freedom from every internal and external constraint. (Boerma 1979:69)

The New Testament records other clear illustrations of community togetherness. Acts 4:32–37 and 6:1–6, and 1 Timothy 5:3–16 (also Didache IV 8) indicate how such solidarity was expressed through the holding of material goods in common, the founding of a diaconate and care for widows, so that there were no needy among them. This gave individuals a sense of belonging in a community, and hence a feeling of security both spiritually and materially. Spiritual communion was particularly stressed at the Lord's Table instituted by Jesus himself, as an act of remembrance of him, the Savior, who set them free from bondage. This Communion implied a deep sharing in, and a belonging to, the life they received by grace from the Lord.

Biblical community-mutuality is a fundamental principle for a healthy cohesive society, affirming that every individual person is created by God and is part of the divine purpose.

> Faith in God as creator leads to respect for the other person as a worthwhile individual, even outside the bounds of tribe, family

and people. Faith in God as Creator is thus more than a familiar, formal belief. It has direct consequences for our behaviour towards one another. . . . This knowledge that God is creator affects not only relations among God's people but also their relationships outside [with aliens and non-Christians]... [Every individual, no matter who,] is in the image of his maker. Any infringement of human rights is an infringement of God's purposes and thus an infringement of God himself. The society God wants is a society based on the equality of man. Inequality is a violation of God's will. (Boerma 1979:69–70)

Community measures for combating poverty are part of God's plan for human beings. For this very purpose, human beings take their identity from within communities; *one is* because *another is*. God intends individuals to relate not only to him, their Creator, but also to one another. Communities need to be viewed as whole entities, so as to ensure a healthy and fulfilled life for each individual. This is a view development agencies ought to adopt if their efforts to eliminate poverty are to succeed.

Individual Self-confidence

Transforming external causes of poverty (structures, institutions, the rich and powerful), although essential, is not enough. Poverty in the Bible is considered evil when it subjects its victims to contemptuous treatment by their oppressors. The poor, as a category, but more so as individuals, find themselves acquiescing to such second-rate status and begin to believe that life is meant to be like this, that nothing can be done to change things for better:

Poverty is like a disease. It stigmatizes and humiliates. The poor man has to fall back on himself, and at the same time he becomes reserved. He begins to doubt his own capacity. . . . He no longer believes in change. (Boerma 1979:76)

Constant oppression and deprivation so blunts normal expression that dull acquiescence and hopelessness come to characterize the poor. Chances for change are very remote; the poor individual is helpless to save himself. The Bible calls this condition helplessness, or being lost or dead in sin, or tired from labor and heavy burdens. These states demand external help for individual empowerment, if the poor are to be emancipated into full involvement in society as equal human beings and not remain poor and despised. The poor need to be liberated from all that incapacitates and debilitates them personally—whether resulting from oppression, or inner feelings of apathy, hopelessness, worthlessness, dejection, inferiority, self-contempt, or sickness.

Old Testament Law details how the community is to help the needy so that they may continue as contributing members of society rather than as dependents. The prophets' message, in particular, advocated justice in all structures of society to ensure the well-being of everybody. The psalms (e.g., 3, 5, 6, 34) depict the poor crying to God. And God hears, rescues and restores them.

In the New Testament, Jesus champions the cause of the poor, identifies with the poor, and meets them on their level. He offers them no charity and does not see their poverty as an end in itself when he inaugurates God's kingdom, which he announces as belonging to the poor. He attracts the poor to himself, frees them from their afflictions and sends them home well and whole, often with the words "your sins are forgiven, go and sin no more"; "your faith has made you whole"; "take up your bed and walk"; "be made clean." At each encounter with the needy or the poor Jesus pronounces a holistic restitution of the individual. He releases them from both physical and spiritual causes of their impoverishment, so that they may fulfill the Law's demands, especially of loving their neighbor. This was the practice the disciples of Jesus followed (e.g., Acts 3:1–8).

Jesus insisted that those he set free should go back to their communities and become contributors to the well-being of the community (Luke 8:39; Mark 5:19). In other words, biblical liberation is total, making them liberators too. It is not simply a change of circumstances by which the liberated may become, in their turn, new oppressors.

One fact on which the Bible is not silent is that the struggle against poverty is a difficult and dangerous undertaking. The prophets often incurred the wrath of the oppressors they uncompromisingly challenged. For this same reason Jesus was put to death by the rulers of the establishment of his day.

In summary, it is clear that the Bible employs a rich vocabulary to tease out the different nuances, causes and effects of poverty. The Bible recognizes the dual nature of poverty—spiritual and material—and affirms that

God in his nature as a God of justice and love is concerned with all the poor, not only the poor in spirit. He cares when people enslave and oppress others. God helps the indigent poor, champions the powerless poor and exalts the humble poor (Stott 1984:220).

The Bible views poverty as a result of both internal and external causes, related to acts of the individual and to natural calamities and systemic structural paradigms. The Bible requires total transformation to bring structures, communities and individuals into line with God's will and purpose. Through righteousness, justice and equity, the poor are enabled to become fully human, enjoying the life God intends for them, as well as to become good stewards in sharing with others the resources God gives them as agents of his justice and love.

PART II

CONCEPTUAL ANALYSIS OF EMPOWERMENT

6

Power and Rural Development

One could set up an endless parade of great names from Plato and Aristotle through Machiavelli and Hobbes to Pareto and Weber to demonstrate that a large number of seminal social theorists have devoted a good deal of attention to power and the phenomena associated with it.
—Ronald A. Dahl, "The Concept of Power"

I n rural development, *power* has two faces; on the one hand, its abuse or misuse can lead to powerlessness, and on the other hand, its proper use leads to empowerment. The social sciences discuss power in terms of social relationship, that is, the power of some over others. But power may exist as both "power to" (capacity to attain ends) and "power over" (power over "self and over nature as well as the power of men over other men" [Wrong 1979/88:2]).

Definitions and Interpretations of Power

Definitions of power basically fall into the two categories of power mentioned above. Hobbes defines power as "man's present means to any future apparent good" (Hobbes 1958:78). And Parsons views power

> primarily as a facility that makes possible the attainment of collective goals to which a normative commitment has been made. . . .

99

Power then is generalised capacity to secure the performance of binding obligations by units in a system of collective organisation when the obligations are legitimised with reference to collective goals. (Parsons 1967:308)

These definitions, to which others could be added, clearly treat power as a means or "power to" but do not preclude "power over." The implication is that power-holders and others who seek power desire it not necessarily as an end in itself but as a means to the attainment of gain, glory, or other goals.

For Hobbes, power in a world of scarcity is "a means of acquiring scarce possessions and reputation in the eyes of others and, having acquired these, they must continue to augment their power for strictly defensive reasons in order to retain what they have won" (quoted in Wrong 1979/88:219). Where a conflict of interest arises between two equals, the two "become enemies; and in the way to their end, which is principally their own conservation, and sometimes their delectation only, endeavor to destroy or subdue one another" (Hobbes 1958:105).

Power, according to Wrong, is more often sought as a means to other satisfactions such as wealth, sexual gratification, prestige and a wide range of valued experiences in general" (Wrong 1979/88:220, 236). Similarly, Lasswell views power both as an end in itself and as a means for achievement of other values, including wealth, prestige, respect and privilege. His idea of a political man is one who

pursues power as a means of compensation against deprivation. Power is expected to overcome low estimates of the self, by changing either the traits of the self or the environment in which it functions. (Lasswell 1948:39)

In the context of rural development, power is desired in order to acquire the means and capacities to satisfy needs and wants, where these are "conditions of deficit requiring action to alter the actor's relation to objects in his environment if the deficit is to be eliminated" (Wrong 1979/88:219). This has important bearing on third-world countries where rural development is an important undertaking in the midst of scarce resources. Power as a means of access to resources is vital for empowering the rural poor, who often lack power for accessing resources.

"Power over," within the perspective of social relations, is here extended to cover the power people have over self, nature, or their environment. Those who define power as "power over" include Bachrach and Baratz: "Power is relational, as opposed to possessive or substantive. . . . One cannot have power in a vacuum, but only in relation to someone else" (Bachrach and Baratz 1970:21, 19). Weber gives three interpretations of power: power as legitimate power, which he calls authority; power as influence; and power as dictatorial power *(Macht)*. The third of these is the most commonly quoted, with the expanded meaning that "power *(Macht)* is the probability that one actor within a social relationship will be in a position to carry out his will despite resistance, regardless of the basis on which this probability rests" (Weber 1947:152). In the same school of thought, Russell defines power as "the production of intended effects" (Russell 1938:25). This definition has been viewed by some social scientists as too general. Lasswell and Kaplan, for instance, argue that "power in the political [or economic or social] sense cannot be conceived as the ability to produce intended effects in general, but only such effects as involve other persons" (Lasswell and Kaplan 1950:35). Wrong, too, sees Russell's definition as lacking clarity of relational expression and modifies it thus: "Power is the capacity of some person to produce intended and foreseen effects on others." In this sense, power can be viewed as "equivalent to capability, potency or mastery" (Wrong 1979/88:2, 219).

Some theorists explicitly define power as an instrument for the attainment of personal goals over others' goals. For example, Wrong writes, "Power over others . . . is readily seen as an instrument for the achievement of a wide range of goals. Power is the most universal means, indeed even more so than money because it can command that as well" (Wrong 1979/88:220).

Most of these interpretations of power, in the event of abuse or misuse of power, imply that people who wield power will prevail over and subdue others and render them powerless.

A slightly different interpretation of "power over" views power in relation to "who participates, who gains and who loses, and who prevails in decision-making" (Polsby 1963:55). Power is sought in this case for capacity to participate, for gain and for prevailing in decisions. For rural development, this definition of power is particularly popular among developers who think of empowerment in terms of giving people "power for participation" in decision-making. In essence, they agree that participation must be preceded by empowerment, and that one cannot participate effectively unless one has the power to do so.

Dahl views power in terms of a relation between people, which he expresses in simple symbolic notation as "A has power over B to the extent that he can get B to do something that B would not otherwise do" (Dahl 1957:202–3). Lukes develops Dahl's view: "A exercises power over B when A affects B in a manner contrary to B's interests. . . . A may exercise power over B by getting him to do what he does not want to do, but he also exercises power over him by shaping or determining his very wants" (Lukes 1974:34, 23). What Lukes implies is that A has power over B by "prevailing in the resolution of key issues or by preventing B from effectively raising those issues," as well as "through affecting B's conceptions of the issues altogether" (Gaventa 1980:12). Bachrach and Baratz expand on this by treating A and B not as individuals, but as groups involved in systems, where A becomes a group of power-holders who manipulate systems to have their way against B, a powerless group. For rural development, B would be the poor, the powerless, who are overpowered by A, who are rich and powerful. Bachrach and Baratz introduce an element of "mobilisation of bias," by which the powerful shut the powerless and their issues out of decision-making arenas.

> Political systems and sub-systems develop a "mobilisation of bias,"
> a set of predominant values, beliefs, rituals, and institutional pro-
> cedures ("rules of the game") that operate systematically and con-
> sistently to the benefit of certain persons and groups at the expense
> of others. Those who benefit are placed in a preferred position to
> defend and promote their vested interests. . . . The primary method
> for sustaining a given mobilization of bias is nondecision-making.
> A nondecision . . . is a decision that results in suppression or thwart-
> ing a latent or manifest challenge to the values of the decision-
> maker. (Bachrach and Baratz 1970:43, 44)

Nondecision-making, they explain, is a means by which the demands of the powerless are eliminated even before they reach the decision-making arena, or, if they should reach it, are destroyed before a decision is to be made.

The point here is that the barriers powerless group B faces, through mobilization of bias, are wielded by power-holders, group A, upon decision-making in political arenas, and are sustained through nondecisions. Such nondecisions may be expressed in several ways: (1) in the form of force; (2) by threat of negative or positive sanctions, "ranging from intimidation . . . to co-optation"; (3) the "invocation of an existing bias of the political system—a norm, precedent, rule of procedure—to squelch a threatening demand or incipient issue," which may involve the manipulation of symbols, or name-calling; and (4) "reshaping or strengthening the mobilization bias" through establishment of new barriers or new symbols "against the challengers' effort to widen the scope of conflict" (Bachrach and Baratz 1970:45–46). These processes are frequently reported in many rural areas where rich, powerful landowners or moneylenders prevail in issues of oppression against the landless or debtors.

Other interpretations of "power over" view power as an instrument of rule. Sugden states, "Rule owes its existence to the instinct of domination." He quotes three writers: First, Voltaire, who said power "consists in my making others act as I choose." Second, Bertrand de Jouvenal, who stated, "To command and be obeyed: without that there is no Power—with it no other attribute is needed for it to be. . . . The thing without which it cannot be: that essence is command." And third, he quotes Moltmann's definition of power as "the means whereby we get something by force" (Sugden 1974:1).

These interpretations assume what Parsons calls the "zero-sum" concept or phenomenon, "which is to say that there is a fixed 'quantity' of power in any relational system and hence any gain of power on the part of A must by definition occur by diminishing the power at the disposal of other units, B, C, D . . . " (Parsons 1963:232–33). In other words, they regard power *in a society* as a fixed quantity resource (almost analogous to land)—but different from capital or knowledge as resources. This "constant sum conception of power" assumes that "being fixed in overall quantity, any gain to one unit must imply a loss to another unit. Thus, if some have more power, others must have less" (Gamson 1968/71:108–9; see also Barnes 1988:17). This explains why the powerful will often oppose any moves toward empowering those whom they dominate. They fear that some of their power will be taken away when those they dominate become empowered, leaving them less powerful.

"Power over" can be sought and held onto by individuals or groups and abused by being used to subdue, oppress or destroy others for the security of the power-holders and their possessions.

> Even though men may be of peaceable disposition and "content
> with a moderate power," they have to seek continually more power
> in order to secure the advantages they have already attained or
> else they will be deprived of what they have by the less successful
> who in a world of scarcity are prepared to "kill, subdue, supplant
> or repel" them. (Wrong 1979/88:219)

David Prior expands this idea that the desire for "power over" is inherent in human nature, quoting first, the Roman historian Tacitus, "The
lust for power, for dominating others, influences the heart more than
any other passion"; second, the German philosopher Nietzsche, "Wherever I found a living creature, I found the unconditioned will to power,
to overpower"; and third, Russell, who agreed, "Of the infinite desires
of man the chief are the desires for power and for glory" (Prior 1987:12).

These views portray "power over" as more or less undesirable, because when people dominate others, such domination is more often than
not accompanied by oppression, manipulation, exploitation and other
dehumanizing treatments. But "power over" can at times be desirable.
In rural development powerless individuals and groups need to take
power over their own inertia, environment and systems, as well as over
other people and groups, in order to meet their needs. The poor need

> to confront the people, the institutions and the relationships that
> seek to use one as an object to be disposed of, as a pawn in their
> own game. The persons thus confronted may be landowners, or
> money lenders, or employers, or bureaucrats, or politicians, or
> corrupt judges; and the institutions may be co-operatives or credit
> societies, or political or even families. (Elliott 1987a:78)

This view expressed is recommended for any efforts to empower the
poor, with a cautionary warning that the poor in their turn must not
abuse the power they acquire.

For the process of empowerment to occur, "power to" is desirable because it directly empowers to have access to resources, to be capable of
attaining goals and to satisfy needs. A necessary condition though, is that
such power be equitably distributed in the community. "Power over," as
we have seen, is beset with dangers of abuse like oppression and the creation of powerlessness, the very antithesis of empowerment. However,

when used responsibly with accountability, "power over" as exercised over others is desirable for order and for getting things done. In addition, "power over" is also desirable as power over self (to overcome personal inertia) and power over institutions, systems and nature—but not for exploitation.

Power in African Rural Society

One legacy of colonial history in Africa is a dualistic mode of development that gave birth to the *modern sector* (predominantly the domain of government or state and its apparatus) and the *traditional sector* (the domain of the local community). In the language of center and periphery, the modern sector is the center and the traditional sector is the periphery. In power dynamics between center and periphery, the center becomes dominant over the periphery. In every African state the government wants full control of both sectors. The state has sought to integrate the traditional or rural sector into the modern sector, which operates under the market (cash) economy, and into the political and cultural system of the state. This process of incorporation carries on, despite divergences of the two sectors' objectives.

In the rural sector local communities wish to increase family and household welfare, productivity and income, as well as viability and well-being. They also want access to resources of the center. The state meanwhile seeks, on its own terms, a viable rural economy, loyal rural communities and local contributions to long-term national growth and productivity. Barbara P. Thomas-Slayter says the terms under which these rural communities are incorporated into the market economy and larger political sphere of the state shape the communities' capacities for effective action and for demanding accountability (1994: 1484). Some rural communities, Thomas-Slayter continues, try to retreat into the kinship support systems of the "economy of affection" documented by Hyden (1980). But this is not viable for many rural communities, since the state, fearing loss of control, has tended to become more authoritarian, "emphasising its control functions more than its support functions" (Thomas-Slayter 1994:1484). For most African countries (see, e.g., Holmquist and Ford 1992; Ndi 1993; Sithole 1993; Knight 1991), governments tend to penetrate and take control rather than empower local rural communities, despite some benefits the latter approach could bring. Empirical evidence asserts that a strong association exists between sustainability of projects and local involvement. Thomas-Slayter quotes two studies illustrating this. The first is an analysis by the World Bank of 25 projects specifically showing that a major contribution to sustainability came from the development and support of grassroots organizations (IBRD 1985). "Project beneficiaries gradually assumed increasing responsibility for project activities including decision-making with a high degree of autonomy and reliance (Thomas-Slayter 1994:1481). The second study, by Ghai, further explores the same issue with analysis of nine projects in which formation of local organizations was basic to project success (Ghai 1989).

The behavior of the state in African countries has been noted to "lean overwhelmingly toward an urban bias" (Thomas-Slayter 1994:1484). This is lamented by a number of writers; for example, Jonathan Barker, who writes, "A development oriented state has yet to appear in Africa" (1989:204). Even examples cited in some African countries of local people's participatory development, such as the District Focus and Harambee approaches in Kenya, and the *ujamaa* socialist approach to people's participation in Tanzania, have been analyzed to be either non-threatening at the state level or a combination of "bureaucratic authoritarianism and technocratic development" (see Thomas-Slayter 1994:1484, and Samoff 1989:13). Decentralization in many parts of Africa has served as a cover for increased lack of governance; fragile institutions; constant unresolved issues concerning responsibility, authority and accountability; and corruption and/or control by government and rural elite. African politics has been called an authoritarian legacy of colonialism, characterized by "life presidents, military rule, and patrimonial styles" (Thomas-Slayter 1994:1479). This has not brought about transfer of control over resources to communities as a whole (Esman and Uphoff 1984; see also Thomas 1985; Sandbrook 1985; Olowu 1989; Yeager 1989). Yet despite authoritarian governments in African countries, there are power bases along which local communities operate.

Power Bases in African Rural Communities

In African rural communities, according to Mbithi, it is assumed that there is maximum flow of information and feedback between an actor and recipient of power. . . . Thus if one asks a local Maragoli farmer "who runs this sub-location?" one expects the respondent to have certain issues in mind, to evaluate certain holders of power resources, to review certain incumbents of important offices and come out with a balance sheet which shows the power centre. (Mbithi 1974:157)

It is therefore erroneous to conclude that local bureaucratic arms of government wield maximum power with unchallenged compliance. There are inherent ambiguities and multiple power relationships within any given rural community. Mbithi identifies five operational bases of power from his study of the Kikuyu, Kamba and Mbere communities in Central and East Kenya:

- Coercive or Force Power—the expectation that the recipient will be punished if he fails to conform to the influence attempt. In the cases Mbithi examined, punishment included fines, confiscation of stock, imprisonment, and so forth.
- Reward Power—the recipient's expectation that the power agent has the ability to mediate rewards to him.
- Legitimate Power-Compliance—stemming from internalised values, that the actor has "legitimate" right to influence and that the recipient has obligation to accept this influence.
- Referent Power—compliance based on the recipient's identification with the actor.
- Expert Power—compliance which varies according to the recipient's perception of the actor's extent of knowledge within a given area of meaning.

In these categories of operational power, no distinction is made between authority and influence. When authority is seen as legitimate power, and influence as the form of compliance based on psychological change due to changes in recipients' values and aspirations, then both can be defined under the broader definition of power—the capacity to control.

These power bases can be summed up as traditionally legitimate modes of compliance and discipline operative in rural African communities. Mbithi states that tradition forms the most important basis for legitimate use of power in rural Kenyan settings, and this could apply to other African rural communities. Tradition provides group structures, along which power bases operate. Two such group structures, identified by Mbithi among the Kamba, tend to apply to many other tribal and ethnic groups: age groups and kinship groups.

- Age Groups—These recruit membership on the basis of sex and age to form an age set. Those who can belong to such groups have been circumcised together, attended dances together, or left school after attending primary school together, for example. Age groups have no hierarchy of authority or elected leaders. Members act in informally recognized roles, such as the jester, the opinion leader, the judge, the prosecutor, even the general. Also, the senior age-group member exercises the role of mentor and disciplinarian to young members.
- Kinship Groups—The most important functional kinship group is the clan. A clan is usually part of a tribe, members of which are related or in some way connected by means of a common bond, such as a totem or claim to common descent. The chief obligation among clan members is to help one another, especially in paying traditionally imposed fines for manslaughter. This obligation to help is most strictly observed among clan members who are also neighbors and includes obligation to share in bridewealth duties, rituals and proceeds; and to share in imposing family discipline, especially among young age groups. Members often display open unity and love, although friendship boundaries may transcend these bloodlines, which mixing between the sexes in a given clan is kept to a minimum. The kinship group has a more clearly defined hierarchy of overall control than other rural groups; its structure is shown in Table 6–1.

In these group structures, authority relationships develop only in a group because only group values legitimize the exercise of social control, and only group norms serve as an independent basis for enforcing compliance. This ensures against individual selfish motives and abuse of power creeping into the system. The weakness in these traditional modes of power is the requirement of expected duty or obedience regardless of the quality of leadership; there are, in addition, constant values conflicts between individuals and the group.

When these traditional structures are considered within a context where modern structures are also operative—the normal order of things today—multiple power relationships characterize any rural community, resulting in conflicts of goals.

How Should Power Be Structured in a Rural Society?

To explore how power is structured in society, the most elaborate classic discussion on power structures available offers some parallels for analytical application to development situations.

Clan Hierarchy	
Clan Chairman for Locality who convenes the	
General Clan Assembly for Locality	Convenes mainly for major interclan disputes, such as land cases, incest, manslaughter, feasts and disciplinary action.
which elects and empowers the	
Clan Committee for Locality	Reviews minor family disputes.
which coordinates	
Age-Group Assemblies	Coalesce mainly as bases for work groups; coalitions of close age-grades or members of different age-grades from different localities.
which are broken down into	
Clan Age Groups	Mainly work groups, entertainment groups, training groups.
which are regulated by	
Family and Household Heads	Ongoing family leadership.
who are responsible for	
Family Members	Reciprocity among siblings and half-siblings.

Table 6-1: Kinship Group Hierarchical Structure (source: Mbithi 1974, 178).

The Elitist View of Power

An elitist view of power is popularly connected with Mills and Dahl (Bachrach and Baratz 1970:3; Kornhauser 1961:252; Anderson 1984:169). Power is concentrated in the hands of a few, who determine all major policies for the unorganized masses, who are construed to be submissive and can be manipulated, as they are "incapable of engaging in effective communication and political action" (Kornhauser 1961:258). In other words, power is viewed as highly centralized, monolithic and coherent.

The elitists maintain that every human institution contains an ordered system of power structure that "is an integral part and mirror image of the organization's stratification" (Bachrach and Baratz 1970:4). This position receives criticism, mainly from the pluralists, who maintain that "nothing categorical can be assumed about power in any community." Polsby continues:

> If anything, there seems to be an unspoken notion among pluralist researchers that at the bottom nobody dominates in a town, so that their first question is not likely to be, "Who runs this community?," but rather, "Does anyone at all run this community? (Polsby 1960:475)

The elitists generally assume that the structure of power tends to be stable over time. The pluralists object to this on the grounds that power

> may be tied to issues, and issues are fleeting or persistent, provoking coalitions among interest groups and citizens, ranging in their duration from momentary to semi-permanent. . . . To presume that the set of coalitions which exist in the community at any given time is a timeless stable aspect of social structure is to introduce systematic inaccuracies into one's description of social reality. (Polsby 1960:478–79)

Kornhauser summarizes the elitist argument that "power tends to be patterned according to the structure of interests in a society. It is shared among those whose interests converge, and divides along lines where interests diverge." He maintains that Mills sees the power elite as "a reflection and solidification of a 'coincidence of interests' among the ascendant institutional orders" (Kornhauser 1961:257).

The assumption often made is that there is only one such structure, and that all units may be ranked vis-a-vis one another. Units
higher in the hierarchy have power over units lower in the structure, so there is a one-way flow of power. (Kornhauser 1961:261)

Mills himself maintained that the power elite did not merely rest on the
coincidence of interests among power-holders, but also on the "psychological similarity and social intermingling" of those in power, which is
based on their shared codes and values as well as material interests that
arise from such grounds as similarity of social origins, religious affilia-
tions and education. In other words, they share a common way of life
and therefore possess both the will and the opportunity to integrate
their lines of action, which at times involves "explicit co-ordination"
(Mills 1956:19–20).

According to Mills, the favored ways of exercising power in the power
elite are the concentration of power in a small circle and the use of
manipulation. Power may be thought to reside in the public and its
elected representatives, but in reality it comes to reside in the hands of
those few who direct the key bureaucracies; eventually those few who
wield power are neither responsible nor accountable for their power.
When this happens, Mills contends, even politics will no longer involve
genuine political debate; the result of all this is a severe weakening of
democratic institutions (Mills 1956:316–17).

The Pluralist View of Power

Political scientists are the main proponents of the pluralist view; to
them, power is widely diffused in societies. The pluralist view concerns
itself with the exercise of power rather than with its source. Power is
viewed as more amorphous and indeterminate. In the pluralist view
there is no decisive ruling group, rather "an amorphous structure of
power centering in the interplay among interest groups. The lower
level of the pyramid comprises a more or less unorganized public, which
is sought as an ally (rather than dominated) by interest groups in their
maneuvers against actual or threatened encroachments on the juris-
diction each claims for itself " (Kornhauser 1961:254). Where the elitists see the ascendancy of the power elite, the pluralists see the opposite
tendency toward dispersal of power among a plurality of organized
interests.

One criticism leveled against the pluralist view is that this view encourages weak leadership.

> If . . . power tends to be dispersed among groups which are primarily concerned to protect and defend their interests, rather than to advance general policies and their leadership, and if at the same time politics has declined as a sphere of duty and self-interest, then there will be a *severe weakening of leadership*. (Kornhauser 1961:260)

D. Riesman extends this criticism by arguing that the "indeterminacy and amorphousness" of power in pluralism inhibits the development of leadership.

> Where the issue involves the country as a whole, no individual or group leadership is likely to be very effective, because the entrenched veto groups cannot be budged. . . . Veto groups exist as defense groups, not as leadership groups. (Riesman 1953:257, 248)

A counter argument is that "the dispersion of power among a diversity of 'veto groups' operates to support democratic institutions even as it inhibits effective leadership"; this in itself is desirable, although "the long-run prospects of a leaderless democracy are not promising" (Kornhauser 1961:261).

Power for the pluralists involves manipulation under the guise of mutual tolerance for one another's interests and beliefs. Riesman's view was that manipulation takes place because each group is trying to hide its concern with power in order not to antagonize other groups. He contends that power relations are in the form of "monopolistic competition, [where] rules of fairness and fellowship dictate how far one can go" (Riesman 1953:247).

The Two Views and Rural Development

These two views of power, elitist and pluralist, provide two different ways of viewing how power is distributed in society, especially in American society. How do these models apply in the context of rural societies in developing countries? It would appear that the elitist model applies to situations where the society is characterized by the majority of the population being illiterate, lacking critical self-awareness, being inarticulate (and hence acquiescent), powerless and poor; while a minority is educated, very articulate and hence holds positions of authority and decision-making through which they exercise power over the rest, and can accumulate wealth and prestige for themselves. The pluralist model seems applicable to situations where most people in a society are educated, articulate, self-aware and critically aware of their situation, and are capable of decision-making as well as critical assessment of leaders; in other words, in situations in which the majority possess some measure of effective power and are not powerless and poor.

According to John Prior Lewis, rural development takes place in an environment of dualism, a concept he introduced and defined as

the coexistence of modern and traditional methods of production in urban and rural sectors; the coexistence of wealthy, highly educated elites with masses of illiterate poor people. (quoted in Todaro 1989:81)

In terms of the dependency development models, such coexistence is between the centers and the peripheries (Forbes 1984/86:67f.). Lewis's analysis of dualism and the dependency models seems to provide an explanation for the fact that the elitist model has dominated rural development in developing countries and has led to the creation of dependency and powerlessness among the rural poor. Basic to that situation was a development process that involved, among other things, the transfer of technology, capital, skills and modern methods of development to rural areas through the agency of the educated elite working as government extension workers or agency field workers. Where masses of the rural poor are illiterate and powerless, as is the case in most developing countries, these educated elite implement blueprints of preplanned activities set up by the government or development agencies by merely soliciting rural people's "participation," a synonym for their labor, without an agenda to make them architects of their own development.

There is an increasing general outcry for a change to something akin to the pluralist model of power structure, wherein the poor masses acquire power that would enable them to undertake effective control of their own development. In some countries such change is already taking place; for example, in Kenya and the Philippines the struggle for self-reliance and people power is no longer mere rhetoric but a practical reality through which power is becoming more dispersed than concentrated. Wherever it is taking place, however, this struggle is more or less intense, because power-holders are not ready to share their power. In the places where such a struggle has occurred, it has been played out in different arenas, such as education, trade unionism, women's movements, liberation theology, even revolutionary or terrorist activities and coups d'etat. Some of these arenas of struggle, like terrorism, revolution and coups, are negative, using methods that are destructive to society as a whole or in part; others end up with mere "change of seats," where those that were powerful are rendered powerless while some of the formerly powerless become powerful, as in coups or military takeovers, and some trade unionist or women's movements. A few, however, are positive and constructive in their overall effects, including education and liberation theology.

Power and Powerlessness

"Power to" and "power over" may be distinguishable when considered technically, but practically the distinction tends to disappear. Once a person has power, it is hardly likely that he or she will wield it at only one of these levels; rather, the person is more likely to wield this both as "power to" and "power over."

Consider Hobbes. He defines power as "power to," which he expresses as "man's present means to any future apparent good" (Hobbes 1958:78). But when he develops his thesis, there is a clear progression from "power as capacity to attain ends to power over other men" (Wrong 1979/88). In fact, Freud, who later expanded on Hobbes, brings out more clearly Hobbes's view of power as two-tiered and dangerous:

> Men are not gentle, friendly creatures wishing for love, who simply defend themselves if they are attacked. . . . Their neighbor is to them not only a possible helper or sexual object, but also a temptation to them to gratify their aggressiveness on him, to exploit his capacity for work without recompense, to use him sexually without his consent, to seize his possessions, to humiliate him, to cause him pain, to torture and to kill him. . . . Who has the cour-

age to dispute it in the face of all the evidence in his own life and in history? (Freud 1958:60–61)

This is clearly both "power to" and "power over." In the present experience of many developing countries of the world, including Eastern Europe, the struggle to hold onto power and to acquire more at the expense of lives or of rendering others absolutely powerless is fully realizing this quotation. Abuse of power is the surest means of creating utter powerlessness of the masses. Most of the time the root of power abuse is that "positions of power are usually highly rewarded financially and carry great prestige," such that the "greater the prestige attached to positions of authority and the higher the material rewards" received, the more power is sought after and the more it tends to "overflow scope-specific boundaries" (Wrong 1979/88:250, 226). This seems in line with Lord Acton's well-known maxim, "Power corrupts, and absolute power corrupts absolutely."

Power is also relational. The relationship, however, is asymmetrical, meaning there are relatively few power-holders and many power-subjects. Dependency on power-holders reduces opportunities for the powerless to resist or challenge the expansiveness of the power of the powerful. Groups thus rendered powerless through inherent power inequality develop a sense of inferiority and acquiescence; they become locked into what Freire calls the "culture of silence." The powerless, "having internalized the image of [the powerful] and adopted [their] guidelines, [become] fearful of freedom" and lose the ability to struggle against their inferior state of powerlessness (Freire 1972/90:23). Such fear may also result from an anticipated reaction in which the powerful, having greater resources, will invoke sanctions against the powerless.

Any situation in which A exploits B or hinders his pursuit for self-affirmation as a responsible person is one of oppression. Such a situation itself constitutes violence, even when sweetened by false generosity, because it interferes with man's ontological and historical vocation to be more fully human. (Freire 1972/90:31)

This process is most evident in rural areas of developing countries, where the majority of the population is poor and illiterate and there is widespread powerlessness. The majority are rendered powerless by the

few power-wielders, that is, the wealthy and propertied and the educated elite who hold status or job positions which make them powerful
and influential. When resources such as land are scarce, the powerful
amass these for themselves. In cases of the introduction of technology
to curb resource shortages, the powerful benefit more. The Green Revolution in Southeast Asia, where newly introduced technology and increased harvests benefited the rich and powerful more than the poor,
clearly demonstrates this point.

A Biblical View of Power

In the Old Testament power belongs to and is dispensed by God:
"The Lord is king; he is robed in majesty" (Ps. 93:1; also see Pss. 9:7;
47:8; 96:10; 97:1; 99:1; 146:10; and Isa. 52:7). The idea of God reigning
originates from the tradition that God was the reigning king of Israel;
hence, no earthly king was needed. Thus, political power held by tribal
leaders or elders and judges before the period of earthly monarchy in
Israel was delegated power, mediated by God. Hans-Rudi Weber writes,
"God's Spirit would suddenly take hold of a person for accomplishing
mighty acts of liberation or judgment" (Weber 1989:50). However, after the Exodus, when Israel settled in Canaan, God's people felt great
pressures not only for Israel to be like neighboring states, but also to
have a leader who would "save the people from the hand of their enemies round about" (Weber 1989:49). Such pressure mounted until God
agreed to delegate his power through earthly kings. Power thus delegated was to be exercised with stewardship that required a king to be
accountable to God. But this stewardship was not followed by some
kings, who ruled by oppression (1 Kings 12:1–11); they placed their
trust more "in their own diplomacy and military might than in God's
royal power." Such distortion of God-given power, transformed into
manmade autocratic power, was challenged by the prophets. Elijah "confronted Ahab and his foreign wife"; Amos announced judgment on "the
politically successful King Jeroboam II, and on his corrupt and rich functionaries and priests"; and Hosea "restated the Mosaic faith over against
the syncretism and oppression which characterised such man-made
monarchy" (Weber 1989:53).

These kings chose to follow human ways to power rather than God's
commands. This theme is taken up again in the New Testament, with

comparison between the effect of fallen "powers" and the proper exercise of power demonstrated by Jesus.

When Jesus entered the human realm, he introduced God's kingdom, with its requirements. Jesus affirmed that power, both his own and that of earthly rulers as exemplified by Pilate, emanates from God (John 19:11). Paul echoes this when he says, "There is no authority except from God, and those authorities that exist have been instituted by God" (Rom. 13:1). As under the Old Covenant, God vests power in leaders and calls them to be his stewards in exercising it rightly. Jesus demonstrated the proper way to exercise power—not grabbing, but serving humbly, giving himself away, walking the way of the Cross. This contrasted greatly with the way power was exercised in the society to which he came, where power meant getting, grabbing, keeping, snatching, controlling and retaliating.

Jesus used power not as "power over," to dominate and control, but as "power to" serve (Prior 1987:69). This placed him in direct conflict with both religious and political leaders of his society. He spoke out especially about the contradictions of the religious leaders, who held great authority in Jewish society. He challenged the scribes and the Pharisees, bringing a number of charges against them, five of which are discussed by Prior (1987:127–32): they do not practice what they preach, while imposing heavy burdens on ordinary people (Matt. 23:3–4); they run their lives to impress others (Matt. 23:5–7) with the result that they lose genuine God-consciousness, affecting religious acts like praying, fasting, and almsgiving; they are culpably blind leaders, whose insincere behavior encourages "sheer flippancy in making promises and in speaking the truth" (Prior 1987:129); they neglect what really matters to God and engage in trivial pursuits (Matt. 23:23); and they cover up their inner rottenness with a copious display of ritual correctness (Matt. 23:27–28, also 15:19–20).

Jesus called these scribes and Pharisees hypocrites, and he likened their hypocrisy to leaven that affects the whole dough; that is, their lives and teaching were damaging to the whole society. Jesus warns his disciples to stay clear of them.

Although Jesus did not introduce any program or strategy for political liberation, his message "generated a dynamism of socio-political change" (Prior 1987:140; see Acts 17:6–7). This placed him in direct confrontation with political rulers, both "the totalitarian rule of Rome and the more local authority of the Herods" (Prior 1987:140). Jesus' confrontation with political authorities is presented at its climax, after he has been arrested and brought before the rulers for interrogation. In humble submission to his Father's permissive higher will, Jesus submits to these misguided earthly authorities: "When I was with you day after day in the temple, you did not lay hands on me," he says to them. "But this is your hour, and the power of darkness!" (Luke 22:53). Pilate makes the choice to be Caesar's friend rather than God's, and he releases Barabbas, the murderer, instead of Jesus, the righteous, a clear demonstration of the stark difference between right exercise of power from God (represented by Jesus) and selfish, ambivalent, arrogantly exercised human authority (Caesar).

Jesus' power and authority was of a nonviolent nature (Luke 22:52; Matt. 26:52–55). This, too, is in marked contrast to earthly, human powers, whose expected course of action would be retaliation or at least some attempt at self-defense. When Jesus says "when the power of darkness reigns," or when Paul (1 Cor. 2:8) says the powers "crucified the Lord of glory," another dimension of powers is evident. The New Testament also views powers, authorities and rulers not only as human beings but as super-earthly spiritual realities that play a definitive role in the affairs of human beings. Paul emphasizes that the crucifixion of Christ was far more than simply the work of human personalities (Foster 1985:181; see also Berkhof 1962:chap. 2). Paul calls those responsible "forces of evil in the heavenly places" (Eph. 6:12). The New Testament refers to powers as created by God (Col. 1:16), implying that they were originally good, in the sense that God pronounced everything he had made "very good" (Gen. 1:31a). Powers were to be "related to the creative will of God, but they have become fallen and are in revolt and rebellion against God the Creator" (Foster 1985:181).

Jesus seemingly submits to them all and allows these spiritual powers of darkness to inflict the final blow of death on him. Thus, Jesus is in essence inviting those powers to draw out all their devastating ammunition (including death, the final enemy) so that he may demonstrate to them an astounding, final and decisive victory. Writing about this later, the apostle Paul said, "He disarmed the rulers and authorities and made a public example of them, triumphing over them in it" (Col. 2:15). In humbling himself, even to death on a cross (Phil. 2:8), Jesus brought himself to "a place of triumph over every such spiritual (and human) power" (Prior 1987:156).

This integral worldview of power "takes seriously the spiritual insights of the ancient or biblical world view by affirming a withinness or interiority of all things, but sees this inner spiritual reality as inextricably related to an outer concretion or physical manifestation" (Wink 1992:5). Wink explains spiritual "principalities and powers" as

> the inner and outer aspects of any given manifestation of power. As the inner aspect they are the spirituality of institutions, the "within" of corporate structures and systems, the inner essence of outer organizations of power As the outer aspect they are political systems, appointed officials, the "chair" of an organization, laws— in short, all the tangible manifestations which power takes. Every Power tends to have a visible pole, an outer form—be it a church, nation, or an economy—and an invisible pole, an inner spirit or driving force that animates, legitimates, and regulates its physical manifestation in the world. (Wink 1984:5)

Authorities and powers by this measure are not merely the status and physical attributes of human beings but possess very real spiritual dimensions by which they regulate not only human beings but also organizations, institutions and whole structures of society. Wink argues that these powers are profound in nature and, espousing a biblical view, claims that they are "both visible *and* invisible, earthly *and* heavenly, spiritual *and* institutional" (Wink 1992:3). Foster adds, "There are fundamental spiritual realities that underlie all political, social, and economic systems. In back of brutal dictators and unjust policies and corrupt institutions are spiritual principalities and powers" (Foster 1985:182). The implications are that those who wish to see justice and power and authority properly exercised, according to the example Jesus gave, especially for rural development, must not think they are dealing only with physical realities. They must contend also with the spiritual ethos of institutions and structures. This is a formidable task, which Paul expresses very clearly: "For our struggle is not against enemies of blood and flesh, but against the rulers, against the authorities, against the cosmic powers of this present darkness, against the spiritual forces of evil in the heavenly places" (Eph. 6:12). To ignore this reality of institutional life, structures and systems, especially as we address powers in the attempt to empower others, would be at our peril (Wink 1992:6). How to tackle such a problem? According to Yoder,

> The Powers cannot simply be destroyed or set aside or ignored
> Their [evil] sovereignty must be broken. This is what Jesus did,
> concretely and historically, by living among men a genuinely hu-
> man existence. . . . In his death the Powers—in this case the most
> worthy, weighty representatives of the Jewish religion and Roman
> politics—acted in collusion. Like all men, he too was subject (but
> in his case willingly) to these powers. . . . Therefore his cross is a
> victory. . . . Not even to save his own life will he let himself be
> made a slave of these Powers. (Yoder 1972:147–48)

What Yoder points out is the paradoxical significance of the cross. Jesus triumphantly used the very instrument of humiliation, weakness and death employed by those who wielded earthly power to render their powers impotent. Wink explores this in his third volume on power, *Engaging the Powers*. His thesis is that powers are not simply evil that needs to be confronted, combated, or overcome. Rather, because the powers "have been created in, through, and for the humanizing purposes of God in Christ . . . they must be honored, criticized, resisted, and redeemed. Let us then engage these Powers, not just understand them, but to see them changed" (Wink 1992:10). Wink sees the powers through the biblical perspective as created, and thus good, but also fallen, and thus failing to fulfill their creative role; they need redeeming in Christ in the same way fallen humanity needs redeeming.

Thus, the biblical view of power is Christ's way; that is, submission to the will of the God who creates and gives power for his creative purposes. These creative purposes include the empowering of the poor so that they may begin to live fulfilled lives.

Those who exercise power are exhorted to learn from Jesus who, though he was a God and master, came in humility to serve, not to be served; to demonstrate God's love by freeing people from their various bondages—including sickness, demons, sin and oppression—so that they may live and enjoy living as free and fulfilled human beings; to give self-sacrificial service, even dying for the salvation of others; and to exercise power in creative rather than destructive ways (see Foster 1985:chaps. 10, 11).

In power structures within African rural communities, power bases seek to promote generally good conduct, healthy relationships, smooth operations of the clan or groups and families, and benefits for its members.

Clan leaders do not generally exploit their positions for the oppression of their subjects. This notwithstanding, African rural traditional power structures utilize both "power over" and "power to." These structures tend to enforce obedience without question, and conflicts of values between individuals and the group are often not dealt with. When these structures operate alongside modern power structures, multiple power relationships cause goal conflicts that are usually not easy to resolve. The use of power, especially its abuse in the hands of governments and the elite, has created widespread powerlessness, which is at the root of the poverty of the masses of rural people in developing countries.

The systemic ways in which the rich and powerful manipulate the poor and keep them in perpetual powerlessness have to be addressed through empowerment. To this end a framework is needed for an approach to empowerment that challenges the way the rich and powerful use power for oppression. A biblical perspective of power and its exercise delineates an inner spiritual dimension as well as an outer physical manifestation of power. Power in this sense is manifested not simply in individuals but also in organizations institutions, and whole structures of society. Power is created to be used for God's creative and humanizing purposes. But because power is fallen, its exercise and manifestation have tended to produce distorted and destructive effects on its subjects. Power thus needs to be redeemed. Jesus redeems power and exercises it in contrast to the way those wielding earthly power exercise it. Jesus' use of power is marked by humility, servanthood and self-giving sacrifice, not by domination, status and privilege, grabbing, oppression and violence.

7

Powerlessness
in Rural Development

In development, powerlessness is akin to the underdevelopment that has trapped developing countries vis-à-vis industrialized countries. Within developing nations, the rural areas are trapped vis-à-vis urban centers; and among people, the poor vis-à-vis the rich are locked in a form of Weberian "iron cage." Underdevelopment is a form of paralysis, and it affects all of society, both rich and poor. Some writers, like Denis Goulet, attribute underdevelopment not merely to poverty, unsatisfied wants, or minimal opportunities, but above all to "the powerlessness of societies in the face of destiny, of nature, of machine age, of scientific technology, of advanced countries, of processes they cannot understand" (Goulet 1985:44). Goulet divides the problems that make societies powerless into two categories: problems of nature, and problems of modernity.

Problems of nature seem to apply only to the situation of developing nations, rural areas and poor people. The reason is that "knowledge, wealth and the experience needed to face the problems of nature with some degree of confidence" is lacking (Goulet 1985:44). However, when problems of modernity are considered, it is not only developing or poor societies that are powerless; even technologically advanced societies show a measure of powerlessness. This powerlessness, affecting not only the poor but also the rich (though differently), accounts for some of the persistence of poverty.

In rural development powerlessness is commonly discussed and increasingly recognized in the fight against poverty. At present, most considerations of powerlessness relate this term only to the rural poor or the poor in developing nations. Yet all international development agencies, including the World Bank, agree that the fight against poverty is a global problem, because the thinking and activities of the West significantly affect world poverty, in particular rural poverty in developing countries, and vice versa.

The problem of trying to draw a clear demarcation between rich and poor, especially in developing nations where a continuum of conditions exists, has been noted. There is a polarity of conditions, however, that can define, at the one end, conditions for the rich, and at the other end, conditions for the poor. Even when the middle groups are taken into account, the elitist power structure common to developing countries sees to it that the middle groups, although they have a plurality of interests, are often coopted by and become allies of the rich and powerful. In this two-tiered structure, the rich and powerful and their allies (who may be relatively poor) oppress the powerless poor on the bottom tier.

Of the writers on powerlessness, Goudzwaard, Goulet and Freire represent the few who recognize powerlessness not only in the poor but also in the rich. Furthermore, powerlessness does not seem to be recognized in most development processes as an important concept that undergirds the persistence of poverty.

Powerlessness is a concept of vital importance in understanding why poverty persists. Most development programs have not viewed poverty alleviation from the standpoint of the double effect of powerlessness (at best addressing only the powerlessness of the poor), nor have they recognized that powerlessness underlies the persistence of poverty. These programs thus remain ill-prepared to devise appropriate approaches for combating poverty. For a lasting solution to rural poverty the reality of powerlessness underlying the persistence of poverty must first be recognized, and then must be addressed at both levels of the poor and the rich.

Interpreting Powerlessness

Powerlessness is a relational concept, in that it is experienced in relation to situations or to other people, in various forms (social, economic, political) and is found among individuals, groups and communities. Furthermore, powerlessness is functionally significant; without some purposeful engagement or work to be achieved, powerlessness bears no meaning, especially in development.

In development, undue emphasis seems to be placed on socioeconomic and political conditions as causes for the external problems of powerlessness (Friedmann 1992:chap. 2; Goulet 1985:45; Chambers 1983:113). This explains the popularity of strategies that work toward changing these conditions as solutions to powerlessness.

However, in psychopathology bias is toward the internal problems of individual aberration or misperception (Joffe and Albee 1988:53). Emphasis on internal problems has tended to capitalize on "blame the victim" philosophy; since the problem is located within the victim, solutions are sought only for internal problems identified.

Nevertheless, some analyses (such as those of Freire, Gaventa, Chambers) recognize both the external and internal problems of powerlessness. These also fall short, however, in dealing only with those external and internal problems created by natural causes. As yet, little has been presented on causes of powerlessness resulting from modernity in poverty-alleviation in development.

The Vocabulary of Powerlessness

The term *powerlessness* as applied to people has synonyms—*weakness, helplessness, hopelessness, ineffectualness, impotence*—all of which primarily mean "lacking in strength, power, vigor, drive or motivation." *Powerlessness* can also mean "lacking legal or other authority." The connotation is a state of inhibited human existence that is unpleasant and unsatisfactory.

The concept is reflected in other terms: vulnerability (Goulet; Chambers); acquiescence (Gaventa); marginalization (Gran); oppression, domination, dehumanization, culture of silence, and fatalism (Freire). Other frequently used descriptives are derived from these: passivity, dependency, exploitation, susceptibility and inertia.

In Chambers's analysis of interlinked factors underlying the deprivation trap, he applies both powerlessness and vulnerability to interpret the term. He views powerlessness as contributing to poverty "in many ways, not least through exploitation." Powerlessness limits or prevents access to resources from the state, legal redress for abuses, and ability to dispute wages or interest rates; and it entails weakness in negotiating the terms of distress sales, and only feeble influence on government to provide services for poorer people and places. It reinforces physical weakness. . . . Powerlessness also makes the poor more vulnerable to sudden demands [such as loan repayments or threats of bribes in disputes, of prosecution, fine or imprisonment]. (Chambers 1983:113–14)

Goulet defines vulnerability as the

inability to defend oneself against wounds. An individual is vulnerable when he is exposed to injury, societies when they have no adequate defense against the social forces which propel them into processes of change. (Goulet 1985:38)

A situation of acquiescence, according to Gaventa, is one in which social deprivation prevents issues from arising, grievances from being voiced, and interests from being recognized; an oppressed community does not rise up when conditions dictate, but instead acquiesces (Gaventa 1980:3). He leans on Freire when describing powerlessness:

In situations of highly unequal power relationships . . . the powerless are highly dependent. They are prevented from either self-determined action or reflection upon their actions. Denied this dialectic process, and denied the democratic experience out of which the "critical consciousness" grows, they develop a "culture of silence." "The dependent society is by definition a silent society." The culture of silence may preclude the development of consciousness amongst the powerless thus lending to the dominant an air of legitimacy. . . . In the sense of powerlessness it may also encourage a susceptibility among the dependent society to internalization of the values of the dominant themselves. (Gaventa 1980:18)

The powerless here are portrayed as not possessing an authentic voice; their voice becomes merely an echo of the voice of the dominant. Further, because the powerless have been socialized into compliance, their definitions of reality—political, social or economic—are in essence those of the dominant groups or government.

Freire characterizes oppression as dehumanization. He argues that man's vocation is to be fully human, but that this vocation is constantly negated and thwarted by "injustice, exploitation, oppression and the violence of the oppressors; affirmed by the yearning of the oppressed for freedom and justice, and their struggle to recover their lost humanity" (Freire 1972/90:20).

> Dehumanization, which marks not only those whose humanity has been stolen, but also (though in a different way) those who have stolen it, is a *distortion* of the vocation of becoming more fully human. . . . Indeed, to accept dehumanization as an historical vocation would lead either to cynicism or total despair. The struggle for humanization, . . . for the affirmation of men as persons, would be meaningless. This struggle is possible only because dehumanization . . . is *not* a given destiny but the result of an unjust order that engenders violence in the oppressors, which in turn dehumanizes the oppressed. (Freire 1972/90:20–21)

Such dehumanizing, Freire contends, is accompanied by a conditioning of the thought structure of the oppressed by contradictions of the concrete, existential situation that shapes them. The oppressed internalize the image of the oppressor, adopt the oppressor's guidelines, and become fearful of freedom. Faced by this particular problem of existential duality—in which the powerless are at the same time themselves and the oppressor—and constituted by a dialectic conflict between opposing social forces, the oppressed become entrapped into Freire's "culture of silence." In this state they are "forced to mimic the dictates of their paternal overlords to have 'authentic' voices of their own" (Gleeson 1974:365). The oppressed become fatalistic about their situation; they can do nothing about their poverty. They begin to believe it is their fate. Or, in a distorted view of the Divine. they may believe their poverty to be the will of God. At the personal level, self-depreciation sets in. The internalized image of the oppressor, telling them they are good for nothing, know nothing, are capable of learning nothing, are lazy and unproductive, convinces them of their unfitness and hence of their inferiority before their bosses, who seem to know and run things.

The Powerlessness of the Poor

The poor are victims who suffer the consequences of powerlessness. They are left out of the progress race and are powerless to catch up. Powerlessness of the poor can be defined as lack of human fulfillment or development for an individual and for people as groups or communities, resulting from socialized deprivation and conditioned inertia, as well as from lack of ownership of, or even access to, resources and social-economic-political power to control their own affairs and the development process. Internal problems at the level of the psyche and human development and external problems of a socioeconomic and political nature are interrelated in the context of powerlessness among the poor.

What seems to be happening in efforts to address the powerlessness of the poor is that attention is focused on the external problems of powerlessness but little attention is paid to internal problems. "Development in any meaningful sense must begin with, and within, the individual. Unless motivation comes from within, efforts to promote change will not be sustainable by that individual. They will remain under the power of others" (Burkey 1993:35). Burkey illustrates the image graphically, using the analogy of a building, with economic and political development forming the columns that support social development, which forms the girder of the building; all these structures stand upon the foundation of personal (human) development (Burkey 1993:38).

It often seems easier, especially given the tools of modernity, to identify and address the social, economic and political problems of powerlessness, considered to include: (a) lack of basic human resources, and social and physical infrastructure—food, clothing, shelter, education and training, health services and facilities, clean air and water, energy, transport and communication, physical security; (b) lack of ownership of or access to production resources—capital, land, credit, inputs, skills, entrepreneurship, technology and markets; and (c) lack of political power to participate in decision-making; that is to claim rights, to affect one's own development, to choose accountable local leaders and government representatives, and to share in political power for democratic planning and just, equitable and efficient allocation of communal resources in the community (Burkey 1993:chap. 2).

This list provides conceptually definable and researchable problems. It compares closely with the list that the International Fund for Agricultural Development compiled of underlying factors of poverty (see the Introduction herein). By contrast, internal problems have seemed elusive and difficult to define and address. If internal problems can be defined, then they can be addressed. Are they definable?

Defining Internal Problems of Powerlessness

Internal problems arise in the shaping of the consciousness through power relations. Powerlessness is "an adaptive response to the exploitative situation" (Gaventa 1980:92). This is well illustrated by a comment from a spokeswoman for a group of female factory workers in the crumbling Soviet Union. Asked by a television interviewer, "Now that you are free, what do you intend to do with your freedom?" the woman replied, "We have been under bondage for so many years, all our lives, we have forgotten what it means to be free. How do we know what to do with freedom?" (ITV documentary, 2 September 1991).

Internal problems tend to cause people to be dependent, to lack self-confidence, to have low self-esteem accompanied by an inferiority complex and low morale. The powerless suffer from an identity crisis. They hardly know who they really are; they take their identity from someone else. What they do, they do at another's bidding, and they find making decisions difficult. In such circumstances people tend to believe "they cannot do much to affect their circumstances, alleviate their misery, or build a better world for their children" (Joffe and Albee 1988:54). This may reflect a true perception of the situation, but when accepted as a destiny, it amounts to people receiving and believing in a poor image of themselves. Psychologists agree that a poor image about oneself is destructive; (a) it paralyses potential; (b) it creates pessimism and fatalism; (c) it ruins relationships; and (d) it makes a person unable to function well in society (Seamands 1981:49–56).

In other words, self-image—constituted by a whole system of symbols and feelings, both mental and emotional, that have been put together about the self—influences "actions and attitudes, and especially relationships with other people" (Seamands 1981:59, 60). Thus, self-image is a vital element in social change. It is futile to attempt any change directed toward improvement of conditions of the poor merely by changing their external conditions, like physical appearance or environment, without affecting the internal situation of self-image. Yet external change seems to be the modus operandi of most development efforts.

Having stressed the importance of recognizing internal problems, however, it should be said that a balanced treatment of the two sets of problems is the way ahead, since they are interrelated. Governments and aid agencies either forget or ignore this basic interrelationship (see Burkey 1993:38). In addition, in addressing powerlessness, it is important to identify the nature of the powerlessness experienced in the particular situation being considered.

Maintenance of Powerlessness

These mechanisms are inferences from the relational conditions between the powerful rich and the powerless poor:

1. *The ever-increasing gap between rich and poor:* This is exploited in the name of modernity, which has set the pace of progress in such a way that the rich have no time for the poor as human beings and may consider it a waste of resources to help the poor, since they likely will never catch up anyway. After all, it is the fault of the poor that they remain poor, and besides, those same resources are needed to keep pace with progress. The poor, left as victims, *are* helpless to catch up. The gap goes on increasing.

2. *Acts of bargaining and decision-making:* In key issues vital to the life of the community and its individual members, the poor persistently lose. The cause of failure may be lack of skills and political resources like votes, jobs or influence, which they could bring into the bargaining act, set alongside the effectiveness with which the powerful wield these resources through personal competence, political experience and organizational strength.

3. *The mobilization bias:* The poor are unable to overcome the mobilization bias of the powerful. The power-holders can program predominant values, beliefs, rituals and institutional procedures to operate systematically and consistently to their benefit (Bachrach and Baratz 1970:43), so that the poor are rendered powerless to raise any issues that might safeguard their position.

4. *Anticipated reactions:* The powerless may opt to remain powerless in anticipation of negative response to any efforts they may make. Studies have shown that often the powerless, "confronted by [the powerful] who has greater power resources decides not to make demands upon [the powerful] for fear that the latter will invoke sanctions against the former" (Bachrach and Baratz 1970:46). The powerless choose not to confront the powerful in order to avoid repercussions that may be unbearable.

5. *Processes of socialization and internalization:* Social legitimations are developed around the powerful and instilled as beliefs or roles or images in the powerless (Gaventa 1980:15). Through socialization, the powerless have no alternative but to develop a thought structure conditioned by the situation of their socialization or shaping. The powerless internalize the beliefs, roles and images of this socialization, which become deeply established in their innermost being (Freire 1972/90:24). The normal consequence is that the powerless one, as Freire puts it, "looks inward and decides that it is totally unable to cope with its misery: it concludes that it is impotent" (Freire n.d.:3). Often the powerless begin to treat their powerlessness as fate and destiny: "Nothing can be done about it."

Powerlessness of the Rich and Powerful

The poor are powerless victims; the rich are powerless victors. They do not suffer the same consequences of poverty and deprivation resulting from powerlessness, but their powerlessness—their helplessness to change things to improve the situation of the poor—contributes to the perpetuation of poverty. The way they suffer personally, however, is in some loss of their humanity.

Dehumanization . . . marks not only those whose humanity has been stolen, but also (though in a different way) those who have stolen it. [This] is a distortion of the vocation of becoming more fully human. (Freire 1972/90:20–21)

There is a sense here of a conditioning of the rich, too, to feel that their position of power and domination is a "given," like that of the poor, and that there is no need to alter the status quo. This has led to a systemic blindness in the rich that dictates that the situation cannot be any other way, breeding a form of helplessness to change.

Another aspect of the powerlessness of the rich is defined within the concept of modernity. There is a sense of powerlessness that Goudzwaard, supported by other writers, has identified as a reality in the lives of many people in industrialized nations. This sense of powerlessness is closely connected with the total faith industrial societies have placed in progress. As Eberhard Ernst puts it: "The West has learned to live by *faith* in progress, in *hope* of progress, and out of *love* toward progress" (quoted in Goudzwaard 1984:151). Progress has turned out to be a form of religion providing "propelling all-embracing visions which direct persons in everything they feel, think and do." The influence of ideas of progress has become inescapably "noticeable in the architecture of [Western] society" (Goudzwaard 1979:xxii). The connection of progress to powerlessness, which undergirds the poverty of the poor, is that industrialized societies, copied by third-world elites, are so consumed in the race for progress that they have neither space nor instrumentality for the poor. Given that alleviating poverty requires global attention, "progress" contributes to the persistence of poverty, since it consumes attention and creates a form of powerlessness that renders people hopeless or inert in the face of poverty.

As an extension of the philosophy of the Enlightenment, human progress through scientific and technological processes has created a sense of powerlessness among people of industrialized nations by affecting and taking control not only of consciousness or the thought process, words and actions of the rich and powerful, but also of organizational and institutional structures. Technology and production "pulverise everything in their path: the landscape, the natural environment, history and tradition, the amenities and civilities, the privacy and spaciousness of life, beauty, and the fragile, slow-growing social structures which bind" people together, creating a situation in which people in the West "no longer understand the system under which [they] live. . . . The system has been permitted to assume unchallenged power to dominate [people's] lives, and now rumbles along, unguided and therefore indifferent to human life" (Reich, quoted in Goudzwaard 1979: 153–54). This is similar to Wink's (1992) discussion of powers (see chap. 6 herein). From a biblical perspective, the powers of modernity, like all other powers, are fallen and seek to dominate but can be redeemed.

Other writers have come to similar conclusions. Lapp draws an analogy between today's industrial society and a train gathering speed on a track with "unknown switches and unknown destinations." He adds, "No single scientist is in the engine cab and there may be demons at the switch. Most society is in the caboose and looking backward" (Lapp, cited in Goudzwaard 1979:153). Lowith, commenting on the fate of progress, states:

> An uncanny coincidence of fatalism and a will to progress presently characterise all contemporary thinking about the future course of history. Progress now threatens us; it has become our fate. . . . [we are] set free and yet imprisoned by our own power. . . . Power itself goes on progressing; we can no longer stop it or turn it around. (quoted in Goudzwaard 1979:153)

Schiller likens Western societies' efforts to pursue further economic progress to riding a tiger. "The tiger simply goes his own way and might lead us to a fatal destination. However, to jump off would be even more dangerous. Therefore, we continue our uncontrollable ride, clinging to the back of what might become our ruin" (quoted in Goudzwaard 1979:154).

What all these authors express is how powerfully the forces of modernity through progress are claiming superiority over social structures and human beings, who are left fearful and uneasy. This profound feeling of helplessness and insecurity has caused human beings to begin to believe that these forces of progress, expressed through science, technology and economics, are independent entities that have taken control of institutions, social structures and human beings. Such hopelessness removes from modern society the power to change things.

If this is the effect of modernity in Western societies, it goes without saying that these forces in their turn have effectively spread the impact of modernity to less developed countries. One accompanying feature of modernity is urbanization. In less developed countries, urban centers are copies of the West in all human, social, institutional and national systems. All the forms of powerlessness identified in Western societies can be found among the educated elite, the rich and the powerful in less developed countries, who mostly live in urban centers. How does the powerlessness of the rich affect the poverty of the poor?

Impact of the Powerlessness of the Rich on Poverty

Alleviation of poverty, as indicated, is a task to be tackled globally by the joint forces of the industrialized nations and the less developed countries, of the rich and poor. In this task the powerlessness of the rich should not be viewed as an isolated phenomenon that has no effect on the poverty of the poor. Powerlessness as a pervasive phenomenon affects relations among people. It creates alienation and estrangement between the rich and the poor. If progress goes on progressing like a "speeding train," what option does this leave if one is to survive? One option many have chosen is to keep pace. This has automatically implied no time for others, especially the poor, whom the speeding train either leaves behind or who fall off. Even if the poor try to "walk" by use of indigenous and traditional methods, or to "run" by application of appropriate technology, organizations and institutions, they will not catch up.

The consciousness, words and actions of the rich are affected by values dictated by progress. In the realm of development the message of economics is that increased personal incomes is the best guarantee for happiness in life—in short, *materialism.* Market forces set producers against consumers (the latter being easily manipulated) and determine winners and losers. The winners are always hardworking and deserve their profits; as for losers (the poor), it is their fault for not working hard, a fallacy conveniently believed by many, for it is well known how hardworking the poor can be, even amid hostile conditions. Meanwhile, the pace, direction and extent of progress in science and technology, the glamorous opportunities, the institutional and social structures set up, and the amount of resources needed for research in these areas available in the West, leave no space and no time for the poverty problems of less developed countries and groups of the poor.

The game here is human progress, which has come to be defined in terms of success in the economic sphere, as well as the scientific and technological spheres. This success defines the value placed on human beings. The more successful they are, the more worthy they are to receive the world's attention and economic, scientific and technological resources to address their problems. This scenario is easily one of overt negligent powerlessness, in which the poor are valueless and of no use in the world of success; let them suffer and die. It is "survival of the fittest" and "the best for a better world"—in short, *Darwinianism.*

Powerlessness of the State

The state can also be powerless to change things for the good of the poor. Government policies either do not treat alleviation of poverty as a priority or may be directly harmful to the poor through taxation, pricing, land distribution and restricted access to capital and credit. Or government planning policy for economic development may be biased toward the modern sector at the expense of the traditional rural sector, where most of the poor live. Further, frequent political conflicts and civil strife have meant destructive wars and have consumed government resources so that no time or resources are left for the poor. Finally, external pressures caused by international processes exert exorbitant demands on the resources and time of governments of developing countries, either for payment of external debt or for administering World Bank and IMF-imposed structural adjustment programs.

The IFAD summarizes these problems (see the Introduction herein) as processes that create and perpetuate poverty: domestic policy biases, rural/urban dualism, political conflicts and civil strife, and international processes. These combine in varying degrees to undercut developing countries' ability to attend effectively to the poverty of their nationals. Further implications include these governments' inability to provide social services, welfare, infrastructure and effective rural development programs.

8

Empowerment
in Rural Development

The need to alleviate poverty in the contemporary world is undeniable, not only in rural development programs of developing countries, but in the development programs of the world as a whole. The international development community does not need further evidence than to see how the world recession of the early 1990s and the increasing turmoil of wars, lack of governance and famine (which cause massive destruction and misuse of development resources) have increased the devastating impact of poverty on a number of nations, both developing and developed. The World Bank, for example, devoted the whole of its 1990 annual report to the topic of poverty, implying that it still regarded poverty as among the highest issues on the development agenda at the end of a century of "progress."

Alleviation of poverty, even when undertaken within a rural development program, needs to remain on national and global agendas. The main point of rural development in most developing countries is alleviation of poverty. "Rural Development . . . requires government action and is of such global import that it would postulate the existence even of a world government" (Carmen 1990:52). Likewise:

> It is not only within nations that we need to give priority to Rural
> Development. World growth, and world development, must also
> be based on a strategy of rural development. And for the world,

the rural areas are the developing nations. Everything which I have said in relation to the implications of a strategy of rural development within nations can be applied to the international economic and political relationships. The only exception—and it is an important one—is we have no world government which can make decisions and enforce them. (Nyerere 1979:11)

Alleviation of poverty through rural development cannot be left either to rural areas alone or to developing nations on their own. This would be tantamount to condemning the process of development simply to a redistribution of poverty rather than elimination of poverty. Alleviation of poverty needs all peoples of the world and their national governments, as well as non-governmental agencies, to join in the effort.

Unless rich people and rich nations are challenged to face up to their moral responsibility and accountability—not only to the poor, but also in the just sharing of the world's resources—empowerment of only the poor will hardly alter the present status quo, especially the increasing gap between the rich and the poor. The world capitalist system with its deeply entrenched structures, which give a warrant to the rich to go on amassing material possessions at the expense of the poor, must be addressed. Empowerment of *both* rich and poor is imperative.

The Concept of Empowerment

Empowerment has existed in the minds and literature of advocates of alternative development for almost as long as the process of rethinking development has existed. *Empowerment* became an accepted term in development vocabulary particularly after the World Conference on Agrarian Reform and Rural Development (WCARRD) in 1979, where emphasis was placed on the importance of the transfer of power in development (Oakley 1991:9). However, not until the late 1980s and early 1990s did empowerment in development receive direct and increasing prominence, particularly among nongovernmental organizations (NGOs), grassroots efforts (projects) and also some international development agencies. These avenues initially popularized the concept more explicitly through sectoral strategies of development for, for example, women (UNICEF 1986); education (Kronenburg 1986); organization (Mehta 1988; Linthicum 1991); and health (Werner 1988).

The more a concept like empowerment becomes understood, the more its application gains ground at all levels of development, including the integrated level, which in essence can be viewed as holistic empowerment. A new awareness in development circles of the crucial importance of empowerment in the entire process of development stresses a sociopolitical goal of "the equalising of power and basic rights" (Werner 1988:1). This seems to be a recognition that the poverty of people is based on powerlessness—a lack of power rendering them not only "weakened economically, socially and politically," but also "blinded to their own strengths and abilities" (Fernando 1988:10) to engage in development programs that could empower them to take control and bring about desired social change. The challenge for empowerment is, therefore, to respond to powerlessness in all its forms in all development activity.

Interpreting Empowerment

Despite having been part of development vocabulary for many years, the concept of empowerment has not been well defined.

Some see empowering as the development of skills and abilities to enable rural people to manage better, have a say in or negotiate with existing development delivery systems; others see it as more fundamental and essentially concerned with enabling rural people to decide upon and take the actions which they believe are essential to their development. (Oakley 1991:9)

Both the development of managerial and negotiating skills and abilities and development of decision-making and action-oriented capabilities are encapsulated in this quotation. "Empowering participatory approaches are characterised by enabling processes" (Kronenburg 1986:265). Elliott also interprets empowerment as a process "committed to enabling (or training) communities" (Elliott 1987a:58).

It follows from these definitions that lack of skills, abilities and hence initiative often force the poor into dependency relationships with outsiders, not only for decision-making concerning their development activities, but also for management and control of the whole development process. This renders the poor powerless and fosters those inimical processes that keep them perpetually poor. Poverty alleviation seen from this perspective will rightly require an empowerment approach that focuses on providing the poor with skills, abilities and initiative. In a specific situation these may constitute critical factors in the poverty in question, and this action may be adequate. But more often, where there are innumerable other factors related to and creating the powerlessness that underlies poverty, this view is too narrow and limited and will prove insufficient to bring about desirable empowerment.

Interpretation of empowerment as a *process* (of empowering, of bestowing or releasing power—and a *state* (of being empowered, possessing power) has two implications; namely, that empowerment involves the prior existence of absolute or relative powerlessness in an individual or group, and that empowerment is mediated by an outside intervention. Furthermore, empowerment as a process is viewed to be gradual, occurring through a buildup from event to event and involving a fundamental change in both self-concept—the way the individual or group perceives itself— and in relationships with other individuals or groups in the society.

Another view describes empowerment as *organization*: the poor need both to be organized and to have organized mediating structures to enable them to become more resourceful in their development efforts. Mehta (1988) and Linthicum (1991) characterize the organizing of the poor as empowering. Mehta views the poor as "scattered and unorganized"; he argues that organizing the poor, though a task "beset with formidable problems," is the way by which latent capabilities of the poor come to the surface and can be utilized creatively (Mehta 1988:174). Linthicum views community organization as a

> process by which people of an . . . area organize themselves to "take charge" of their situation and thus develop a sense of being a community together. It is . . . [an] effective tool for the poor and powerless as they determine for themselves the actions they will take to deal with the essential forces that are destroying their community and consequently causing them to be powerless. (Linthicum 1991:31)

Once organized, the poor can have a tremendous power of collective action and can overcome dependency as they gain power to build up alternatives that supply their needs. Community organization, Linthicum states, empowers the poor "to meaningfully encounter, cope with and sometimes change . . . structures and systems" (Linthicum 1991:31). Additionally, the resulting collective leadership rids them of overbearing elitism. "Collective efforts are very important in this respect which alone can sustain the organisation and cement the unity of the poor to fight against corruption and other illegal practices" (Mehta 1988:185).

Peter L. Berger and Richard John Neuhaus also view empowerment through mediating structures. These are institutions that they define as "standing between the individual in his private life and the large institutions of public life" (Berger and Neuhaus 1984:251). Their position is that modernization creates a "powerlessness in the face of institutions controlled by those whom [the poor] do not know and whose values [the poor] often do not share." Modernity's megastructures include the modern state itself, large economic conglomerates of capitalist enterprise, big labor unions, and the growing bureaucracies that administer wide sectors of society, as in education and organized professions. Because the rich and powerful often have ways to resist the encroachment of megastructures that the poor do not have, they contend that the organizing of mediating structures would take account of the needs of the poor as a "principal expression of the real values and the real needs of the people in society." They see mediating structures as a paradigm that "aims at empowering the poor" and "at spreading the power around a bit more—. . . where it matters, in people's control over their own lives" (Berger and Neuhaus 1984:256).

Organization certainly is one of the important elements of empowerment. But on its own it is not sufficient; other elements need to accompany organization for a complete or holistic empowerment process.

Other interpretations have tended to equate empowerment with participation. At worst, they make empowerment nothing more than an advanced state of, or the end result of, participation, which therefore does not deserve treatment as a separate approach. Participation to some has become a catch-all strategy that can take care of anything that might fall under any analysis of empowerment.

Participation and empowerment are closely related and could be (and have been) at times loosely used interchangeably. In fact, the concepts of popular participation put forward by advocates such as Rahman (1984) and the UNRISD dialogue (1983) contain the major elements of an empowering approach. Despite these discussions equating empowerment with participation, there are identifiable distinctions, not least of which deals with measurability. Both concepts are difficult to measure, but analysts of participation generally use empowerment as the measure, or the criterion of effectiveness of participation. In terms of priorities in alleviation of poverty, empowerment comes before participation, because in a situation of underlying powerlessness, one needs to be empowered in order to participate. One cannot participate effectively when powerless.

The last interpretation of empowerment considered here treats empowerment as the third and best approach by NGOs in development. First was the welfare approach, in which delivery of services to specific groups was made with no concern for empowerment of the local communities; second came the development approach concerned with supporting projects to increase the productive capacity of self-reliance. The third approach, in which Elliott treats development in terms of empowerment, "sees poverty as a result of political processes and is therefore committed to enabling (or training) communities to enter those processes" (Elliott 1987a:58). This view of empowerment narrows the perspective to political processes. But Elliott also views empowerment as a process that cannot be reduced to "something that can be delivered or bought"; neither can it be "reduced to a project" (Elliott 1987a:59). This view of empowerment as a process is the major sense in which empowerment is treated and developed in the next section.

Empowerment as a Process

As a process, empowerment involves the following features:

- Empowerment is a people-oriented process; as such it has a moral focus on relations among individual persons, families, households and communities, and it draws its values from that sphere (Friedmann 1992:33).
- Empowerment is a vital and integral element of development geared toward the building up of internal and external abilities and initiatives of rural people and communities in order to enable them to play an active part in the alleviation of poverty.
- Empowerment is a distinctive process for achieving authentic sustainable development.
- Empowerment is a gradual learning process, progressing from the simple and known to large and more complex activities.
- Although empowerment must be a grassroots process, based at a specific location and social group, like a village or community, it requires catalytic and facilitatory external intervention.

- Empowerment requires a strong government to bolster its grassroots efforts, including grassroots political activity.
- Empowerment distinguishes itself from impersonal processes responsive to the principle of economic growth efficiency and seeks the empowerment of households and their individual members through their involvement in socially and politically relevant actions (Friedmann 1992:33).

In order to achieve all of the above, a holistic empowerment process needs to incorporate different and varied elements, such as: (a) building up personal self-esteem, dignity, identity, confidence and a sense of belonging for individuals and groups in a community; (b) equipping the rural poor with capabilities and skills for decision-making, action, management, negotiation and production; (c) acquiring just access to productive resources, rights and development power; (d) satisfying the spiritual needs of the people, especially enabling them to enter into a personal relationship with their Maker; (e) challenging existing (local, national and international) structures and institutions to create space for appropriate structures and mediating institutions and organizations to foster development efforts of the poor; (f) challenging conditioned behavioral constructs and the actions of the rich in order to make them responsive to the poor; and (g) instituting mechanisms guided by ethical principles for conscious identification of and opposition to inimical and inhuman effects that inhibit empowerment.

Holistic Empowerment

The term *holistic* is an adjective from the noun *holism*, which means "the theory that reality is made up of organic or unified wholes that are greater than the simple sum of their parts" (Universal Dictionary). Holistic empowerment thus presupposes that empowerment can subsist in part. Indeed it is only in part that current efforts are being deemed as empowerment. In particular, a number of sectoral activities (such as health, women, and others) are carried out by NGOs under the banner of empowerment. This conveys an idea that there exists in development circles a pervasive negative view toward the integral wholeness of development work, although there is much talk, and even in some quarters the practice, of integrated development. In other words, what is currently taking place in the name of empowerment amounts to *parts* of empowerment. And because of being only *part*, their impact has been relatively insignificant and easily negated by the deep-rooted countervailing forces of poverty. What is needed, especially in the context of sustainable development, is holistic empowerment; that is, an empowerment that will be greater in its impact on those countervailing forces than the simple sum of the parts of empowerment that are being achieved. What does this desirable holistic empowerment amount to?

Holistic empowerment can be understood as a three-tiered integral process. The first tier concerns the individual person; the second tier concerns the community; and the third tier concerns structures. An empowerment process should treat each individual as a whole person with tripartite needs of a material, spiritual and social nature. The community in development is often conceived and treated as composed of only the poor. However, a community as a whole entity is composed of an entire population (consisting of the rich, the poor and those in between), including a local leadership, all of whom need to be addressed by an empowerment process. Structures are, for example, cultural and traditional, legal, socioeconomic, political or governmental, institutional, organizational and international. Summoning these structures to respond positively and to foster a development process that enhances human flourishing is the task of empowerment.

Holistic empowerment, therefore, requires the integral empowerment of whole persons, communities as complete entities, and a range of structures that affect the individuals and their communities. This integral view of empowerment is what governments in developing countries need to adopt and seek to implement for their development plans. NGOs in their turn should be made to comply with what contributes to holistic empowerment to assist these countries to attain sustainable development.

The Case for Empowerment[1]

Empowerment as an alternative approach seeks changes in existing approaches to development that include focus on people, the politics of

---

[1] Material in this section draws heavily on Friedmann 1992:31–36 and is presented in terms that highlight positive characteristics which empowerment seeks to achieve and which distinguish empowerment from mainstream neoclassical approaches to development.

inclusive democracy, appropriate economic growth, gender equality and sustainability or intergenerational equity. What all this means is that empowerment seeks to break away from conventional models emphasizing efficient economic growth. Real empowerment stresses appropriate economic growth optimizing use of resources over several broad and competing objectives; namely, inclusive democracy and incorporation through empowerment of excluded sectors of population in the wider processes of societal development, and sensitivity to the social and environmental costs of its production investment.

Holistic empowerment seeks to center on people and their environment rather than on production and profits. Its basic unit of analysis is the household, not the firm of the neo-classical model. Mainstream neo-classical economic models assume a person who is a rational, utility-maximizing being, with a built-in moral calculus, and declare that the market's rules of competition dictate that whatever promotes one's material interest will also further the interests of all individuals together. Empowerment as an alternative seeks to be sensitive to moral ethics and to view people as natural, moral human beings with moral obligations who, although they compete, work together (here, the competition referred to is "healthy" competition rather than the "cut-throat perfect competition" of the theory of competition, which implies conflict and absolute self-interest). Empowered people may relate to each other according to a complex moral code that determines cultural responses; as moral beings, they not only have *wants* and *desires*, but also have *needs* of a psychological nature, namely, needs for affection, self-expression, and esteem that are not available as commodities but arise directly from human encounters or relationships.

In addition, empowerment as an alternative seeks to acknowledge other human *needs* and the established rights of people and to empower people through the satisfaction of those needs and the acquisition of those rights.

Empowerment as an alternative recognizes the importance of the microsphere of political and territorial life in its intrinsic diversity; it thus seeks decentralization and participatory decision-making in development and historical continuity in territorial development, and it seeks to remove structural constraints on the possibilities for local development. At the same time, empowered communities are enabled to support or establish a strong state that is agile, responsive and accountable to its citizens in order to implement those policies that require a state apparatus. Such a strong state would be based on an inclusive democracy "in which the powers to manage problems that are best handled locally have been devolved to local units of governance and to the people themselves organized in their communities" (Friedmann 1992:35).

In neo-classical models production takes place away from home—in the factory, field or office—and households are treated as consuming units that provide accommodation and leisure for workers and the biological reproduction of labor. Consumption is considered a private and individualized activity, while production is a public activity subject to state regulation. Empowerment as an alternative, according to Ekeh, contrasts with this view and treats households as essentially productive and active units that thrive on cooperative actions and community relations that are governed by a fundamental ethical principle of reciprocity that underlies all social conduct (quoted in Friedmann 1992:33).

According to Friedmann, empowerment as an alternative form of development seeks to empower individuals and communities in their pursuit of appropriate development in three basic kinds of power: socioeconomic, political and psychological. Socioeconomic power "is concerned with access to certain 'bases' of household production, such as information, knowledge and skills, participation in social organizations, and financial resources" (Friedmann 1992:33). Increase in socioeconomic power for a household increases its access to resource bases as well as its ability to produce wealth. Political power is concerned with "access of individual household members to the process by which decisions, particularly those that affect their own future, are made" (Friedmann 1992:33). This power confers on local people the power to vote, to have a voice, and to engage in collective action. Friedmann describes psychological power as a sense of potency for the individual: "Where present, it is demonstrated in self-confident behavior. Psychological empowerment is often a result of successful action in the social or political domains, though it may also result from intersubjective work" (Friedmann 1992:33). Increased sense of personal potency contributes positively to a household's strength for increased struggle in the arenas of socioeconomic and political power (Friedmann 1992:33).

Friedmann expresses here one of the major tasks with which empowerment is concerned, that is, the distribution of power. To bring this about, confrontation with power-holders whose positions become threatened is inevitable and necessary. Empowerment involves disturbance of the status quo in order to bring about desired social change. An empowerment approach to development aims not only at a genuine and lasting improvement of people's conditions, but also is a political struggle for power for individuals and communities.

Friedmann observes a sequence in empowerment through distribution of power in which political empowerment appears to require a prior socioeconomic empowerment, through which effective participation in politics becomes possible. In other words, gains in socioeconomic power must be translated into effective political power to enable the formerly powerless to consolidate a sustained development process. The location of power in the community in this context must be diffused in the hands of the people in the community, more or less in a pluralistic mode, and not located in an elite, which would be the antithesis of empowerment.

Empowerment further seeks to encompass world resource and power imbalances, and to address these in such a way that the rich and powerful nations work together with poor nations to alleviate poverty. If poverty is to be eliminated, a new global redistribution agenda for resources and power needs to be drawn up that directly addresses the increasing gap between the rich and powerful and the poor and powerless. Anything less will continue to perpetuate poverty in poor societies and poor nations, and all lesser attempts at poverty alleviation will result in merely redistributing poverty.

If empowerment is a people-oriented process that requires a moral focus for relationships of individuals in community, then without a moral focus, even if holism is featured, an empowerment alternative may not prove effective or sustainable. But such a moral focus needs ethical principles to guide it. Such ethical principles, especially if applied to an approach that is to relate to widespread conditions, need to be grounded in some absolutes to avoid the common problem of relativism in application. It is on this basis that this study suggests the application of biblical ethical principles on the grounds that the Bible asserts itself as the Word of God, the Creator, to his creation for the ordering of life and its issues, among which is development (see chaps. 2–5 herein).

9

Development Agency Structures and Development Projects

Development projects constitute a vital component in the development process, as tools in the hands of development agencies. To a large extent the structures and projects devised by development agencies determine the outcome of the development process in general, and specifically of rural development in less developed countries. Different causes, including strategies, have been blamed for the unsatisfactory results of development, but scarcely ever is the blame placed on the structures of development agencies and the process of development projects, or their design and implementation requirements. To explore the manner in which the structures of development agencies and the project process can be obstacles in the development process, this chapter traces the forces that have shaped the structures of agencies and created the characteristics that development projects have assumed, and it offers a brief account of the development experience of less developed countries in their relationships with such organizational structures and development project processes.

Influence of Past Strategies

Because theory and strategy in development are closely related (Hettne 1990:3), development strategies throughout the history of development have been influenced by various dominant theories. Strategies in their turn influence development policies, which determine the nature and outcome of development projects, the means by which policies are implemented by development agencies (Griffin and Knight 1990:2; Rondinelli 1983a:3). Development experience in less developed countries indicates that the dominant theories, and hence strategies, that have held great sway in their processes have been foreign, mostly of Western or Eurocentric origin (Hettne 1990:5, 36; Lewis and Kallab 1986:6; Wignaraja 1984:7; Todaro 1977/89:42; Schneider 1988:1).

In the 1940s, 1950s and early 1960s the dominant Western development philosophy was *mechanistic positivism*, which sought to solve less developed countries' development problems through rationalistic approaches. These in turn treated less developed countries' problems with *predetermined universalism*, that is, with uniformity or little distinction (Todaro 1977/89:63; Martin and Kandal 1989:6).

> Theorizing about development was more or less mechanical application of the main body of theory of whatever discipline to the countries of the Third World under the assumption the differences between . . . problems . . . was one of degree rather than of kind. (Hettne 1990:1)

Eurocentric theories were applied in developing countries not only in a mechanistic manner but also without consulting the less developed countries regarding their needs and priorities (Hettne 1990:5). Development was simply imposed, top-down; it was generally believed that development could be "induced or imposed" (Mountjoy 1963:27), a point re-emphasized by Sen: "These countries [were] expected to perform like wind-up toys and 'lumber through' the various stages of development single-mindedly" (Sen 1983:748). Julian Laite has described developmentalism in terms of modernization, in which less developed countries, as underdeveloped states, make progress toward becoming developed states, as exemplified by Britain and America. Included in this modernization, during global reconstruction after World War II, were such processes as urbanization, industrialization and democratization, where the latter entailed the "rupture of traditional value systems and the inculcation of striving after personal motivation" (Laite 1984:190).

Wallerstein gives a more graphic description of developmentalism:

This perspective assumed that all states were engaged in "developing" . . . that their progress along this path could be measured quantitatively and synchronically, and that on the basis of knowledge derived from such measurements, governments could in fact hasten the process, which was a highly commendable thing to do. Since these states were proceeding down parallel paths, *all* states were intrinsically capable of achieving the desired results. The only serious intellectual question was why so many resisted doing so. (quoted in Gran 1983:8)

Associated with this view was the belief that development was transferable and imitative (Wignaraja 1984:4; Hettne 1990:76; Singh 1988). If the experience of the developed countries, along with some resources, were transferred to the developing countries, the gap between industrialized and less developed countries would be narrowed, and less developed countries would catch up. The consequences, Wignaraja argues, "may have helped to create 'soft' societies, impoverish rural areas and increase the dependence" of less developed countries (Wignaraja 1984:4).

Rationalism dominant in the analysis of development models asserted that

complex social problems [could] be understood through systematic analysis and solved through comprehensive analysis . . . [that] exhaustive analysis [would] lead to a concise definition of problems, and generate alternatives from which optimal and correct policy choices [could] be made . . . [that] models or theories of social change [could] be constructed in problem definition and policy formulation, that these policies will respond adequately to human needs and that there is a direct relationship between government action and social problems. (Rondinelli 1983a:2)

This view was later criticized and labeled one of the causes of failure in past development strategies to identify adequately and address less developed countries' development problems. Gran, for example, recognized that one cause of failure was the choice made of the "state or society as the unit of analysis, as though each nation-state were a relatively autonomous unit," rather than analysis of a unit such as "mode of production," which would encompass "ways of understanding people as they act and relate to each other" (Gran 1983:9).

The resulting dissatisfaction led to new trends in development that placed emphasis on growth and modernization. These were to characterize post-independence strategies of development.

Emphasis on Growth and Modernization

Thinking discussed above laid the foundations for the development experience in most developing countries after independence, including the rise of development planning, development projects, and the state or government as chief actor in the development process. These features are still prominent in development in less developed countries—in particular development projects—although the role of the state as chief actor has been supplemented and in crisis even supplanted by NGOs.

Development objectives, according to dominant thinking, were founded upon economic growth. Results were measured primarily in economic terms governed by the laws of economic efficiency for allocation of resources. Economic growth became the central theme of modernization theories and strategies of development in the 1950s and 1960s. A common belief was that newly emerging, less developed nations were backward and underdeveloped, and hence needed an urgent inflow of experience and resources, especially capital, from developed countries—and that the lack of these was constraining development. Inflow would somehow lift these countries out of the doldrums of underdevelopment and set them on the road to "progress" (Lewis and Kallab 1986:5; Wignaraja 1984:3). Economic growth was equated with progress and viewed as a linear process by a majority of writers, following what Rostow called the five stages of growth (1960:3). The five stages were successive, and each country supposedly had to pass through each stage in order to ensure growth (Todaro 1977/89:63; Martin and Kandal 1989:6). Hettne argues that Rostow's doctrine played an important political role in the late 1950s and 1960s and made a great economic contribution within the tradition of modernization theory. It also represented a "typical expression of a western development paradigm in its capitalist form," encompassing the traditional society stage; the pre-takeoff stage; the takeoff stage; the road to maturity stage; and the mass-consumption-society stage (Hettne 1990:63). Rostow's theory later came under heavy criticism.

Optimism was still expressed in the possibility of finding shortcuts in the long historical process of development experienced by developed economies, and achieving desired results, especially improved standards of living, much more quickly (Robinson 1964:x; Mountjoy 1963:26). Achievement of quick results became a goal, in the belief that "rapid economic growth" was sure to take place with "central planning and control of the economy [by government] as a top-down process with emphasis on industrialisation, modernisation and urbanisation" (Wignaraja 1984:3). A strong link was thus formed between the planning process and government bureaucratic control. "The planning process in most developing countries tended to be coupled . . . with proliferating direct controls and proliferating bureaucracies to administer them" (Lewis and Kallab 1986:6). This led to a technocratic approach to development.

Technocratic Planning and Organizational Bureaucracies

After the mid-1960s the planning process and development projects became increasingly the focal instruments of the development process in the hands of development agencies. Development projects came to be regarded as specialized enterprises requiring technocrats, trained bureaucrats and well-educated political leaders. This in turn strengthened the technocratic approach, which later became entrenched in the planning and administrative machinery of less developed countries.

With the emphasis on efficiency and control, it was hoped that well-planned and well-executed projects of investments and innovations, coupled with adequate supports and controls for implementing government economic policies, would allow developing economies to overcome stagnation (Mountjoy 1963:27; Rondinelli 1983a:5). In other words, it was believed that economic development could be induced or even imposed as a top-down process through the technocratic apparatus. Goals were determined by governments, which became responsible for coordinating and planning projects deemed necessary for the attainment of these goals (Mountjoy 1963:27).

Systems approaches had to be introduced, because they were both compatible with "macro-economic concepts of development prevalent in the strategies of the 1950s and 1960s" and effective for "reducing uncertainty and increasing influence of technocrats" (Rondinelli 1983a:5). The outcome, however, was unfavorable, because although "politicians and administrators embraced control-oriented planning and management techniques," these techniques were "either ineffective or inherently incapable of reducing uncertainty" (Rondinelli 1983a:5), especially as the development process became increasingly more complex and uncertainty became more widespread. Adoption of systems-approach principles was consistent with the conventional notion that "planners and government [needed] strong power to plan; that planning has to be 'imperative' in nature"; and that without centralization and strong executive control to impose it, the plan was doomed (Benveniste 1972:27).

At another level, a rationale for a systems approach put forward by Benveniste was that, first, the governments in less developed countries did not control all major factors "affecting economic and social change," and second, the organizations or entire governments in less developed countries were unable "to function in an environment that had become too uncertain" (Benveniste 1972:24). Consequently, "the trend toward quantification and the introduction of technocratic methods of analysis wrapped national planners and foreign experts in the mantle of authoritativeness, [in which] their tools became their power" (Rondinelli 1983a:6).

The technocratic model thus took the reins of the development process through bureaucratic control of the scientific experts or technicians involved. This technocratic model was also rationalist. One assumption was the existence of an authoritative and objective decision-making process whose actions could, if carried out correctly, ameliorate economic and social adversities (Rondinelli 1983a:3). As such, much trust had to be placed in the technocrats' ability to plan and implement projects and to apply the virtues of the planning process by use of systems and statistical analyses. With these as tools, the technocrats were meant to foresee trends and problems of the future and hence remove such obstacles to progress as uncertainty and wasteful resource allocation. This they would supposedly accomplish by careful forethought and timely action.

The consequence of this technocratic approach was that "knowledge and power to control it become concentrated in the hands of those with the technical skills necessary to understand the language and methods being used" (Edwards 1989:118). The premise that development consists of transfers of skills, information and technology "creates a role for the expert as the only person capable of mediating" not only the transfers between persons or societies, but more so, the transfer of development as a process from "developed" to "underdeveloped" nations (Edwards 1989:118), and within less developed countries, from progressive modern/urban sectors to lagging traditional/rural sectors. The "trickle down" process was also presumed to occur.

This technocratic approach met with criticism, in particular from development thinkers concerned with rural development. One such well-documented criticism, by Robert Hummel (1977), critiqued the technocratic model in terms of bureaucracy in organizational structures. Salient features of his argument, presented in Gran (1983:16–17) are summarized below:

I.   General Features of a Technocratic Model:
   • The internal workings of modern technocratic bureaucracy are basically alien to and quite distinct from particularly the rural community and its social structure.
   • The gap between technocratic bureaucracy and the rest of society is quite wide.
   • The imperative within the system is control.
   • Its essential nature is rationally organized action.

II. Five Aspects of Organizational Bureaucratic Behavior:
   (a) As a Political Entity:
   • It is an authoritarian, hierarchical control instrument.
   • It replaces the needs of people with the needs of systems.
   • It hires functionaries instead of citizens.
   • It requires the application of management instead of functional representative leadership.
   (b) As a Cultural Entity:
   • It replaces social norms with operational codes.
   • It replaces ethics with effectiveness and material efficiency.
   (c) As a Psychological Instrument:
   • It creates new forms of dependency.
   • Role and work identity replace person and personality.
   • Conditioning takes the place of socialization.
   • Teamwork is more rewarded than [individual] skill.
   (d) As a Communication Instrument:

- It changes the way people think and the words they use.
- It replaces dialogue with command.
- It replaces causal reasoning with analogous (causal) reasoning.
- It develops specialized secret (esoteric) language to prevent external supervision.

(e) As a Social Entity:

- It turns people into cases or objects.
- It turns social action into functions.

The result is dehumanization and powerlessness, which is more acutely experienced by marginalized rural people.

> Without the initial institutional support given to recruits into bureaucracy, clients must learn a new language, tune in to new norms, bow properly to immense institutional power, understand and flatter the bureaucratic personality, and try to become a "case." Paradoxically, especially in welfare bureaucracies, only to the extent that clients surrender their humanity, are they given the bare promise of material support by which to uphold that humanity. (Hummel 1977:17)

Gran shows how Hummel's argument pinpoints what the "irresolvable dilemma" in the essential nature of organizations—their tendency to control. "If the essential nature of organisations . . . is to seek to control, how can one use them as a tool for liberation that is implicit in a participatory society and participatory development?" (Gran 1983:17)—or in an empowering approach to development?

Organizational structures, governmental or nongovernmental, are important to development. They not only form the apparatus for planning development, but they also provide the arrangements behind development projects by which plans are implemented. But when these structures become technocratic and bureaucratic, they dehumanize the process of human development. Gran points out the ways in which organizational culture and its imperatives have discouraged participation by the poor in project procedures (Gran 1983:chaps. 9 and 10). Empowerment requires nonbureaucratic and nontechnocratic organizational structures.

Disaffection with the bureaucratic and technocratic modes of the organizational structures of development agencies influenced the birth of new organizational structures, which have come to be popularly known as nongovernmental development organizations.

Non-Governmental Organizations (NGOs)

The birth of NGOs as new development organizational structures was part of the post-growth/modernization paradigmatic trend that marked the mid-1970s onward (see the Introduction herein). Much thinking was directed to finding alternative development approaches for less developed countries that would both avoid past constraints and be more relevant in addressing less developed countries' development problems. This thinking—increasingly dominated by neo-populist theories with "normativist" rather than "positivist" orientations, and a focus on the "content" rather than the "form" of development—included such themes as people-centeredness, redistribution, self-reliance, participation, holism, empowerment and sustainability. These themes, as embodied in the new development alternatives, were considered to need completely different development agency structures rather than only governmental structures. Since current belief was that the government or state had become part of the problems of development, the alternative path should bypass the government in its development process (see Friedmann 1992:6). NGOs fit this task. At the World Development (WD)/Overseas Development Institute (ODI) symposium "Development Alternatives: A Challenge for NGOs" of March 1987, in London, one conference subtitle assigned to NGOs the responsibility of being "Promoters of Alternative Development Strategies" (Drabek 1987:x).

NGOs fall into two distinct categories: Northern and Southern. Northern NGOs are sometimes also known as international NGOs and are based in industrialized countries. Southern NGOs, also known as local or indigenous NGOs, are based in less developed countries. This division has tended to determine the nature of the roles played by these NGOs. Northern NGOs in particular are commonly assigned the roles of (1) fund-raising for meeting human needs in the South; (2) educating the public in the North on global issues, especially regarding the nature and seriousness of poverty; and (3) through lobbying and advocacy, influencing the policies of both Northern and Southern governments and international development institutions to respond positively toward alleviation of poverty and toward developmental needs of the South. Southern NGOs, for their part, are assigned (1) close encounter with the poor, involving raising awareness among the poor; (2) enhancing the self-confidence of the poor; (3) increasing the participation of the poor in critical decision-making that affects their lives; (4) making resources available to the poor; (5) furthering awareness of the poor about wider socioeconomic and political structural problems underlying their poverty; and (6) empowering the poor to take action to confront these problems (Smith 1987:88).

NGO structures are believed to possess certain virtues in the development process that are superior to government bureaucratic structures, especially in responding to rural poverty in less developed countries. Although NGOs are heterogenous—that is, they show diversity in "their operating styles, management practices, and development philosophies" (Gorman 1984:2)—some general features are common to all. In a study of 75 projects funded by the United States Agency for International Development (USAID), Judith Tendler (1982) discusses some of these features. She prefers to view these features or themes not as proven standards of NGO self-assessment, but rather "as 'articles of faith' by means of which NGOs motivate their staffs and define a distinctive territory" (Brown 1990:6). Tendler herself questions whether any NGO can substantiate the empirical validity of these claims.

Tendler's seven themes, as outlined by Brown (1990:5–6), follow:

1. *Reaching the poor*: NGOs claim a particular ability to reach the poor, and tend to perform better in social targeting than do international donors and host governments whose performance discredits them.
2. *Participation*: Claimed participation of the poor is an inherent element in NGO projects, while such participation is low in the activities of larger donors and the state.
3. *Process vs. outcome*: NGOs claim ability to involve the poor in a learning process whereby they become involved in sustainable and "self-reliant" development, rather than in task performance or simple promotion of economic growth, as characterises the processes of larger donors and governments.

4. *Contrast with the public sector*: NGOs emphasise a process of "people-centred" development, free from political and bureaucratic considerations which preoccupy Third World governments and their institutional partners. This view of development causes NGOs to minimise the importance of "purely monetary considerations, and provides the basis of their critique of the excessively economistic approach of " governments and larger donors.

5. *Flexibility and experimentation*: NGOs claim certain essential virtues for the promotion of development needs, particularly of the poor in less developed countries. These virtues include their smaller size, their freedom from bureaucratic constraints, their flexibility, their responsiveness to specific needs of the poor at the local level, and their ability to experiment with alternative ideas and practices.

6. *Institution-building*: NGOs claim a unique capacity for building institutions suited to less developed countries' development, especially at the grassroots level.

7. *Cost*: NGOs claim that their members' commitment, accompanied by a strong sense of voluntarism and greater structural flexibility, allows NGOs to reach the poor at a much lower cost than is required by larger institutions and governments.

Fowler (1990) expands Tendler's list of comparative advantages of NGOs to include NGOs' ability (1) to choose the proper mix of assistance—educational, technical, material; (2) to employ long-term, strategic perspectives and time scales; (3) to undertake people-centered identification and research; (4) to utilize indigenous knowledge and other local resources; (5) to learn from and (re)apply experience; (6) to analyze and identify with the reality of the poor; (7) to motivate and retain personnel; and (8) to promote sustainable development (Fowler 1990:11).

Fowler believes these comparative advantages derive their strength from NGOs' independence from governmental agencies. The quality of relationships NGOs create with the poor tend to be "unambiguous, equal and supportive" of the poor, unlike the dominance of authoritative control relationships from the government. Second, NGOs can design and structure their organizations according to situations and development tasks they select with the poor in mind. By contrast, a government's need to control and direct makes it necessary to create "hierarchical bureaucratic structures which rely on uniformity, standardisation and rigidity," working with staff that "cannot avoid ambivalent relationships with poor people" (Fowler 1990:12).

The empirical validity of these claims remains questionable and requires more research study. But they suggest ideals needed for any organizational structures that would hope to execute alternative development approaches such as empowerment. Because of the heterogeneity of NGOs, individual NGOs will necessarily show strengths and weaknesses at different points. Therefore, the ideals, treated together, must not be sought in any one individual NGO, but rather in an amalgam of NGOs.

NGOs, even as an amalgam or in total, are not without weaknesses. In particular, these weaknesses regard evaluation of their activities. In the practical area there is the problem of the small size of NGO grants and their impermanence in the field. In the ideology of NGOs there is difficulty with measuring the social development processes in which NGOs are involved, such as empowerment. In strategy constraints include fund-raising (especially where fund-raising is related to fund-spending); multiple constituencies with different, broad and varied interests and influences; and the voluntaristic nature of NGOs (Brown 1990:8–9). These and other weaknesses can limit the effectiveness of NGOs in facilitating development.

The very name they bear, "non-governmental," implies there is still an official role for government-based, direct funding for development in less developed countries. Data on the growth of NGOs in the 1980s show that "in 1986 [NGOs] based in the 26 countries of the OECD were responsible for $5.3 billion worth of assistance to the developing countries" (Brown 1990:3). However, this amounted to only 14 percent of total overseas development aid and was only 0.048 percent of gross national product (GNP) of donor countries. Although such a figure is impressive in terms of the size of the NGO sector, it indicates a very large area left to be filled by governments and other larger donor institutions.

NGOs need to know their comparative strengths compared to government agencies, and to concentrate on these areas. These would be primarily at the micro-level of development, where governments are weak or tend to lack the "interest, technical skills or capacity to play an effective role as an agent of development" (Fowler 1990:12). Insofar as NGOs are forcefully claiming the development of less developed countries as their responsibility, while at the same time there is need for the involvement of both governments and NGOs in the development process, NGOs must shoulder the burden of lobbying and educating both governments and larger international donor institutions to assure that appropriate development alternatives are not stifled.

An initiative that some fear could stifle the development effort of NGOs if applied in conventional manner is the project process. New development alternatives have influenced the creation of new organizational structures, but the project process also needs to be examined.

Critique of Development Projects

Development projects in the hands of development agencies have assumed characteristics that seem to have become obstacles to development, particularly to rural development.

Development projects, like the planning process, have their origin in growth-maximizing development models. Projects and planning together still play a central role in development. "Sound development plans require good projects, just as good projects require sound planning. . . . Projects provide an important means by which investment and other development expenditures foreseen in plans can be brought into focus and realised" (Gittinger 1982:5). Rondinelli supports this, stating that projects "have become the primary means through which governments of developing countries attempt to translate their plans and policies into programs of action. No matter how comprehensive and detailed development plans seem to be, they are of little value unless they can be translated into projects . . . that can be carried out" (Rondinelli 1983a:3). In addition, Rondinelli sees projects as channels of resource investment and aid by governments and international assistance organizations.

The important role of development projects in the development process is emphasized by many. Wignaraja states that the project approach is "deeply rooted in the current operations of most governments, donor agencies and . . . integrated rural development programs" (Wignaraja 1984:5).

But what is "a project"?

The Conventional Project

James Price Gittinger defines a project as consisting of "a whole complex of activities using resources to gain benefits" (Gittinger 1982:3), or as a kind of investment activity in which financial resources are expended to create capital assets that produce benefits over an extended period of time. He develops the definition further with an almost exhaustive list of the characteristics of a project, an activity on which money is spent in "expectation of returns and which logically seems to lend itself to planning, financing, and implementing as a unit" (Gittinger 1982:3). Distinct features mark it:

- The smallest operational element prepared and implemented as a separate entity in a national plan or programme.
- A specific activity with specific beginning and ending points and objectives.
- A unique activity noticeably different from both preceding and succeeding similar investments.
- Something around which a boundary can be drawn.
- An activity with a specific geographic location.
- An activity with a specific target or clientele group to reach.
- A well-defined sequence of investment and production activities that are quantifiable, and to which money value is attached.
- An activity with a specific group of benefits that are identifiable, quantifiable and for which money value is determinable.
- A useful tool for phasing long-term programs.
- An activity financed through a specifically defined financial package.
- An activity subject to an analysis of the financial results and economic justification, i.e., cost-benefit analysis. (Gittinger 1982:3–4)

Before Gittinger, Hirschman had offered a similar but less detailed definition:

The development project is a special kind of investment. The term connotes purposefulness, some minimum size, a specific location, the introduction of something qualitatively new and the expectation that a sequence of further development moves will be set in motion. (Hirschman 1967:1)

Morgan considered the basic elements common to all conventional projects to be:

1. Disciplined conceptual "dis-aggregation" of complex or ill-defined problems into discrete tasks for which resources can be mobilized and targeted.
2. Specific time boundaries within which projects begin and end according to a funding schedule and work plan.
3. Preprogrammed activities in which the resources, contracting, procurement, training and anticipated outcomes are all planned or designed.
4. Applied economic and systems analysis used in the appraisal of a project idea to determine whether it is economically viable or rational according to other technical criteria.
5. Standardized reporting procedures for monitoring, control and evaluation. (Morgan 1983:330)

Other writers express similar views of projects: "purposive interventions that are commonly used to accelerate economic development" (Cernea 1985:4); "defined narrowly as financial investments or broadly as organized activities for promoting social and economic change" (Rondinelli 1983b:308); "discrete activities, aimed at specific objectives with earmarked budgets and limited time frames . . . are also likely to be targeted on specific geographic areas and aimed at particular beneficiary groups" (Honadle and Rosengard 1983:300).

Enshrined in all these interpretations is the central idea that development projects are controlled, manageable investments and discrete activities whose behavior is usually assumed to create a momentum for continued widespread economic progress. However, the experience of the developing countries has commonly been the reverse of this.

Evolution of the Project Process

Early projects placed primary emphasis on physical investment. This gave rise to a mechanistic notion of a project based on "scientific and engineering experience in the industrial countries of the west" (Morgan 1983:330), which prescribed the modus operandi of its application in less developed countries. Such a notion led to creation of "structures for converting inputs into outputs" (Uphoff 1990:1402). The basic assumption was that by simply investing resources, desired results were obtainable in some predictable ratio of outputs to inputs. In other words, the rationalist confidence position held that "desired outcomes can be designed" (Uphoff 1990:1402).

The mechanistic project notion entailed what became known as the project cycle, which defined carefully orchestrated and controlled stages of the project process. These stages, as formulated by Baum, were:

Stage 1:   project identification;
Stage 2:   preparation;
Stage 3:   appraisal;
Stage 4:   implementation; and
Stage 5:   evaluation (Baum 1978; Cernea 1985:7).

Each stage requires sizeable physical effort, financial resources, and expertise (Uphoff 1990:1401), since they are subject to systematic and rigorous procedures to develop and improve them, especially their mathematical content. In addition, they are controlled by technocratic experts such as politicians, planners, administrators, managers and consultants (Cernea 1985:7; Chambers 1988:4).

The whole project process now demands use of the methods and procedures of engineering and economic statistical analyses—including cost-benefit analysis, linear-programming models, network scheduling, and planning-programming-budgeting systems, as well as application of blueprints or preplanned solutions for problems. These methods, procedures and blueprinting practices render the project mode attractive to the Western world's private corporations, which deal with physical construction projects (Rondinelli 1983a:5).

In this sense, projects are better suited to the construction of physical "things" rather than the development of people (Chambers 1988:3). However, evolution of the project process with regard to its application to human situations seems to have involved wholesale direct application of the whole procedure of "thinking, values, methods and behaviour which fit and work [best] with things . . . to people with whom they fit and work less well" (Chambers 1988:3).

The project mode's attraction rests on two basic assumptions: first, that it reduces the basic investment problem of uncertainty; and second, that it is supposedly the most cost-effective mode for allocation of investment resources, since most investors in their quest for profit maximization seek "to do more with less" (Uphoff 1990:1402).

But what has been the experience of less developed countries with project development?

Development Experience of Less Developed Countries

In the 1960s Western international lending institutions came to regard projects as easily transferrable to bureaucracies in most developing countries. Since the dominant belief was that the development process itself was transferable, it was only logical to regard one of its means— the project process—to be so too. Consequently, in less developed countries experience with the project mode of development, particularly in the early days, involved mere adoption of the mechanistic Western notion of the project with its straitjacket, blueprinting practices and procedures involving large capital investments and rigid methods of planning and control. These practices have tended to become deeply entrenched in the less developed countries' systems, "set in bureaucratic concrete" (Uphoff 1990:1401). Set styles remain characteristically top-down, timebound and mechanistic, despite imperfect knowledge and constantly changing conditions (Chambers 1988:3).

Initial Emphasis on Physical Structures

The mechanistic notion of projects suits the construction of physical objects and structures. It is not surprising that early project goals in less developed countries were defined primarily in physical, material, and economic terms. Initial projects concentrated on construction of physical infrastructure, facilities and industrial structures (Rondinelli 1983a:5; Chambers 1988:3). Early project efforts in less developed countries by governments and international aid agencies, chiefly the World Bank, were predominantly in areas such as irrigation, electric power generation and transmission, transportation and communication, and basic industry (Gran 1983:59; Hirschman 1967:4).

Two notable analyses were carried out separately by Hirschman and King, both of whom studied the World Bank's experience with development projects in less developed countries. Hirschman included eleven projects, all large scale: four irrigation, three transport/communication, two electric power, one related to industry, and one livestock agricultural. King's study involved thirty cases of which seventeen were electric power, nine were transport, and four were basic industry projects (Chambers 1978:211 and 1988:3). All these projects were capital intensive in nature and concerned with structural, physical results. Neither of the two studies included any projects of social concern, such as human resource development or small decentralized projects intended to benefit the rural poor. The reason for this may lie in the dominant influence that certain disciplines had on the development process at the time.

Initial Dominance of Science and Economics

From the emphasis the mechanistic model placed on such disciplines as engineering and statistical economics, the project process acquired planning and control properties that called for specialized skills and other requirements such as "architectonic quality of design" to ensure good results. "Normal professionalism" and its ingrained biases (especially against the poor), says Chambers, lead to hierarchical classification, according to those biases, of professional disciplines involved in the development process and development projects. The combined effect of these biases assigns to "engineering a higher status [and makes it] carry more weight than agronomy; and economics than sociology or social anthropology." Chambers stresses that "high normal professional status coincides with the professions and disciplines . . . which are dominant in the early phases of the evolution of both institutions and projects" (Chambers 1988:3). For this reason, Chambers points out, the World Bank and other aid agencies are dominated by engineers and economists.

Engineers and economists were seen to have more to contribute to the project process than the non-economic or "soft" social sciences that study people, cultures and societies (Chambers 1988:4; Cernea 1985:3). Engineering and economics remained predominant even past the early phases of projects, in accordance with what Chambers calls "the law of prior bias," stating, "what comes first in a process sets patterns and takes most" (Chambers 1988:3). Cernea contends that even in (planned) rural development, physical scientific disciplines preside over the process, while the vital and necessary social science disciplines concerned with people are only marginally engaged.

Among the social science disciplines, economics became dominant and still exerts greater influence on the development project process than other social science disciplines, so that a serious imbalance now exists. Cernea, in his defense for inclusion of sociological variables in the project process, argues that such an imbalance has resulted in repeated failures that have plagued development programs and projects, as they have been sociologically ill-informed and ill-conceived. It is "precisely sociological knowledge and analysis that can help conceptualise the socio-structural issues involved" in project and program analysis (Cernea 1985:6). It becomes clear that for projects and programs to succeed, socio-structural and institutional variables, including those variables from other essential human and social science disciplines that constitute a desirable multidisciplinary model for rural development, cannot be ignored. This is particularly true in the case of alternative development approaches that call for multidisciplinary models of development.

PART III

EMPIRICAL ANALYSIS

10

A Case Study: Development Agencies and Holistic Empowerment

The original aim was to survey 12 development agencies whose work included rural poverty alleviation, particularly looking at East Africa as a case study. *The Third World Directory 1993*, "a comprehensive guide with information for development organisations" (Stubbs 1993), provides a wide variety of information including the objectives of each organization; the nature of its work; geographical areas it covers; total budget, people working on projects and publications; and particular fields of activities with which it is involved.

Seven nonreligious and seven Christian agencies were selected from the directory list, taking into account the possibility of some agencies declining to be included in the study. "Christian agencies" here refers to agencies adhering to the Christian gospel and endeavoring to demonstrate gospel objectives and priorities as part and parcel of development in their project activities. Eight agencies responded positively, and dates to visit them for interviews and material were fixed.

Individuals interviewed were engaged in policy-making in the particular agency, familiar with its work in East Africa, and well-informed about its operations in the field there. Some difficulties arose regarding vocabulary. Certain terms employed in the research were either understood differently or were not used at all by the respondents. For example, a number of respondents interpreted the word *empowerment* in terms of political power, as in giving the poor political power for decision-making. Understood this way, empowerment was not what some of these agencies would engage in because of restrictions by either the Charity Commission or church bylaws forbidding participation in political activities. Some Christian agencies also felt the term *justice* was political, and hence the word did not figure in their activity descriptions. A term avoided by the nonreligious agencies was *stewardship*, because it was perceived as a religious term (although one agency treated it as meaning care for the environment). The non-Christian agencies were not very keen on discussing biblical principles or anything perceived as religious. Terms including *human dignity, identity,* and *justice* were understood from parallel definitions rendered by the nonreligious agencies from humanistic philosophical thinking.

Agency Profiles

In Britain, of about 200 agencies involved in development, about 20 percent are "religious"; the majority of these are Christian (Stubbs 1993), and include Tearfund, World Vision UK, Emmanuel International and Y-Care International. Secular agencies include Oxfam, ActionAid, ACORD, and APT Design and Development. These agencies declare in their constitutions that they are nonreligious, meaning they have no affiliation with any particular religion or specific religious sect. The eight mentioned agreed to participate in this study of holistic empowerment.

These eight agencies, being based in Britain, fall in the category of Northern NGOs, sometimes known as international NGOs, based in industrialized countries, as opposed to Southern NGOs, which are based in and indigenous to less developed countries. As noted earlier, this division between Northern and Southern tends to determine the nature of the roles played by these NGOs.

Size

A key difference among the agencies is size, measured in terms of annual incomes and expenditures. In Britain, there are five well-known NGOs:

Save the Children Fund	£100M
Oxfam	£73M
Christian Aid	£42M
ActionAid	£25M
CAFOD	£23M

(Annual figures here and following are for fiscal year 1991/92 [Stubbs 1993] unless otherwise noted.)

Among the four nonreligious agencies surveyed, two figure in this list: Oxfam, the second largest, and ActionAid, the fourth largest. When these two are compared with the other two nonreligious agencies surveyed, ACORD and APT Design and Development—each with an annual income of £0.4M—the divergence in size among NGOs is readily apparent.

The four Christian agencies studied exhibited more moderate differences in size:

Tearfund	£20M
World Vision UK	more than £11M
Emmanuel International	almost £5M
Y-Care International	almost £3M

The size of an agency tends to determine the influence it wields, especially at macro-levels of involvement, that is, interacting with national governments and international development institutions. For example, as discussed more specifically later in this chapter, Oxfam and ActionAid, individually and in collaboration with other British or European agencies, engage more than the other agencies in development issues that concern governments or international development institutions.

Size also tends to determine the scope and extent of agency activities and geographical coverage. In general, the larger the agency, the wider the scope and the greater the extent of activities. Available information suggests the following picture: Oxfam in 1992/93 allocated more than half its budget to Africa (about 29 countries) (Oxfam 1992–93). Of this amount (not counting emergency grants), more than £1.7M was allocated to 63 project activities in Kenya, more than £1.1M to 52 project activities in Uganda, and about £0.4M to 47 project activities in Tanzania. ActionAid programs aim to "promote a sustainable level of subsistence for all members of the community by focusing on poor families" (ActionAid 1994:3). These communities are situated primarily in rural areas, varying in population from 10,000 to more than 100,000. ActionAid work reached about 2 million of the world's poorest people (ActionAid 1994:4). ActionAid's presence in East Africa covered only communities in Kenya and Uganda.

ACORD's presence in East Africa was mainly in Tanzania and Uganda. In Tanzania it operated in only one area, Biharamulo, where it worked with local farmers' groups and individuals, providing them with seeds, tools and training. The aim was to make them self-reliant, to plant their own trees, rear and care for their own livestock, and cultivate their own crops. In Uganda, ACORD had three programs in which it worked with a total of 520 producer groups (ACORD 1993:26), although it worked in joint efforts in two other programs with other agencies.

APT Design and Development (APT) worked in all three East African countries. The work concentrated on six main areas: technical training, business and management training, savings and credit development, strengthening of local NGOs, effective resource management, and supporting the development of government policy. Training was sometimes organized and funded by bigger bodies, such as the Commonwealth Secretariat, on a regional basis, and APT supplied the teaching staff and facilitators. APT's small size suits it to the nature of the tasks it carries out.

Among the Christian agencies, the larger agencies can provide figures of coverage of activities while the smaller agencies seemed to lack such figures. Tearfund only funded partner projects; during the time period surveyed, in Kenya it funded 20 projects, in Tanzania 15, and in Uganda 15. The size and population coverage of these projects was not given.

World Vision International has several offices in different industrialized countries; it funded more than 120 projects in Kenya, 100 projects in Tanzania, and 80 projects in Uganda. These figures are much higher than those provided by Tearfund, although Tearfund is larger than World Vision UK, because the World Vision figures include projects funded by all of its offices.

Emmanuel International is of moderate size and had projects only in Tanzania and in Uganda during the time surveyed. In Tanzania, the work had not been continuous, but an effort was being made to set up some long-term work, and already a local partner, with a local person to coordinate the work, had been identified. In Uganda, Emmanuel International had two programs. One program was divided into five project activities; the other was also divided into five, but with a different mix of project activities. Emmanuel International thus funded 10 project activities in Uganda.

Y-Care International is also a relatively small agency; it funded project activities in all three East African countries, but figures showing the extent of these activities were not available.

Comparison of these agencies revealed disparity in data-recording procedures and availability of information. Generally speaking, the larger the agency, the better the data-recording systems and the more easily available any required information.

Operations and Funding

Another difference among these agencies concerned operationality and funding functions. An agency is considered operational if it directly initiates programs with local people and communities without the mediation of local agencies. It is a funding agency if it provides funds (for development purposes in the South) to another agency (usually a local agency) that actually spends the money on activities with communities at the grassroots level. Most agencies in this study—the two exceptions being ActionAid and ACORD—were funding agencies only, at least technically, working through the intermediation of local agencies on the ground. ActionAid and ACORD combined both funding and operationality functions. Some writers assign to all Northern agencies merely a funding role, but these case studies reveal that some Northern agencies, such as those mentioned, participate in both direct operations and funding.

Funding agencies work in partnership with local agencies. The initiative in most cases comes from the local agency, which applies to a Northern agency for funding of its project activities. The Northern agency responds in accordance with criteria by which the local agency is assessed for compatibility in partnership. In some cases a Northern agency takes the initiative and makes itself known to local agencies—as in the case of APT Design and Development. Then, through negotiations and detailed discussions, agreements to work in partnership are reached. These partnerships take different forms, three of which were described by Tearfund (in *Good News to the Poor*, 13):

- *Horse and Rider:* A form of partnership in which the "rider," who holds the reins, is in charge and decides the course of things; the "horse" simply complies. The Northern agency is likened to the rider, for it has the resources; hence, it is in charge, and determines the course of the development process with which the local agency, the horse, has to comply.
- *Cow and Milker:* A partnership in which the "milker" (local agency) tries to get as much "milk" (assistance) from the "cow"(Northern agency) as possible.
- *Two Oxen:* An ideal partnership (unlike the previous two), in which "two oxen" (agencies) are yoked together to perform the same task.

In the last form, because both share the same objective, any comparative advantages possessed by one is applied for the good of the other, for effective accomplishment of the common objective. This form will perhaps become more attractive to agencies in light of common evidence suggesting that the other two forms of partnership usually fail to achieve desired outcomes effectively.

None of the Christian agencies reviewed here was operational, at least in the technical definitions of its projects. This may suggest that Christian agencies view the development task of the South as an undertaking that requires partnership. As discussed, effective partnership recognizes the value of local knowledge and resources, and institutional and organizational capabilities, all of which may need empowering as they are built upon and improved. This is not to say operational agencies cannot contribute toward institution-building; they can, especially in areas where no local institutions exist. The danger some have foreseen is that where local agencies already exist, proliferation and duplication could lead to waste of effort and resources with meaningless competition and confusion.

Policies, Strategies and Activities

The eight agencies' policies, strategies and activities for rural development all claimed to combat poverty. This poverty-orientation marks a significant departure from past strategies, which laid much emphasis on economic growth and modernization (as described in chapter 9 above).

A closer look at the agencies reveals, however, some variability in their strategies and policies. Some agencies adopted different strategies and policies for each country in which they operated. This was particularly true of the relatively large agencies undertaking large operations that could create a significant impact in a country; such agencies included Oxfam, ActionAid, and World Vision UK, as well as ACORD acting as an operational agency. These agencies tried to take account, first, of each recipient national government's strategies and policies; second, of different priorities assigned to critical development problems addressed in each country; and third, efforts in place, in order to avoid duplication, particularly with the recipient national government's own effort, and wasting of resources. The variability revealed within the agencies' policies and strategies was significant, demonstrating that there was no uniformity within situations of poverty in which the agencies were working. This again marks an important departure from past strategies, which tended to treat situations in developing countries as more or less uniform, treating development as set stages to growth rather than solving specific problems of development that differ from situation to situation and need different response strategies.

In other cases, a Northern agency adopts its Southern partner agency's strategies and policies as long as functional compatibility for partnership, on the basis of other desirable criteria, is established. This approach was adopted mostly by funding agencies of moderate and smaller sizes: Tearfund, Emmanuel International, Y-Care International, and APT Design and Development. Such an approach recognizes that development is neither transferable nor a top-down undertaking, but a task in which those who need assistance should be allowed to determine what direction development should take, with some negotiated facilitation.

Of course, these general descriptions fail to account for the real-life nuances in operations and strategies described by each agency. But in general, differences in the underlying philosophies adopted by different agencies affected the approaches these agencies followed in their activities. Oxfam, for example, states that its main objective is "to relieve poverty, distress and suffering in any part of the world" (Oxfam 1989:1); it therefore followed an approach guided by three imperatives: gender sensitivity, sustainable livelihoods and basic rights. These key imperatives differentiated it from other agencies.

ActionAid believes its raison d'être is "to help children, families and communities in the world's poorest countries to overcome poverty and secure lasting improvements in the quality of their lives" (ActionAid 1994). To achieve this, it followed an Integrated Rural Development approach to guide its activities. The integrated approach is the undertaking of a number of activities in any particular area, simultaneously, in order to respond to various aspects of the poverty facing people in that area. This approach is chosen over the single-activity approach in order to prevent counterproductive pressure from unaddressed sectors in a multifaceted, poverty-infested situation. Of course, a situation of poverty can still be addressed through one activity, at a single point of entry.

ACORD considered its main role, as a consortium, "to help establish or strengthen local, non-governmental structures with a view to promoting self-reliant, participatory development" (ACORD 1993). As an operational agency working in devastated areas where local structures might not exist, ACORD adopted an approach focused on the use of rural development workers, whose task was to build up local organizations around specific activities.

APT Design and Development "is dedicated to the alleviation of poverty and to promoting the growth of local economies in less developed countries; by providing specialist support for the training and development of small-scale enterprises" (APT 1984–93:3). APT believes that the growth of numerous small businesses makes for a healthy and sustainable economic basis in developing countries, and thus it adopts an approach that targets not the poorest of the poor but the enterprising poor, those who work hard but cannot make ends meet.

The Christian agencies were unified by an underlying conviction that they are called to respond to both spiritual and physical needs of the poor. For example:

> Tearfund believes the Gospel of Jesus Christ is concerned with both the spiritual and physical needs of people. Tearfund seeks to enter into partnership with churches and Christian groups anxious to promote both aspects of this Gospel and who share . . . the biblically based beliefs (in *Introducing Tearfund*, 1).

Such groups and churches are carefully screened according to detailed criteria before they can be accepted as compatible partners to work with Tearfund. Then together they attempt to meet the needs of the people around them, as part of their primary call to fulfill Christ's mission of sharing the Good News in the world.

World Vision UK works through established structures and churches, which take responsibility for identifying areas of work to be facilitated by World Vision UK field teams. The gospel is shared with great sensitivity and dialogue (World Vision UK interview).

Emmanuel International's mandate is "to encourage, strengthen and assist churches worldwide to meet the spiritual and physical needs of the poor in accordance with the Holy Scriptures" (Emmanuel International 1993). It places emphasis on motivation and enablement of national evangelical churches worldwide to meet the physical and spiritual needs of the poor in their communities and around the world by sharing and utilizing available resources in accordance with Holy Scripture (Emmanuel International SCW:1).

Y-Care International, being small and in its early years, relied heavily on YMCA national councils to identify projects and Christian partners to work with, although there is a bias toward youth and women's work, and general community participation (Y-Care International interview).

A noticeable difference arose between the nonreligious agencies and the Christian agencies here. Among the nonreligious agencies, the underlying philosophies vary widely. This may be accounted for by the plurality of views accommodated by secular humanism. The Christian agencies, in contrast, each applied Bible-based philosophies that, though allowing variety in approach, unifies them in their objectives to carry by word and deed Christ's Good News to the world's poor.

When these policies and strategies are translated into actual activities, some dissimilarities among the agencies become even more apparent, chiefly because of different emphases placed on different activities each agency undertakes. Being Northern agencies, these agencies operated at both micro- and macro-levels. At the micro-level, operations required activities that involved interacting directly with local agencies and local people and communities being assisted at grassroots level. At the macro-level, operations required encounters with national governments (both Northern and Southern) and with international development bodies, organizations and institutions in order to try to make these different agents responsive to the task of combating poverty.

The non-Christian agencies all claim to provide humanitarian material assistance for the poor; because they are nonreligious, they are not concerned with spiritual needs. On the other hand, the Christian agencies attempt to provide both material and spiritual assistance to the poor, recognizing that human beings have both physical and spiritual needs. This Christian effort to meet both physical and spiritual needs has become known as a *holistic approach*.

Macro-level activities include lobbying, advocacy, research for correctly informed presentations, and education of the public on the nature, causes, effects and intensity of poverty. These activities are usually directed toward national governments and their development bodies (both Southern and Northern), the international development bodies, agencies and institutions, such as the European parliament, the European Economic Commission and Union, the World Bank, the IMF, USAID, the UN and its organizations, and the like. All eight agencies were involved in such activities to varying degrees. The smaller agencies tended not to get as deeply involved, either because of lack of staff or because they considered themselves too small to be heard or to influence multinational institutions. They can, however, provide research material from their own experience to larger agencies or to a joint resource pool to help in lobbying and advocacy work. Y-Care International reported lobbying the government of Brazil through the International Committee of Refugees on the activities of the death/murder squads against street children.

The larger agencies, in their turn, participated in all these activities as individual agencies or through consortia with which they worked in collaboration to create a stronger force and make a greater impact on the subject of their activities. Oxfam and ActionAid, at one and the same time, worked independently in these areas and were also part of a number of consortia for advocacy and lobbying. For example, both were members of a consortium of the five largest NGOs in Britain formed to lobby the British Parliament; they are members of Euro Step, which comprises 22 NGOs from 15 European countries, who lobby the European Parliament and EEC and EU to seek justice and equal opportunities for people in the North and South at the European level; they are members of ICVA (International Council of Voluntary Agencies), an independent international association of NGOs active in humanitarian assistance and sustainable development. The ICVA also undertakes advocacy work before the UN and other international bodies and institutions on issues of common concern to its members.

This involvement at the macro-level is as important as activities at the micro-level, because all these agencies, speaking from their experience, cited macro-level problems as major obstacles to development—including poor national government policies; lack of good governance; rampant wars and conflicts; the structural adjustment programs of the World Bank and the IMF; international trade; the dumping of European products in less developed countries' markets (for example, the dumping of beef by the European Union in West African countries—ACORD reported having lobbied successfully against this practice through Euro Step for the state of Mali).

Involvement at the macro-level can be characterized as the domain of Northern NGOs, but the agencies did report certain limitations imposed on them, some by the Charity Commission in Britain. Southern NGOs are involved less in interagency lobbying on the international scene, as they would be more bound up with their national governments, whom they would need to represent and please by their activities. To a lesser extent, Northern NGOs may also be restricted in the extent of lobbying in which they can be involved because, for some of the agencies, a greater percentage of their income comes from the official sources against whose policies (or lack of policies) they lobby.

The major contribution of macro-level NGO activities is that they cause governments and large international development institutions to be less complacent and to be more aware of the need for moral accountability in their policies and activities. In other words, the agencies surveyed took the ethical aspect of development seriously.

The Project Process

As discussed in chapter 9 above, the blueprint approach to development projects placed pressure on donor agencies "to move too much money too quickly in time-bounded, pre-planned projects in pursuit of short-term results" (Korten 1984:177). Such a process, from beginning to end, relied on experts and expert knowledge and was carried out in a more or less mechanical manner better suited to construction of physical or material objects than the undertaking of people development.

On examining the project processes of the eight agencies included in this study, an alternative approach to the project process emerges. In almost every case, the process begins with an invitation from local agencies (or local governments) representing local people. The project, from beginning to end, becomes a joint undertaking between local people (or beneficiaries) and agency personnel. Korten refers to this alternative approach as "the learning process approach," which he contrasts with the "blueprint approach" (Korten 1984:182).

In this alternative approach, initial activity involves the application to each case of Rapid Rural Appraisal (RRA) or Participatory Rural Appraisal (PRA) exercises for assessing the real needs of the local people and setting priorities. These exercises necessarily involve the participation of local people and recognize local people's knowledge as important. This approach deviates widely from the blueprint approach, in which the expert alone carries out feasibility studies and determines the priority of needs for the local people, independent of their participation.

After prioritization of needs under the learning process approach, decision-making and implementation of activities is undertaken by agency personnel, again with the local people's participation. The process is usually not time-bound; rather a long-term perspective is adopted. This helps in cases where time is required to allow learning to take place for the building up of individual, collective and institutional capabilities for sustained action on unfamiliar development problems. The long-term learning curve is essential in order for local people and agency personnel to be able to share knowledge and resources and so "to create a fit between the needs, actions and the capacity of the assisting agency" (Korten 1984:182). In his analysis Korten synthesizes three stages in the learning process approach: the effectiveness stage, the efficiency stage, and the expansion stage.

The effectiveness stage involves initiating working relationships between agency personnel (who will be highly qualified) and the local people; familiarizing themselves with the problems with which they are faced, especially from the local people's perspective; trying out some known and promising approaches for joint action in addressing identified needs with the support of expertise from different fields of "the social, managerial, and related technical sciences" (Korten 1984:184). During this stage errors will be common and input will be high relative to results; also, "it is assumed that rapid adaptive action will be taken as errors in initial assumptions are identified" (Korten 1984:184), this being necessary for the learning to be effective.

The efficiency stage focuses attention on how to do more efficiently that which has been learned in the initial stage. This involves elimination of unproductive activities and reinforcement of simplified problem-solving routines that even the less skilled can join in with confidence; at the same time, the means of learning, testing, refining and applying new methods and skills can be established. These twin efforts are necessary for learning to be efficient.

The expansion stage redirects emphasis to building into the organization "supporting skills, management systems, structures, and values" (Korten 1984:184), with a view to enabling the supporting agency to carry out its prescribed activities on a larger scale. If Korten means the expansion should only take place in the supporting agency, then the expansion would be more appropriate if the local agency were also included, giving it an opportunity to strengthen itself with supporting skills, management systems, structures and values. The work of assisting agencies is also to empower through institution-building the structures of organizations and institutions they assist through their project process.

A final aspect of this alternative approach to the project process is monitoring and evaluation. These exercises, undertaken jointly by agency personnel and local people, are of value to a number of groups for different reasons. First, local people need to know that they are making progress. This can encourage and spur them on to improve activities and extend these to other essential activities which they would never have undertaken without the positive orientation, skills, capabilities and income they may now have. Second, the local agency needs to know the success of its work to be able to attract further assistance and to expand; it also needs to provide evidence to have its viability confirmed by the local people and by the national government (although sometimes the national government can carry out its own evaluation independently to assess the viability of agencies). Third, the assisting agency needs such data for its own management criteria and to satisfy the needs of its funding constituencies.

Exercises should include impact evaluation to establish in definitive terms what effect each of the different actors in the process of development has had. This is important in cases where a number of actors may be involved with the same activity at different levels. For example, Oxfam funded a local NGO, which was involved with local people in some project activity. Impact evaluation should be able to identify, from the outcome of the project activity at any particular time, what specific result was due to the funds from Oxfam, what was due to the activity of the local NGO, what resulted from the people's efforts, and what could have resulted from other independent causes. Although rudiments of impact-evaluation techniques exist, there is need for more research into such techniques and to develop them further. Oxfam and ActionAid both reported that they are active in research to establish methods for impact evaluation. This will yield significantly improved project process evaluation. It will also contribute greatly to complete departure from the blueprint approach, which was concerned with the interests of the funding agency, with evaluation conducted by an expert.

In summary, the learning approach to project process has now become common among the nongovernmental agencies. It seems fair to say that this rethinking of the development process has resulted not only in new agency structures (NGOs) but also in an alternative project process—a definite departure from emphasis on physical impacts of the blueprint approach to an emphasis on people.

Overcoming Powerlessness as an Objective

Powerlessness among people affected by small projects was recognized by all eight agencies in this study as a significant obstacle to be addressed in the alleviation of poverty. However, the agencies differed slightly in their definitions of *powerlessness.*

Defining Powerlessness

Powerlessness is a term in common use. Those who use it, like the agencies in this study, try to adopt a useful interpretation for their own purposes. The result is a plurality of definitions and understandings.

Oxfam defined *powerlessness* as a state in which "people do not have control over the main influences determining their destiny; or lack of access to land, to means of production, to schooling, and to markets" (Oxfam interview). With this interpretation Oxfam considers powerlessness from the side of the poor per se, that is, as a condition of the poor, a malady they suffer as a result of lack of control over influences and destiny, as well as a lack of resources and opportunities. Oxfam did not identify powerlessness in the rich, whom it considers to be powerful.

According to ActionAid, *powerlessness* is defined by "resource poverty which renders people powerless and marginalized. It thus follows that it is those people who are poor in resources that are powerless" (ActionAid interview). ActionAid also views powerlessness from the side of the poor. The poor lack resources and are marginalized, hence they are poor; again, ActionAid views the rich are powerful.

ACORD interpreted powerlessness in terms of vulnerability to the forces of impoverishment. Goulet has defined vulnerability as

> the inability to defend oneself against wounds. An individual is vulnerable when he is exposed to injury, societies when they have no adequate defenses against the social forces that propel them into the processes of change. (Goulet 1985:38)

ACORD saw vulnerability in both the poor and the rich, almost in the same way that Goulet sees it in the weak (poor) and in the powerful (rich). Thus, when ACORD carried out poverty analyses, it undertook vulnerability analysis at the same time in order to establish the incidence of vulnerability in a community with which it starts to work.

APT Design and Development regarded *powerlessness* as "people locked into a state of poverty such that they cannot break out. It also involves inertia and apathy in people; and helplessness which can be a mental state or perceived state" (APT interview). This interpretation is also one that sees powerlessness as a condition only of the poor, who are locked in poverty and characterized by inertia, apathy and helplessness. APT saw this powerlessness as something that can be overcome in the enterprising poor by unlocking the chains of poverty through empowerment. But APT also saw that certain national policies may actually render the rich powerless to respond positively to assist the poor. This powerlessness for the rich is due to external pressure.

The Christian agencies revealed other dimensions of powerlessness in their accounts. Tearfund viewed powerlessness in both economic/political and spiritual terms. To Tearfund, *powerlessness* is expressed in "the numbers of people that are denied access to decision-making, facilities and essentials of life—these essentials include the knowledge of God" (Tearfund interview). Thus, the powerless for Tearfund are those to whom access is denied to decision-making and basic human physical needs, as well as to an opportunity to have a personal knowledge of their Creator. Powerlessness is seen here in both social and spiritual senses, implying that not only those who are economically poor but also those who are economically rich may display a form of powerlessness.

World Vision UK viewed *powerlessness* as

> the absence of power or the ability to effect change. In other words,
> it is the dis-enablement of an individual, family, or community by
> factors outside its immediate control to effect change. When the
> poor are referred to as powerless, what is meant is that power to
> effect change lies elsewhere. This makes power relations in a com-
> munity an essential target in addressing long-term development.
> (World Vision UK interview)

This is a more or less economic-political interpretation. World Vision
UK also saw powerlessness primarily in the poor, because they are the
ones who cannot overcome the barriers to development that stand against
them. But, as a Christian agency, it also acknowledges a spiritual dimension of poverty and observes aspects of powerlessness in the rich
and powerful—that is, their lack of spiritual resources.

Emmanuel International defined *powerlessness* as "deprivation of human rights and basic human necessities, i.e., lack of land rights, lack of
freedom of speech, lack of means to earn a living, ill health, poor nutri-
tion, and high child mortality rates as well as lack of knowledge of God
the Creator" (Emmanuel International interview). This interpretation
treats powerlessness from both social and spiritual perspectives.
Emmanuel International treats knowledge of God as a basic human right
that confers on people spiritual resources that are as essential as the
physical resources for their fulfilled livelihoods.

Y-Care International defined *powerlessness* as an "inability to alter one's
personal circumstances, family situation and that of the community
around; lack of ability to access state systems; lack of ability to access
other sources of support—for example, other agencies; lack of power to
win resources—the kind of resources that can bring about change in
one's own life" (Y-Care International interview). This interpretation is
basically economic/political and refers to lack of ability and power to
access resources and to bring about change. Y-Care International, as a
Christian agency, acknowledged a spiritual side to powerlessness that
all people, whether poor or rich, can display.

In summary, these definitions revealed the agencies' differing views
concerning powerlessness. Apart from ACORD and APT, the other two
nonreligious agencies viewed powerlessness only in the poor, while all

the Christian agencies acknowledged powerlessness also in the rich. Second, all the nonreligious agencies interpreted powerlessness in social terms only, while the Christian agencies interpreted powerlessness in both social and spiritual terms.

Who Are the Powerless and How Are They Powerless?

Who is powerless, as perceived by agencies set up to combat the poverty of the poor? the poor? the rich? the state?

All the agencies studied agreed that the poor are powerless to fight their poverty successfully; otherwise they would not be poor. The poor suffer from internal personal deficiencies, lack of resources and access to them, and external pressures or forces imposed from without.

With regard to the rich, Onora O'Neill is among those secular writers who see a moral obligation for the rich and powerful to meet the basic needs of the world's poor:

> The rich and powerful often see no reason why they should help end distant poverty. This book asks *whether* and *why* development should be pursued, not only by the poor and vulnerable, but the rich and powerful. (O'Neill 1986:xi)

Six of the eight agencies studied agreed that there is a form of powerlessness also among the rich which prevents them from active involvement in the fight against the poverty suffered by the poor. The powerlessness displayed by the rich generally derives from powerlessness due to internal personal deficiencies and/or powerlessness due to external pressures. For example, ACORD's experience shows that even the rich can be vulnerable, and because of this, they are not able actively to fight poverty with and for the poor. APT in turn stated that national government policies have much to do with the powerlessness of the rich to help the poor, even though the rich may be aware of the suffering that poverty inflicts. These two positions, it should be noted, treat powerlessness at the social level only.

The perspective of the Christian agencies combined the social and spiritual aspects. Tearfund's view of the rich was that their excessive reliance on transitory material things, and their lack of recognition of their need to be dependent on God, contribute to their blindness toward the poverty of the poor. This is a form of powerlessness that fosters the perpetuation of poverty. Where society encourages consumerist materialism, people's awareness of the suffering of the poor is dulled.

World Vision UK suggested that the rich lack motivation for helping the poor; in most cases they lack information and education about the situation of the poor, since they are usually far removed from the situation of the poor. The rich, therefore, show a form of powerlessness that contributes to the growth and persistence of the poverty of the poor through both negligence and ignorance, and through active oppression and exploitation of the poor.

Emmanuel International also recognized a form of powerlessness among the rich in which the rich sit back and blame the poor for their poverty; in some cases the rich are blind to the situation of the poor because they think that such a situation is a "given," that nothing can be done to change things.

Y-Care International held a view similar to APT's, that government policies, especially in the case of a dictatorship or military government, can prevent the rich from assisting the poor.

In general, all the Christian agencies agreed that the rich are spiritually powerless because of their spiritual blindness, which causes them to be lacking in the spiritual resources and knowledge that would compel them to help the poor. The rich, therefore, need empowering at both levels, the social and spiritual, to cause them to respond positively to their moral obligation to the poor.

Regarding the state, all the agencies studied agreed that the state in developing countries is powerless to do much to alleviate the poverty of its nationals. State powerlessness arises from its own policies and priorities, and from external pressures. What the agencies note is that the policies and priorities of national governments in developing countries often do nothing to alleviate poverty. Currently the major reason cited by all the agencies for the powerlessness of the states in the countries of East Africa is the external pressures experienced by their governments. Oxfam, for example, stated:

> African governments have been damaged in their capacity to develop and support their citizens through the international policy of "rolling back frontiers of the state." This is where the Structural Adjustment Policy (SAP) strategies and donor policies have pushed these governments into privatization, nationalization,

shrinking government bureaucracy, paying off civil servants, and
so forth, in the name of restructuring their economies. SAPs in
their full blown programs have inflicted untold suffering on the
poor communities. (Oxfam interview)

Research studies conducted in Zimbabwe by Oxfam on the impact of
SAPs on schooling and health revealed that the poor can no longer af-
ford education or medical care.

World Vision UK offered an equally bleak picture:

Governments in developing countries are rendered powerless by
the persistent reliance on foreign aid of up to 80 percent in most
countries, which include Kenya, Tanzania, and Uganda. In these
cases the developing country is forced to adjust national budgets
in accordance *not* with their national priorities *but* with the priorities of the lender(s)—the World Bank, the IMF and Western governments. Meanwhile, these countries' social welfare and social
services suffer reductions of expenditure, or a discontinuation. The
development policies implemented by these countries under the
consultative and advisory services of Western economists give priority to external balances and thereby cease to be effective in alleviating poverty. In some instances, their government policies, even
independent of Western influences, are seen to be inimical to the
poor, especially through taxation, pricing, and land distribution
policies; while development policies are often designed to serve
external markets, being biased toward urban development at the
neglect of rural areas and biased toward commercial farming at
the expense of subsistence farming; with pricing policies that do
not favor farmers and taxation that is usually relatively heavy on
the poor. (World Vision UK interview)

In addition, some of the agencies cited poor governance in most developing countries, especially in Africa, as underlying the wars and conflicts that create instability, which in turn denies these governments (as
well as NGOs) both the time and resources to commit to long-term
sustained alleviation of poverty. What results from such a scenario, especially in Africa, is the further spread and worsening of poverty. Therefore, the state itself needs empowering.

What is missing, however, is a prophetic voice of the Christian agencies to speak out about the spiritual powerlessness of the state. These agencies talked of the neglect of the poor by the state and, in some cases, of the oppressive nature of some of its policies. This should be sufficient evidence for these Christian agencies to have noticed that there is spiritual powerlessness in this. A silent agenda among the Christian agencies seemingly forbids their involvement in political activity and hence in direct confrontation with the state over the issues in question.

The agencies studied agreed that powerlessness, viewed as inability to fight poverty, is not a condition of the poor only. It is also a condition of the rich and the state. Effective empowerment would address powerlessness in the poor, the rich, and the state, at both social and spiritual levels.

How Is Powerlessness Being Addressed?

All the agencies addressed powerlessness at the level of the poor. A manifest view seemed to indicate that the primary task of a development agency, especially NGOs, is direct involvement with the poor, helping them to fight their poverty. These agencies, however, being Northern, are often considered to be relatively little involved with the poor directly (Elliott 1987a:59). But of the agencies included in this study, two were operational (able to initiate project activities directly with the poor); those that fund do so through partnerships with local agencies, so that their personnel are involved together with the local agency personnel in working directly with the poor. These agencies *are* involved with the poor.

All the agencies showed weakness in addressing powerlessness among the rich. Most supported and funded activities were directed primarily to the poor. In the experience of some agencies—for example, ACORD, APT, and World Vision UK—the rich have at times been included in activities with the poor, with the aim of arousing their motivation to be more involved in assisting the poor. The Christian agencies, although they saw powerlessness in the rich, still found it difficult to address. This is because in their agenda resources are too limited to be committed to activities addressing both the poor and the rich, and so priority is given to the poor, or because they simply find it difficult to address the rich or to plan for activities involving them. Not much is documented by the agencies in this area. Agencies need to venture further into this domain.

One area of involvement for which Northern agencies are vital concerns governments and international institutions. Not all the agencies studied, however, felt they had the capacity to engage in matters concerning governments and international institutions. One in particular, Emmanuel International, believes that it is too small to engage in macro-level issues; furthermore, involvement with government is a political activity, which the agency considered to be outside its scope of operations. All other agencies said they become involved in addressing the powerlessness of the state by confronting issues internal to these governments (their policies and priorities), as well as by exerting external pressures to create awareness and elicit positive responses to the alleviation of poverty. One example: In Africa, Oxfam is vociferous in reminding African governments of their key function in providing social and welfare services, education, health, agricultural extension and marketing facilities for the poor. These services cannot easily be placed in the private sector, and the international community should be supporting national governments to help them fulfill their legitimate functions. At the international level the agencies are involved in much lobbying and advocacy against, for example, SAPs, debt-repayment schedules, international trade policies, European agricultural policies of a protectionist nature, dumping European farm products on poor countries' markets and the arms trade.

In addressing state powerlessness the agencies act according to the way such powerlessness is viewed. State powerlessness was viewed from a sociopolitical perspective alone; hence the activities of the agencies were primarily at the sociopolitical level. The Christian agencies seemingly failed to recognize the spiritual aspect of state powerlessness. Activities were confined to addressing government policies and placing international pressure at sociopolitical levels only, but the spiritual problems that would need to be examined for injustices and the inequalities and oppressiveness of regimes to be corrected were not addressed.

Empowerment as an Objective

Empowerment was interpreted by all agencies as "enablement," with slight variations—"to supply with the means, knowledge, or opportunity to be or to do something; to make feasible or possible; and to give legal power, capacity, or sanction to." In essence, such a dictionary definition conveys the full meaning this study gives to the concept of empowerment, which is to provide to rural people and their communities through government and institutions the means, knowledge and opportunity that will allow them to live more fulfilled lives, making it possible for them to take full control of the processes that influence their lives; for people to have the power and capacity (both poor and rich) to do what they were not able to do before, and whatever else that is not only for their good, but also for that of others; and to have the full human rights that are often denied the poor. Such an interpretation differs from simply giving legal power.

Oxfam did not use the word *enablement* directly, but it gave the same meaning in its interpretation of *empowerment:* "To give people control over the main influences that affect their lives and to have greater control, as well as to have access to resources" (Oxfam interview).

According to ActionAid, *empowerment* is "enabling people to be heard; enabling people to exercise control over their own lives. In other words, enabling people to live with dignity; enabling people to be in control, to have their voices heard, and to exercise choice" (ActionAid interview). ActionAid's operational motto is "Giving People Choices."

ACORD defined *empowerment* as "helping people to cope with change by enabling people to have greater influence over processes of change and the way change affects their lives" (ACORD interview). ACORD views empowerment in various ways: in terms of gender empowerment, that is, empowering rural women; technical empowerment; political empowerment; and economic empowerment. ACORD considers these four aspects of empowerment to constitute holistic empowerment; it included no spiritual empowerment.

APT Design and Development gave a brief definition of *empowerment* as "enabling people to break out of the poverty trap" (APT interview).

Tearfund did not use the word *enablement*. It defined *empowerment* as "helping people to recover their human dignity of life on the basis that all people are created in the image of God, and helping them to have opportunities that are denied them, like education, health, income, and relationships with God, and to have other resources" (Tearfund interview).

World Vision UK defined *empowerment* as "enabling people to overcome the barriers that prevent them from progressing to a better and more secure future; to enable people to remove these barriers from all levels at which they exist—personal level, family level, and community level. It is about enabling people to have enough, that is, sufficient food for today and sufficient in store for the day after tomorrow. It is to enable people to take more control over their development. It is to enable people and communities to take control over development decision-making processes" (World Vision UK interview). Empowering the poor, to World Vision UK, has to do with triggering a process that allows the poor not to look elsewhere again, but to know what to do in a particular situation and to be able to do it, and to be able to call in resources and do what they consider appropriate. The poor become empowered when they cease to be constantly dependent on external assistance. This is quite an extensive definition but, like almost all others, it lays emphasis on the poor only. And, though a Christian agency, World Vision UK did not mention the spiritual aspect of empowerment.

Emmanuel International defined *empowerment* as "enabling and helping people to use the potential God has given them so that they are not dependent on 'hand-outs.' This involves helping people to make decisions and to sit on committees" (Emmanuel International interview). Emmanuel International thinks that empowering people by teaching them to be healthy, for example, involves helping them to establish and operate their own clinics. Empowerment to Emmanuel International also meant giving people access to work and employment, and to other resources they need. This definition does mention God, which could be interpreted as dealing with the spiritual aspect of empowerment, but again emphasis is placed on empowerment of the poor only.

Y-Care International did not use the word *enablement*. It sees empowerment as a long-term process of several stages—conscientizing the poor; acquiring technical and production skills and resources for development; engaging in negotiations with those who control the system, such as agency personnel, the rich and powerful, and government bureaucrats and officials; taking decisions for actions to be implemented, and implementing these activities; and acquiring ongoing capacity, capabilities and institutional and organizational structures for sustained development. This is an extensive interpretation of empowerment, but seems also to lay emphasis on the poor, though the rich and the government are mentioned at the level of negotiations, which could be interpreted as a way of empowering the rich and the state. Though a Christian agency, Y-Care International did not mention the spiritual aspect of empowerment.

In summing up, all the agencies' definitions lay emphasis on the empowerment of the poor, with only two mentioning the rich. This is anomalous, considering that powerlessness was identified by six of the agencies as including the rich, and by all of them as also involving the state. Two of the four Christian agencies did not refer to a spiritual aspect of empowerment (which seems to be an anomaly, especially when these two had identified a spiritual aspect of powerlessness), although the other two did.

The implication of partial definitions is often that only partial solutions can be arrived at in the quest for the ultimate empowerment that aims at eliminating poverty.

Objectives, Intervention Strategies and Activities for Empowerment

The agencies generally claimed that their objectives, intervention strategies, and activities for empowerment are the same as those they maintain for rural development in general. However, there are some notable variations.

Oxfam's objective in engaging in empowerment is that the poor may have greater participation in the political process, access to resources, access to information (education, media, information for use in the debate around development choices within the community) and access to markets. Oxfam stated that the empowerment of people is for relief of poverty and for development of accountable institutions. Its policy for empowerment is to enable the poor "to be more and to have more," utilizing strategies formulated according to themes of gender sensitivity, sustainable livelihoods and human rights. The vision and the goal are to create a world where all people have sufficient food and water, roofs over their heads, sustainable livelihoods, access to basic education and health care, their human rights respected, freedom from persecution for their beliefs, right to decide their own future, and suffer no armed conflict.

The activities Oxfam undertakes for empowerment are the same as those it undertakes for addressing poverty in general. These are prioritized within the context of each country, through strategic planning with the participation of the communities concerned. Oxfam's activities are directed first and foremost to the poor, but Oxfam also engages in activities directed toward governments and international institutions, some of which require research for the production of information papers, pamphlets and books. The expected outcomes of these activities depend on the initial objectives, which are made clear and more or less measurable, and which can be evaluated through a reporting system. Oxfam is engaged in developing measurable impact indicators and a methodology for impact measurement in both quantitative and qualitative terms. This will help in establishing the exact contributions of different actors involved in the process of development or empowerment.

ActionAid's objectives, strategies and activities regarding empowerment were also the same as those for development in general. These are directed to the poorest in the communities, but ActionAid work in communities also included the better-off, whose genuine needs are identified and addressed, so long as this does not increase the political power of the better-off and result in greater inequalities. The expected outcome of these activities in relation to empowerment is that people will live with dignity, have control, be able to exercise choice and have security. ActionAid cited an example of work it has done in Bangladesh connected with savings and credit groups consisting mostly of women. This work has helped to allow the poorest among these communities to acquire assets and set up businesses on their own. This is the sort of result ActionAid would like to see spread to all the communities it works with, especially in East Africa. With regard to criteria for measuring the achievements of these activities, ActionAid has systems of monitoring and evaluation. Like Oxfam, ActionAid is at present carrying out studies to establish an impact-evaluation methodology; it was in receipt of an Overseas Development Administration grant for research toward development of such a methodology. In addition, ActionAid's India program has already sponsored a student for a master's research degree in the UK to investigate the assessment of empowerment in development projects. This study was completed in August 1991; its results remain to be tested.

ACORD's objective for empowerment is to help people to take more control of the processes of change affecting their lives and to have the ability to control that change. One of its missions is to empower communities through collective and sustainable use of assets, and the leverage this gives, so as to be able to participate in decision-making on issues affecting their lives (ACORD 1993). Activities for empowerment were the same as those for development in general, and these were prioritized by rural development workers with the full participation of local people. The expected outcome of these activities is that the groups and

individuals assisted will be empowered so that they will be able to continue running their own activities with little, if any, outside facilitation,
so that ACORD can withdraw. ACORD, like Oxfam and ActionAid,
was in the process of developing a methodology for impact analysis.

APT Design and Development's objective for empowerment through
small business development is that the increase in small businesses should
contribute in a very important way to alleviation of poverty in both
short and long term by providing means for the poorest level of society
to become independent, create jobs and generate income and by helping to build an environment in which manufacturing industries can develop and grow—a critical step in promotion of economic growth.
Strategies and activities that APT employed focused on technical training, business and management training, savings and credit development,
strengthening local NGOs, effective resource management and supporting the development of government policy (APT 1984–93:4). These
activities are given priority according to the needs of the business being
helped, and activities are directed to the enterprising poor as well as to
the government in connection with policy issues. The expected outcome of these activities is that the small businesses being helped will
flourish and contribute to the alleviation of poverty and improvement
of living conditions in their immediate neighborhood by generating income, making available affordable products and creating jobs for poorer
members of their communities.

Tearfund's objectives for empowerment are that people will no longer
be denied a relationship with God or access to resources for a meaningful and fulfilled life within the context in which they live. Its strategy is
to empower local churches so that they may be able to empower their
communities. Tearfund does this through funding, consultancy advice,
personnel and prayer. The expected outcome is that the projects these
local churches run should become sustainable without external funding,
with a good level of community participation and community ownership of the project. Tearfund has no specific measuring criteria for its
empowerment activities, apart from monitoring progress of work to make
sure each project is reaching its initially stated objectives.

World Vision UK's objectives for empowerment are the same as for
development in general. The chief aim is to fight poverty by addressing
its root causes. World Vision does not believe in palliative solutions that
tend to deal only with symptoms and aid in the persistence of poverty.
World Vision UK's objectives thus involve helping people and their

communities to remove the barriers that underlie their poverty. World Vision UK uses research activities to develop country-specific strategies in order to synchronize the varying conditions presented by different country situations. The organization is also sensitive to the fact that there has to be a balance between the strategy for which it has opted and the needs of the poor as articulated by them. Activities are prioritized by its field staff with the full participation of the local people. These activities fall under the themes of water, agriculture, health, income generation, adult literacy, education and environment. The expected outcome of these activities is that they become sustainable without external funding. World Vision systematically monitors and evaluates activities.

Emmanuel International's objective for empowerment is to help partner churches in developing countries to strengthen their abilities to sustain work with needy people and communities around them. Intervention strategies for empowerment that Emmanuel International employs involve helping partner churches to become strong in spiritual resources, human resources, outreach strategy resources, administrative resources and material resources. Activities implemented are agreed upon and prioritized by the partner churches with their communities. The expected outcome of these activities is that they will reach the empowerment objective for which they were planned, so that Emmanuel International will be able to withdraw and leave the partner churches to continue the work with their communities. Emmanuel International does not have all the means, especially statistical, for evaluating the degree of empowerment achieved. However, the Canadian government does much of the evaluation of Emmanuel International's work, and Emmanuel International itself has well-formulated computer programs as an aid to the critical evaluation of its relief work.

The objectives for empowerment of Y-Care International include raising the consciousness of the powerless and assisting the poor in identification of their own needs. Prioritization of activities is done by the grassroots communities, facilitated by personnel of the national YMCA's councils. The expected outcome of these activities is that the communities will become capable of sustaining project activities without Y-Care support, so that Y-Care may withdraw. Y-Care does not have a refined methodology for measuring the empowerment achieved by its activities, but it carries out close estimations, primarily by observation; for example, seeing what structures have been established by a project; the extent of representation of the marginalized in decision-making organs; and the skills that have been learned and are being applied effectively.

In summary, these agencies believe that what they are doing in development is really empowerment. But what they are doing in empowerment does not seem consistent with their convictions about who the powerless are, who would need to be empowered. What the agencies say they are doing in terms of empowerment does not tally with the requirements of effective empowerment, which would dictate that the concept should be applied to all the avenues in which powerlessness is identified—the poor, the rich, and the state.

Obstacles cited by the agencies can be grouped as endogenous factors and exogenous factors. Endogenous factors are those obstacles that originate from within the national situations of the people and communities being assisted. Exogenous factors originate from outside the national boundaries of the communities being assisted. Endogenous factors include rigid hierarchical structures within the community; lack of participation (which could result from rigid structures); traditions and superstitions (which could affect participation of women in particular); lack of resources, such as credit or land; lack of access to information; lack of adequate infrastructure; AIDS; lack of support for the marginalized from the rest of the community, especially from the rich and more powerful members of the community; political influence; war, conflict, and instability (in Africa in particular); and national government bureaucratic procedures and policies. These obstacles pose challenges to poor communities, to the rich and powerful, and to the national governments of developing countries. Each of these should recognize its moral duty to redress those obstacles that fall in its area of responsibility in order to bring about desired empowerment and development.

Exogenous factors cited by the agencies as obstacles include dependency on foreign sources of assistance (resulting usually from the manner in which foreign aid is given); unequal partnership (usually to the disadvantage of the recipient); contradictory agency approaches to development (which can create more harm than good); and macro-level issues and policies, especially larger donor policy pressures, such as SAPs and international debt. These factors are directly concerned with international development bodies, institutions and agencies, such as the World Bank, the IMF, the UN and its organizations, Western governments and their development agencies, OPEC, EEC and EU, and the northern NGOs. All these have an important role to play in addressing the obstacles to development and empowerment in developing countries for the ultimate elimination of poverty.

Promoters of empowerment cited by the agencies include acceptance of change by traditional leadership; preparedness of the community to accept change and the pains it brings; enthusiasm of local communities; working with communities as whole units; knowledge of God's purposes in development; participative processes, that is, local people's participation; concentration on people rather than material ends; gender equality strategies; building local groups, institutions and organizations; provision of infrastructural facilities; provision of organized credit and other resources; cross-cultural and intercultural training of team workers for local and in particular for foreign workers; and favorable government policies.

Holistic Empowerment

Holistic empowerment is a concept understood by all the agencies, although they do not all interpret it in the same way. Oxfam's definition of holistic empowerment views the person as a whole, with not only economic and political needs but also spiritual and cultural needs. However, in its activities Oxfam is concerned only with economic and political needs (the latter only to the extent allowed by the Charity Commission), and material needs; it does not attempt to meet spiritual and cultural needs, although for cultural needs it sometimes becomes involved in social cohesion issues. For individual purposes Oxfam's interpretation of holistic empowerment is sufficient, but it falls short in not treating an individual person as a whole, with physical and spiritual needs, and not treating communities as whole entities constituted of rich and poor and not-so-rich and leaders. Effective holistic empowerment involves meeting the needs of the whole person as well as the treatment of communities as whole entities. By this scale Oxfam contributes only partially to holistic empowerment. When asked to rate itself on a scale of one to five (five being very effective) to say how effectively it was contributing to holistic empowerment, it considered its contribution to be fair (score: three).

ActionAid recognizes holistic empowerment to refer to treating people as whole persons with physical and spiritual needs. But in its operations it admits that it deals only with physical needs, and it therefore confesses, for its own assessment, that it contributes only partially to holistic empowerment. ActionAid, like Oxfam, uses only the individual, personal dimension of holistic empowerment and omits the treatment of communities as whole entities. It therefore rates its effectiveness correctly.

ACORD views holistic empowerment as involving a balance among four types of empowerment: economic, technological, physical and environmental. From this vantage point ACORD believes its activities contribute reasonably effectively (rating: four) to holistic empowerment. ACORD's interpretation suits its operations, but it does not consider whole persons, with physical and spiritual needs, or treat communities as whole entities. According to this measure, then, ACORD is contributing only partially to holistic empowerment.

Holistic empowerment for APT Design and Development is more or less the same as holistic development, which means developing a fully rounded, whole organization, community, or person. It can be compared to holistic healing, which involves healing the person in body, mind and soul. This interpretation implies that, in development, the targeted communities or individual persons ought to be treated in such a way that all the needs pertaining to that community or person are addressed, thus treating the unit as a whole; in this way the process of meeting the needs can become holistic. APT confesses that it does not contribute to holistic empowerment because its activities are currently directed only to meeting the physical needs of a few businesses in some communities.

Tearfund views holistic empowerment in the same way it views a holistic ministry or holistic development. In Tearfund's work holistic development involves meeting spiritual, social and economic needs. Holistic empowerment thus demands that the spiritual needs of human beings, which include fellowship with God and with fellow human beings, spiritual life and eternal life, be met alongside social needs, which include community justice, brotherhood and mutual submission, and alongside economic needs, which include basic needs, jobs, productive resources and their equal distribution and management. Tearfund believes its activities are contributing reasonably effectively (score four) to holistic empowerment. This may be fair insofar as holistic empowerment of individual persons is concerned, but it fails to consider treatment of a community as a whole entity.

World Vision UK's view of holistic empowerment involves dealing with the totality of human needs—physical, social, spiritual, psychological and emotional. World Vision UK claims that it contributes to all these aspects of human need, and thus rates itself as contributing reasonably effectively (score: four) to holistic empowerment. Like Tearfund, World Vision may be fulfilling holistic empowerment at the individual personal level, but it failed to attend to the wholeness of communities being assisted.

Emmanuel International treats holistic empowerment in the same way it treats a holistic ministry, which is a foundational principle of Emmanuel International's work. This is interpreted as ministering to the needs of a whole person. Emmanuel International derives this principle from the Bible, which portrays Jesus meeting individual needs of all categories—spiritual, physical and social. Emmanuel International also serves churches worldwide to enable them, in a holistic way, to meet the spiritual, physical and social needs of individuals and communities. The agency also rates itself as being reasonably effective (score: four) in contributing to holistic empowerment.

Holistic empowerment is interpreted by Y-Care International as involving empowerment of mind, body and spirit, a liberating process in terms of meeting physical needs, mental needs (education, representation, decision-making) and spiritual needs. Y-Care thinks its contribution to holistic empowerment is fair (score: three). Y-Care also speaks of the individual, personal aspect of holistic empowerment, but omits treatment of communities as whole entities.

In summary, there is a lack (except in two cases) of recognition that communities or churches also need to be treated as whole entities when empowerment is carried out in communities or in churches.

In their contribution to holistic empowerment the nonreligious agencies are not overtly involved in meeting spiritual needs, as all declare in their constitutions that they are nonreligious. The Christian agencies consciously attempt to meet spiritual needs of the individual.

Ethical Principles

The core of this quest for application of ethical principles in the theory and practice of development economics is concerned with real people and with ethical questions that need answers (Crocker 1991:457). Yet modern economics is "self-consciously 'non-ethical' in character" (Sen 1987:2). Sen considers two origins of economics. He shows how economics first developed historically as an offshoot of ethics and traces this ethic-related tradition of economics to Aristotle. One central issue involved an ethics-related view of motivation is where the problem of human motivation leads to the Socratic question, "How should one live?" The second central issue concerned assessment of social achievement. Aristotle, says Sen, considered the end of social achievement to be attaining "the good for man," adding that it was more notable to attain the end for a nation or city-state than for a single man. Sen goes on to argue that "this 'ethics-related view of social achievement' cannot stop the evaluation short at some arbitrary point like satisfying 'efficiency.' The assessment has to be more fully ethical, and take a broader view of 'the good'" (Sen 1987:4).

A second origin of economics to which Sen refers "is characterised by being concerned with primarily logistic issues rather than with ultimate ends and such questions as what may foster 'the good of man' or 'how should one live.'" The ends are treated as given, and what matters is to find the best way to meet them; and human behavior is viewed as determined by motives that are easy to characterize (Sen 1987:4).

As time has progressed, economics and its applications have increasingly adopted this engineering approach, with the result that modern economics has become distanced from ethics. This, Sen claims, while not writing off the achievements of a nonethical approach, has resulted in the impoverishment of modern economics, and he sees an urgent need to pay "greater and more explicit attention to the ethical considerations that shape human behaviour and judgment" (Sen 1987:9) and to promote explicit application of ethics in development.

Evidence of the Need for Ethics in Development

All the agencies studied responded that ethics was of paramount importance in their operations. Crocker describes development ethics as "the normative or ethical assessment of the ends and means of Third World and global development" (Crocker 1991:457). Goulet's definition is more interpretative:

> Genuine ethics may be defined as a kind of *praxis* which generates critical reflection on the value content and meaning of one's social action. Unlike mere extrinsic treatment of means, ethical *praxis* conditions choices and priorities by assigning relative value allegiances to essential needs, basic power relationships, and criteria

for determining tolerable levels of human suffering in promoting social change. (Goulet 1983:620)

The agencies interviewed in this study all emphasized the need for ethics in their practical operations, but with some noticeable differences. The four nonreligious agencies' ethical guiding principles tended to differ widely from one another. Some sample ethical principles, namely human dignity and identity, stewardship, and justice, were included in the questionnaire.

Oxfam has formulated 12 guiding values and beliefs for its operations; these act as its ethical principles.

1. Oxfam declares that poverty, distress and avoidable suffering, are caused by injustice, and are totally unacceptable.
2. Oxfam believes that most poverty and avoidable suffering are created by people and can be eliminated by human action.
3. Oxfam believes in the essential dignity of people and in their capacity to overcome the problems and pressures which can crush or exploit them.
4. Oxfam believes in justice for individuals to secure their human rights and enhance their dignity.
5. Oxfam believes that empowerment of people is essential for the relief of poverty and the development of accountable institutions.
6. Oxfam believes people have a responsibility to meet the basic needs of others and to respect their human rights.
7. Oxfam believes that relieving suffering is not only in the interests of those immediately affected, but also in the longer-term political and economic interests of everyone.
8. Oxfam believes in a world which has an active, responsible civil society and accountable political institutions at all levels.
9. Oxfam believes that, if shared equitably, there are sufficient resources to meet today's human needs.
10. Oxfam believes that radical changes in the management, use and distribution of basic resources are required to ensure there are sufficient to meet the needs of future generations.

11. Oxfam believes that listening and responding to the voices of the poor is and will remain the source of legitimacy for its work.

12. Oxfam believes that peaceful means are always the preferred method for ensuring an environment in which development, relief and rehabilitation work can take place. It accepts enforced peace-making as justifiable only when peaceful means have been exhausted and life is at risk.

These principles are underlaid by Charity Commission laws, which place limits on what Oxfam (and all other agencies registered with the Charity Commission) can and cannot do. Oxfam, being nonreligious, does not apply religious concepts as such; however, it uses the word "sustainable" in the place of "stewardship." Oxfam believes it is the responsibility of all people (including the rich and powerful) to meet the basic needs of others and to respect their human rights, but in its operations it does not say it works toward enabling or empowering the rich to respond to the basic needs of the poor.

ActionAid considers ethical principles of utmost importance not only to guide design and implementation of project activities but to guide all its work. ActionAid has a statement of values that outlines its ethical principles, and this guides all its operations:

We believe that all human beings are of equal value and have the same rights, but are born into inequality of circumstances and opportunity.

We believe that everybody should be under a moral obligation to remedy this inequality, and to ensure—through selfless action for the common good—that the poor and the disadvantaged are able to realise their potential.

We believe that this moral imperative is further defined by the principles of *mutual respect* and *equity*, which should govern the relationships between people and between groups.

- *Mutual respect* is the recognition of the innate dignity of all human beings, the value of cultural diversity, and the right to exercise choice.
- *Equity* is the principle which constrains the use of advantage for selfish ends in favour of the present and future good.

Each person has the right to expect to be treated and the obligation to treat others according to these principles; these values give us a mandate and a duty to engage in society and respond to the needs of the vulnerable in an accountable manner.

ActionAid, as a nonconfessional charity, does not base these principles on the Bible but claims its principles "are nevertheless Christian in nature, insofar as they refer to human dignity, equity and justice" (ActionAid interview). Like Oxfam, ActionAid's principles are grounded on secular humanism and place a moral obligation on everyone in society (including the rich and powerful) to remedy inequalities suffered by the poor and vulnerable. Although ActionAid states that it also works with the better-off, it does not claim explicitly that it works with them in joint efforts to meet the needs of the poor.

ACORD views ethics as involving an agency going into an area not to make matters worse for the people of that area but rather to make them better. ACORD's ethical goal is to facilitate emergence of accountable, community-based institutions in order to promote suitable economic and social conditions for the poorest people in marginalized areas of Africa. ACORD recognizes human dignity and identity as human attributes that must be upheld in every individual through empowerment. Stewardship, as in the case of Oxfam, is viewed from an environmental angle.

APT Design and Development's ethical stand is that, as far as possible, the enterprises it supports should make maximum use of local human and material resources, avoiding excessive depletion of natural resources, damage to the environment, discrimination against any social group on the basis of race, color, creed or gender, or exploitation of the poor and disadvantaged, directly or indirectly. Human dignity is central to APT's work—enabling people to have a decent quality of life, which gives them dignity; enabling people to look after themselves, and become self-reliant, which also gives them dignity. Justice is within the operations of APT, especially in influencing governments in their attitudes and policies to give everybody a fair deal and a just opportunity.

The four Christian agencies all maintain that their ethical principles are based on the Bible. Tearfund's guiding principles apply the words of Jesus from Matthew 4:4: "man cannot live by bread alone" (in *Introducing Tearfund*:2). Tearfund believes that true life can only be found through faith in Jesus Christ, who came to give life in its fullness. Tearfund is involved in issues of human dignity and identity, and stewardship, but finds justice hard to deal with. Tearfund's experience is that where injustice is perpetrated by the governments or ruling elite, it renders it difficult for an NGO (especially if it is not a large foreign agency) to address such issues, and the poor will find it difficult to escape the impact thereof (Tearfund interview).

World Vision UK's ethical principles allow no discrimination on any grounds, including religious beliefs. Work is carried out with communities by consent, not by imposition. Some of the ethical principles that underlie World Vision UK's work include no proselytizing; no requirement to change people's beliefs; staff commitment to follow a way of life among communities that reflects Christ's likeness; and commitment to a holistic mission that encapsulates evangelism through partnership with local churches (World Vision UK interview).

In World Vision UK work, "human dignity" and "identity" refer to human life uninhibited in the search for fullness and is bound up with self-sufficiency. "Stewardship" refers to sustainable development that is not at the expense of others, and creation of awareness both for one another and for the environment. Justice for the poor and oppressed is very important to World Vision UK, which believes that the struggle for justice is one of the tasks with which the church of God on earth ought to be actively involved (World Vision UK interview).

Emmanuel International's ethical principles are based on the Bible as guide and final authority, including in moral matters, in all its activities. Human dignity and identity, stewardship, and justice feature in Emmanuel International's work. Issues of injustice, however, are dealt with only at the micro-level of operations. Emmanuel International believes it is too small to be involved in macro-level issues (Emmanuel International interview).

Y-Care International, like all the other agencies, applies ethical principles to the operations of all its programs. Y-Care adheres to Charity Commission bylaws. It does not knowingly support anything that would be against the interest of those communities it works with or that would perpetuate inequalities in the areas of its work. Y-Care, as a Christian agency, works in a Christian manner, but it does not work to meet the needs of the Christians to the exclusion of others. People from all religions and faiths are helped, and there is no element of proselytizing. Human dignity and identity feature in its work.

Conclusion

A number of findings arising from this overview. First, no one agency can achieve holistic empowerment on its own. This arises from a second finding, that these agencies exhibit wide differences in size, in their operational statuses, and in their policies, strategies and activities. These differences mean that each agency will exhibit strengths and weaknesses in different areas of its operations. It would be of greater benefit and impact, therefore, if there were coordination of the agency operations, so that each could be encouraged to specialize in its area of strength. Such coordination would no doubt make sure that all areas of operation that contribute to holistic empowerment would receive attention. But the situation at the time of this survey was marked by a lack of coordination; each agency operated autonomously.

Third, the study confirms the emergence of a new approach to the project process. It reveals a departure from the blueprint approach, now replaced by a process approach more suited to the development of people.

Fourth, powerlessness—in the sense of inability to do anything to alleviate poverty—although recognized as underlying poverty and affecting not only the poor but also the rich and powerful and the state, is addressed primarily at the level of the poor by all the agencies. Only a few address the state's powerlessness, and fewer address the powerlessness of the rich and supposedly powerful, despite a moral obligation to be involved in the elimination of poverty of the poor (O'Neill 1986:xi).

Fifth, empowerment is recognized as a means of tackling poverty at its roots. But since no one agency can achieve holistic empowerment, when agencies say they are involved with empowerment, what they actually and literally mean is partial empowerment; that is, they are involved only in some aspects of empowerment. Each agency can only do so much—the capability of each is limited and bounded. The implications of this are significant, especially when the prospects of coordinated efforts seem bleak, although less so for the Christian agencies. Holistic empowerment, in brief, involves recognizing human needs to be of a spiritual, social and physical nature, all needing to be addressed simultaneously. It involves—and requires that communities be recognized and worked with as such—whole entities composed of the poor, the not-so-rich, the rich, and also community leadership and structures. It involves tackling causes of powerlessness at personal, group, community, national and international levels; and establishing attitudes, policies, structures, institutions and organizations that engender empowerment at personal, local, national and international levels.

The scattered nature of agency work, as well as the failure of modernity's value-neutral strategies, has driven efforts to seek establishment of ethics in development. However, relativism in the ethical principles that guide practice can lead to different ends, some of which may do more harm than good. Biblically-based ethics lend advantages to the holism of the Christian agencies. What is needed is coordination of effort by these agencies so that each contribution, however small, may add up to what is required by holistic empowerment.

Recapping Some Implications

Powerlessness is the major underlying factor of the persistence of poverty in general, because the hopelessness of bringing about change for the good of the poor is felt not only by the poor themselves but also by the rich and powerful and the state in the developing countries. In much current analysis, powerlessness, and hence the persistence of poverty, is treated myopically as starting and ending with the poor. Courses of action taken have, therefore, directed whatever solutions have been (and are being) employed, to the poor per se, with the inevitable result that poverty has persisted. But powerlessness also afflicts the rich and powerful and the state. The powerlessness of the rich and powerful is attributed to systemic blindness, which allows the rich to be content with the status quo and also to believe that nothing can be done about the poor, who must accept things as they are. Also, the unwillingness of the rich and powerful to do anything, though they are consciously aware that actions can be taken to bring about change for the good of the poor, basically continues because they believe that the poor are to blame for their condition. Finally, the forces of modernity that have dominated both institutional and social structures of the modern economy, and the consciousness and whole lifestyle of the rich, are such that the rich are rendered powerless to change things to help and benefit the poor.

As regards state powerlessness, the IFAD analysis, especially, identifies factors that can make governments in developing countries powerless to respond effectively to the poverty of their nationals. These factors include biases in the domestic policies of these governments that tend to work against the alleviation of poverty; dualism, which is often biased against the rural traditional sectors, where vast numbers of the world's poor reside; political conflicts and civil strife, which often consume both time and resources of governments; and external pressures caused by international processes, which limit the capacity of these governments to fight the poverty within their boundaries.

A biblical perspective offers possible solutions to these problems in a number of ways. First, regarding holism, the biblical perspective applies holism to people and their needs, but also to communities. People are treated by the Bible in a balanced way, not altogether good and not altogether bad, but able to be redeemed. Biblically, people are human beings with dignity and an identity; they cannot be reduced to the level of objects. According to the Bible, people are created in the image of God, which confers to them human dignity and identity; all are valuable in God's sight. God saw them at creation as "very good" (Gen. 1:31). But due to the Fall, the image of God has been marred, and human relationships with God, with each other and with the rest of creation have been distorted. Human behavior and systems, although not completely damaged, are flawed; human beings are no longer capable of doing the good that really pleases God (or even each other at times). God's punishment for humanity's fallenness is death, but due to God's love for creation, and God's view that humanity is redeemable, God instituted a way of redemption for the fallen creation. This is through faith in the death and resurrection of his Son, Jesus Christ. Humanity is enabled to recover the image of God through Jesus, and by obedience to God's laws of socioeconomic and political ordering of life, is also enabled to recover proper human relationships, behavior, and systems of structures. The implication here is that poor people should be treated neither as though they are totally good and so can be left to undertake improving things entirely on their own, as can be the temptation with the thinking underlying bottom-up approaches; nor as though they are totally so bad that they can do nothing and need experts to take actions for them or direct them in what they should do.

The Bible treats people as having not only material needs but also spiritual needs, which must be met simultaneously in a holistic development of people.

Regarding the community, the Bible, in its desire for justice and equity for a community, treats it as a whole entity consisting of the poor, the rich, those in between, as well as its leadership and structures. Work with communities should address all these different facets for a holistic treatment of communities in development to ensure justice and equity.

In contrast to the modern dominance of economics, it is noted that the biblical modus operandi is holistic. Holism dictates a multidisciplinary approach in development, where more disciplines are employed simultaneously in the process of development. The most noted biblical illustration is of the church (a community), likening it to the body, which has many parts. The body functions best when all the parts are together, each performing its individual role properly. The different disciplines involved in development (each of which has an important role to play in meeting the multiple needs of people and communities) are like the different body parts, which must operate efficiently for an effective outcome. The Bible holds that "God is the ultimate Owner of all creation." Human beings are the responsible servants who are "trusted with a commission to handle rightly the property and affairs of the Divine master" (Thompson 1960:ix-x). Failure to carry out the commission of stewardship by human beings is attributed to, but not excused by, the fallen nature of humanity.

Human beings everywhere accept some form of authority to which they can appeal as a reference point both to explain and to legitimize actions. The Bible presumes to say something authoritative to all human beings, particularly on ethical matters, as a source of moral principles applicable across cultures, even regarding concern for ethical principles to guide development work.

Bibliography

ACORD. 1993. *Annual Report 1993*.

ActionAid. 1994. "Giving People Choices: ActionAid and Development."

Albee, George Wilson, Justin M. Joffe, and Linda A. Dusenbury, eds. 1988. *Prevention, Powerlessness and Politics—Readings on Social Change*. London: Sage Publications.

Alfonso, Felipe B. 1986. "Empowering Rural Communities," in Ickis, de Jesus, and Maru 1986.

Anderson, R. J. 1984. "The Empirical Study of Power." In Anderson and Sharrock 1984, 167–89.

Anderson, R. J., and W. W. Sharrock, eds. 1984. *Applied Sociological Perspectives*. London: George Allen and Unwin.

APT. 1984–93. *APT 1984–1993*. APT Design and Development.

Bachrach, Peter, and Morton S. Baratz. 1970. *Power and Poverty: Theory and Practice*. New York: Oxford University Press.

Barker, Jonathan. 1989. *Rural Communities Under Stress*. Cambridge: Cambridge University Press.

Barnes, Barry. 1988. *The Nature of Power*. Oxford: Basil Blackwell.

Barth, Karl. 1975. *Church Dogmatics* 1/1. Translated by G. W. Bromiley. Edinburgh: T. & T. Clark.

———. 1958. *Church Dogmatics* 3/1. Translated by J. W. Edwards, O. Bussey, and Harold Knight. Edinburgh: T & T Clark.

Baum, Warren. 1978. "The World Bank Project Cycle." *Finance and Development* 4/15, 10–17.

Beisner, Calvin E. 1992. "Justice and Power: Two Views Constrasted." Unpublished paper.

———. 1988. *Prosperity and Poverty: The Compassionate Use of Resources in a World of Scarcity*. Westchester, Ill.: Crossway Books.

Benveniste, Guy. 1972. *The Politics of Expertise*, Berkeley, Calif.: Glendary Press.

Berger, Peter L., and Richard John Neuhaus. 1984. "To Empower People." In Korten and Klaus 1984, 250–61.

Berkhof, Hendrikus. 1962. *Christ and Powers*. Translated by John H. Yoder. Scottdale, Pa.: Herald Press.

Boerma, Conrad. 1979. *Rich Man, Poor Man—and the Bible*. London: SCM Press.

Brown, Colin, and Horst Seebass. 1978. "Righteousness and Justification." In *The New International Dictionary of New Testament Theology*, edited by Colin Brown, 3:352–58. Grand Rapids, Mich.: Zondervan, 1975–78.

Brown, David. 1990. "Rhetoric or Reality? Assessing the Role of NGOs as Agencies of Grassroots Development." *Bulletin 28* (February), 3–10. Reading,

UK: University of Reading Agricultural Extension and Rural Development Department.

Brown, R. M. 1978. *Theology in a New Key—Responding to Liberation Themes*. Philadelphia: The Westminster Press.

Brueggemann, Walter. 1977. *The Land*. Philadelphia: Fortress Press.

Bunge, Mario. 1980. *Cencia Desarrollo*. Buenos Aires: Eiciones Siglo Veinte.

Burkey, Stan. 1993. *People First—A Guide to Self-Reliant Participatory Rural Development*. London: ZED Books Ltd.

Camacho, Luis A. 1985. *Cuando se Habla de Ciencia Tecnologia y Desarrollo*.

Carmen, Raff. 1990. *Communication, Education and Empowerment*, Manchester Monographs, University of Manchester.

Casley, D.J., and LURY, D.A. 1981/87.) *Data Collection in Developing Countries*, Oxford: Clarendon Press.

Cernea, Michael M. 1985. "Putting People First—Sociological Variables." In *Putting People First: Sociological Variables in Rural Development*, edited by Michael Cernea. New York: Oxford University Press.

Chambers, Robert. 1988. "Normal Professionalism and the Early Project Process Problems and Solutions." In *Agricultural and Rural Problems*, Institute of Development Studies.

————. 1983. *Rural Development—Putting the Last First*. London: Longman Scientific and Technical, Longman Ltd.

————. 1978. "Project Selection for Poverty—Focussed Rural Development: Simple Is Optimal." *World Development* 6/2, 209–19.

Chenery, Holis Burney, with Monteks Ahluwalia and Nicholas G. Carter. 1974. *Growth and Poverty in Developing Countries*. London and New York: Oxford University Press.

Chewning, Richard C., ed.. 1989. *Biblical Principles and Economics: The Foundations*. Colorado Springs, Colo: NavPress, a ministry of the Navigators.

Clines, David J. A. 1968. "The Image of God in Man." *Tyndale Bulletin*.

Cook, David. 1992. *Living in the Kingdom: The Ethics of Jesus*. London: Hodder and Stoughton.

————. 1988. *The Moral Maze: A Way of Exploring Christian Ethics*. London: SPCK.

Crocker, David A. 1991. "Toward Development Ethics." In *World Development* 19/5, 457–83.

Costas, Orlando. 1982. "Theological Perspectives: The Gospel and the Poor." In Samuel and Sugden 1982:80–85.

Dahl, Ronald.A. 1957. "The Concept of Power." *Behavioral Science* 2 (July), 201–15.

Daly, Herman E., and John B. Cobb Jr. 1990. *For the Common Good: Redirecting the Economy Towards Community the Environment and a Sustainable Future*. London: Green Print-Merlin Press.

De Santa Ana, Julio. 1977. *Good News to the Poor—The Challenge of the Poor in the History of the Church*. Geneva: WCC Publications.

De Vaux, Roland. 1968. *Ancient Israel—Its Life and Institutions*. London: Longman and Todd.

Development Dialogue. 1994. Volume 1. Uppsala: Dag Hammarskjold Foundation.

DNTT [*Dictionary of New Testament Theology*]. 1976. Volume 2.

Dodd, Charles Harold. 1946. "Natural Law in the Bible." *Theology XLIX*, 161–67.

Drabek, Anne Gordon. 1987. "Development Alternatives: The Challenge for NGO's." *World Development* 15 Supplement.

Edwards, Michael. 1989. "The Irrelevance of Development Studies." *Third World Quarterly* (January), 116–35.

Elliott, Charles. 1987a. *Comfortable Compassion—Poverty, Power and the Church*. London: Hodder and Stoughton.

———. 1987b. *"Some Aspects of Relations Between the North and South in the NGO Sector"* in DRABEK, A. G. (1987).

———. 1987c. In *World Development*. Supplemental volume 15.

Emmanuel International SCW. N.d. *Serving Churches Worldwide*.

———. 1993. "Emmanuel International Strategic Plan 1991–2001: Review and Revision."

Engel, James R. 1988. "Ecology and Social Justice: The Search for a Public Environment Ethic." In *Issues of Justice—Social Resources and Religious Meanings*, edited by W. R. Copeland and R. D. Hatch. Macon, Ga.: Mercer University Press.

Escobar, Samuel. 1982. "How Do We Interpret the Bible? The Gospel and the Poor" in Samuel and Sugden 1982:97–106.

Esman M. J., and N. T. Uphoff. 1984. *Local Organizations: Intermediaries in Rural Development*. Ithaca, N.Y.: Cornell University Press.

Fernando, Suman. 1988. "Empowerment for Development." *CONTACT* 102 (April), 10–12.

Fletcher, Joseph. 1960. "Wealth and Taxation: The Ethics of Stewardship." In Thompson 1960: 204–27.

Forbes, D. K. 1984/86. *The Geography of Underdevelopment: A Critical Survey*. London: Croom Helm.

Foster, Roger. 1985. *Money, Sex and Power: The Spiritual Disciplines of Poverty, Chastity and Obedience*. London: Hodder and Stoughton.

Fowler, Alan. 1990. "Doing It Better? Where and How NGOs Have a 'Comparative Advantage' in Facilitating Development." *Bulletin 28* (February), 11–20. Reading, UK: University of Reading Agricultural Extension and Rural Development Department.

Freire, Paulo. 1972/90. *Pedagogy of the Oppressed*. London: Penguin Books Ltd.

———. N.d. "Conscientization." Unpublished paper.

Freud, Sigmund. 1958. *Civilization and Its Discontents*. Garden City, N.Y.: Doubleday Anchor Books.

Friedmann, John. 1992. *Empowerment: The Politics of Alternative Development*. Cambridge, Mass.: Blackwell.

Gamson, William A. 1968/71. *Power and Discontent*. Homewood, Ill.: The Dorsey Press.

Gaventa, John. 1980. *Power and Powerlessness—Quiescence and Rebellion in an Appalachian Valley*. Oxford: Clarendon Press.

Ghai, D. 1989. "Participatory Development: Some Perspectives from Grassroots Experiences." *Journal of Development Planning* 19.

Gittinger, James Price, ed. 1982. *Economic Analysis of Agricultural Projects*. Baltimore, Md.: John Hopkins University Press.

Gleeson, D. 1974. "Theory and Practice in the Sociology of Paulo Freire." *UQ* (Summer), 362–71.

Gorman, Robert F. 1984. *Private Voluntary Organizations as Agents of Development*. London: Westview Press.

Goudzwaard, Bob. 1984. *Idols of Our Time*. Translated by Mark Vander Vennen. Downers Grove, Ill.: InterVarsity Press.

———. 1980. "Toward Reformation in Economics." Paper presented in an Interim Course at the Institute for Christian Studies. Distributed by The Association for the Advancement of Christian Scholarship, 229 College Street, Toronto, Ontario, Canada M5T 1R4.

———. 1979. *Capitalism and Progress: A Diagnosis of Western Society*. Grand Rapids, Mich.: Eerdmans.

Goulet, Denis. 1985. *The Cruel Choice: A New Concept in the Theory of Development*. New York: University Press of America.

———. 1983. "Obstacles to World Development: An Ethical Reflection." In *World Development* 2/7, 609–24.

Gran, Guy. 1983. *Development by People—Citizen Construction of a Just World*. Special Studies. New York: Praeger.

Griffin, Keith B. 1989. *Alternative Strategies for Economic Development*. London: Macmillan.

Griffin, Keith B., and John Knight. 1990. *Human Development and the International Development Strategy for the 1990s*. London: Macmillan.

Gunatilleke, Godfrey, Neelan Tiruchelvan, and Radhika Coomaraswamy. 1988. *Ethical Dilemmas of Development in Asia*. Lexington, Mass.: Lexington Books.

Gutiérrez, Gustavo. 1974. *A Theology of Liberation*. London: SCM Press.

Hall, Douglas John. 1990. *The Steward—A Biblical Symbol Come of Age*. Grand Rapids, Mich.: Eerdmans.

———. 1986. *Imaging GOD—Dominion as Stewardship*. Grand Rapids, Mich: Eerdmans.

Hall, T.C. 1904. "Relativity and Finality in Ethics," *Ethics* 14 pp.150–161.

Hay, Donald A. 1989. *Economics Today: A Christian Critique* Leicester: Apollos, InterVarsity Press.

Hettne, Bjorn. 1990. *Development Theory and the Three Worlds*. London: Longman Scientific and Technical, Longman Ltd.

———. 1988. *Development Options in Europe*. Gottenburg, UNU: European Perspectives, Project Paradigm Papers.

Hirschman, Albert O. 1967. *Development Projects Observed*. Washington, D.C.: Brookings Institution.

Hobbes, Thomas. 1958. *Leviathan*. Indianapolis, Ind.: Bobbs-Merrill.

Hobson, George H., Jr. 1989. *Towards a Doctrine of Providence: A Response to Contemporary Critique*. Mansfield College, Oxford. D.Phil thesis.

Holmquis, F., and M. Ford. 1992. "Kenya Slouching Toward Democracy." *Africa Rights Monitor* 3, 96–111.

Honadle, George Holmes, with Jay K. Rosengard. 1983. "Putting 'Projectized' Development in Perspective." *Public Administration and Development* 3, 299–305.

Hughes, Philip Edgcumbe. 1983. *Christian Ethics in Secular Society*, Grand Rapids, Mich.: Baker Book House.

Hummel, Robert. 1977. *The Bureaucratic Experience*. New York: St. Martin's Press.

Hyden, G. 1980. *Beyond Ujamaa in Tanzania: Under-development and the Uncaptured Peasantry*. London: Heinemann.

IBRD. 1985. *Tenth Annual Review of Project Performance Audit Results*. Washington D.C.: World Bank.

IFAD (International Fund for Agricultural Development. 1993. *The State of World Rural Poverty: A Profile of Africa*.

———. 1992. *The State of World Rural Poverty: An Inquiry into Its Causes and Consequences."* Rome: IFAD.

Jeune, Chavannes. 1987. "Justice, Freedom and Social Transformation." In Samuel and Sugden 1987:218–25.

Joffe, Justin M., and George Wilson Albee. 1988. "Powerlessness and Psychopathology." In Albee et al. 1988.

Johnson, Luke T. 1981. *Sharing Possessions*. Philadelphia: Fortress Press.

Jones, D., and H. Conn. 1978. "Who Are the Poor?" *Evangelical Review of Theology* 2/2 (October), 215–35.

Kaye, Bruce Norman, and Gordon J. Wenham, eds. 1978. *Law, Morality and the Bible*. Leicester: InterVarsity Press.

Kirk, Andrew J. 1979. *Liberation Theology: An Evangelical View from the Third World*. Basingstoke: Marchall, Morgan and Scott.

Knight, V. C. 1991. "Growing Opposition in Zimbabwe." in *Issue* 20.

Kornhauser, W. 1961. "'Power Elite' or 'Veto Groups.'" In Lipset and Lowenthal 1961: 252–66.

Korten, David C. 1984. "Rural Development Programming: The Learning Process Approach." In Korten and Klauss 1984:176–88.

Korten, David C., and Rudi Klauss, eds. 1984. *People Centered Development: Contributions Toward Theory and Planning Frameworks*. West Hartford, Conn.: Kumarian Press.

Kronenburg, Josephus Bernardus Maria. 1986. *Empowerment of the Poor: A Comparative Analysis of Two Development Endeavours in Kenya*. Amsterdam: Koninklijk Instituut voor de Tropen.

Laite, Julian. 1984. "The Social Realities of Development," In Anderson and Sharrock 1984:190–214.

Lasswell, Harold Dwight. 1948. *Power and Personality*. New York: W. W. Norton.

Lasswell, Harold Dwight, and Abraham Kaplan. 1950. *Power and Society*. New Haven, Conn.: Yale University Press.

Lewis, John Prior, and Valeriana Kallab. 1986. *Development Strategies Reconsidered*. Paris: OECD.

Linthicum, Robert C. 1991. *Empowering the Poor: Community Organizing Among the City's "Rag, Tag and Bobtail."* Monrovia, Calif.: MARC.

Lipset, S. M., and L. Lowenthal, eds. 1961. *Culture and Social Character*. New York: Free Press of Glencoe.

Lukes, Steven. 1974. *Power: A Radical View*. London: Macmillan.

Lutz, Mark A., and Kenneth Lux. 1988. *Humanistic Economics: The New Challenge*. New York: Bootstrap Press.

Martin, Michael T., and Terry R. Kandal, eds. 1989. *Studies of Development and Change in the Modern World*. New York: Oxford University Press.

Maslow, Abraham Harold. 1954. *Motivation and Personality*. New York: Harper & Row.

Mbithi, Philip M. 1974. *Rural Sociology and Rural Development: Its Application in Kenya*. Kampala, Nairolbi, Dar es Salaam: East African Literature Bureau.

Mcgrath, Joanna, and Alister E. McGrath. 1992. *The Dilemma of Self-Esteem: The Cross and Christian Confidence*. Wheaton, Ill.: Crossway Books.

Mehta, Prayag. 1988. "Organizing for Empowering the Poor." In *Social Development: A New Role of the Organisational Sciences*. Edited by Pradip N. Khandwalla. New Delhi: Sage Publications.

Midgley, James, with Anthony Hall, Margaret Hardiman, and Dhanpaul Narine, eds. 1986. *Community Participation Social Development and the State*. London: Methuen.

Mills, C. Wright. 1956. *The Power Elite*. New York: Oxford University Press.

Mitchell, Basil. 1967. *Law Morality and Religion in a Secular Society*. Oxford: Oxford University Press.

Morgan, Philip. 1983. "The Project Orthodoxy in Development: Re-evaluating the Cutting Edge." *Public Administration and Development* 3, 329–39.

Mott, Stephen Charles. 1992. "The Partiality of Biblical Justice: A Response to E. Calvin Beisner." Unpublished paper.

———. 1984. *Jesus and Social Ethics*. Bramcote, Notts: Grove Books.

———. 1982. *Biblical Ethics and Social Change*. New York: Oxford University Press.

Mountjoy, Alan Bertram. 1963. *Industrialisation and Under-developed Countries*. London: Hutchinson and Co. Ltd.

Nicholls, Bruce. Ed. 1991. *Mission as Witness and Justice: An Indian Perspective*. New Delhi: TRACI Publications.

Ndi, N. J. F. 1993. "Cameroon: Democracy at Bay." *Africa Demos* 3/1.

Niebuhr, Reinhold. 1956/60. *An Interpretation of Christian Ethics*. New York: Meridian Books.

———. 1941. *The Nature and Destiny of Man: A Christian Interpretation*, Volume 1, *Human Nature*. London: Nisbet.

Nixon, Robin. 1978. "The Universality of the Concept of Law." In Kaye and Wenham 1978:114–21.

Nurnberger, Klaus. 1978. *Affluence, Poverty and the Word of God*. Durban: Lutheran Publishing House.

Nyerere, Julius. 1979. "On Rural Development." *Ideas and Action* 128.

Oakley, Peter. 1991. *Projects with People*. Geneva: ILO.

———. 1987. "State or Process, Means or End? The Concept of Participation in Rural Development." Reading Rural Development Communication Bulletin 21, 3–9. Reading, UK: University of Reading Agricultural Extension and Rural Development Department.

Oluwo, D. 1989. "Local Institutes and Development." *Canadian Journal of African Studies* 23/2, 201–31.

O'Neill, Onora. 1986. *Faces of Hunger: An Essay on Poverty, Justice and Development*. London: Allen and Unwin.

Outka, Gene Harold. 1972. *AGAPE: An Ethical Analysis*. New Haven, Conn.: Yale University Press.

Oxfam. 1992–93. *Oxfam Grants List 1992–1993*. Oxford: Oxfam.

———. 1989. "Oxfam—An Interpretation." Paper approved by Council of Management (28 January).

Oxford Declaration on Christian Faith and Economics. 1990. In *Transformation* 7/2 (April/June). Also available at http://users.churchserve.com/nz/bibpp/oxford.htm.

Parsons, Talcott. 1967. *Sociological Theory and Modern Society*. New York: Free Press.

———. 1963. "On the Concept of Political Power." In *Proceedings of the American Philosophical Society* 107, 232–62.

Pearse, Andrew, and Matthias Stiefel. 1979. "Inquiry into Participation—A Research Approach." *UNRISD*/79/C.14 (May). Geneva.

Perkins, Harvey. 1982. "The Poor and Oppressed." in Samuel and Sugden 1982.

Pilgrim, Walter. E. 1981. *Good News to the Poor*. Minneapolis: Augsburg Publishing House.

Polsby, Nelson W. 1963. *Community Power and Political Theory*. New Haven, Conn.: Yale University Press.

———. 1960. "How to Study Community Power: The Pluralist Alternative." *Journal of Politics* 22, 474–84.

Prior, David. 1987. *Jesus and Power*. London: Hodder and Stoughton.

Rahman, Muhamed Anisur. 1984. *Grassroots Participation and Self-Reliance in South and Southeast Asia*. A paper prepared for the World Employment Programme of the ILO. New Delhi: Oxford and IBH Press.

Ramirez, E. R. 1988. "Etica y Tecnologia," In *Revista Comunicacion* 3/2.

———. 1986. "Desarollo y Etica." *Revista Comunicacion* 2/2.

Rawls, John. 1974. *A Theory of Justice*. Oxford: Oxford University Press.

Riesman, D. 1953. *The Lonely Crowd*. New York: Doubleday Anchor.

Robinson, Edward A. G., ed. 1964. *Economic Development for Africa South of the Sahara*. International Economic Association. London: Macmillan.

Rondinelli, Dennis A. 1983a. *Development Projects as Policy Experiments: An Adaptive Approach to Development Administration*. London: Methuen.

———. 1983b. "Projects as Instruments of Development Administration: A Qualified Defence and Suggestions for Improvements." *Public Administration and Development* 3, 307–27.

Rooy, Silvio. 1980. "Righteousness and Justice." In *Justice in the International Economic Order*. Grand Rapids, Mich.: Calvin College.

Rostow, Walt Whitman. 1960. *The Stages of Economic Growth*. Cambridge: Cambridge University Press.

Russell, Bertrand. 1938. *A New Social Analysis*. London: George Allen and Unwin.

Samoff, J. 1989. "Popular Initiatives and Local Government in Tanzania." *The Journal of Developing Areas* 24, 1–18.

Samuel, Vinay K. N.d. "The Gospel of Transformation." An unpublished paper.

Samuel, Vinay K., and C. Sugden. 1991a. *AD 2000 And Beyond: A Mission Agenda*. Oxford: Regnum Books.

———. 1991b. "Biblical Social Justice and Christian Involvement." In Nicholls 1991.

———, eds. 1987. *The Church in Response to Human Need*. Oxford: Regnum Books.

———, eds. 1982. *Evangelism and the Poor: A Third World Guide*. Oxford: Regnum Books.

Sandbrook Richard. 1985. *The Politics of Africa's Economic Stagnation*. Cambridge: Cambridge University Press.

Scheef, Richard L., Jr. 1960. "Stewardship in the Old Testament." In Thompson 1960, 17–37.

Schneider, Bertrand. 1988. *The Barefoot Revolution*. London: IT Publications.

Schrey, Heinz Horst, Hans Hermann Walz, and Walter Alexander Whitehouse. 1955. *The Biblical Doctrine of Justice and Law*. London: SCM Press.

Seamands, David A. 1981. *Healing for Damaged Emotions*. Wheaton, Ill.: Victor Books.

Segal, Jerome M. 1987. "What Can the History of the Idea of Progress Tell Us About What Development Should be?" Paper presented to the First International Conference on Ethics and Development. San Jose: University of Casta Rica, June 7–13.

Sen, Amatyr. 1987. *On Ethics and Economics*. Oxford: Blackwell.

———. 1983. "Development: Which Way Now?" *Economic Journal* 93 (December), 745–62.

Sen, Amatyr, and M. C. Nussbaum. 1989. "Internal Criticism and Indian Rationalist Traditions." In *Relativism, Interpretation and Confrontation*, ed. Michael Krausz. Notre Dame, Ind.: University of Notre Dame Press.

Sider, Ronald J. 1977. *Rich Christians in an Age of Hunger*. Downers Grove, Ill.: InterVarsity Press.

Singh, Narindar. 1988. "The Apean Way and the Endogenous Path," in Hettne 1988:41–60.

Sithole, M. 1993. "Is Zimbabwe Poised on a Liberal Path? The State and Prospects of the Parties." *Issue* 21.

Smith, Brian H. 1987. "An Agenda of Future Tasks for International and Indigenous NGOs: Views from the North." In Drabek 1987:87–93.

Steidlmeier, Paul. 1987. *The Paradox of Poverty: A Reappraisal of Economic Development Policy*. Cambridge, Mass.: Ballinger.

Stivers, Robert L. 1984. *Hunger, Technology and Limits to Growth: Christian Responsibility in Three Ethical Issues*. Minneapolis, Minn.: Augsburg Publishing House.

Stott, John R. W. S. 1984. *Issues Facing Christians Today: A Major Appraisal of Contemporary Social and Moral Questions*. London: Marshall Morgan & Scott.

Stubbs, Lucy. 1993. *The Third World Directory 1993*. London: Directory of Social Change.

Sugden, Chris. 1991. "What Is Good About Good News to the Poor?" In Samuel and Sugden 1991a:56–81.

———. 1974. "Violence and Revolution." M. Phil. thesis. London: Oxford University.

Tearfund. 1992. *Introducing Tearfund*. London.

———. *Good News to the Poor*. A Tear Fund Profile Booklet.

Tendler, Judith. 1982. "Turning Private Voluntary Organizations into Development Agencies: Questions for Evaluation." AID Program Evaluation Discussion Paper No. 12. Washington, D.C.: USAID.

Thomas, Barbara P. 1985. *Politics, Participation and Poverty: Development through Self-help in Kenya*. Boulder, Colo.: Westview Press.

Thomas-Slayter, Barbara P. 1994. "Structural Change, Power Politics and Community Organizations in Africa: Challenging the Patterns, Puzzles and Paradoxes." In *World Development* 22/10, 1479–90.

Thompson, Thomas K., ed. 1960. *Stewardship in Contemporary Theology*. New York: Association Press.

Todaro, Michael P. 1977/89. *Economic Development in the Third World*. New York and London: Longman.

UNICEF. 1986. "Community Participation: Now You See It, Now You Don't." In *UNICEF News* 124.

UNRISD. 1983. *Dialogue About Participation: 3*. Geneva: UNRISD/83/C.31.

Uphoff, Norman Thomas. 1990. "Paraprojects as New Modes of International Development Assistance." *World Development* 18/10, 1401–11. Oxford: Pergamon.

Van Der Walt, Tijaart. 1980. "God's Call for Justice." In *Justice in the International Economic Order*. Grand Rapids, Mich.: Calvin College.

Vogeler, Ingolf, and Alfred De Souza, eds. 1980. *Dialectic of Third World Development*. Montclair: Allanheld, Osmun.

Von Waldo. 1970. "Social Responsibility and Social Structure in Early Israel." *The Catholic Biblical Quarterly* 32, 182–204.

Weber, Hans-Rudi. 1989. *Power: Focus for a Biblical Theology*. Geneva: WCC Publications.

Weber, Max. 1947. *The Theory of Social and Economic Organisation*. Oxford: Oxford University Press.

Weisband, Edward, ed. 1989. *Poverty Amidst Plenty: World Political Economy and Distributive Justice*. Boulder Colo.: Westview Press.

Werner, David. 1988. "Empowerment and Health." In *CONTACT* 102 (April), 1–9.

Westermann, Claus. 1984. *Genesis 1–11: A Commentary*. London: SPCK.

———. 1974. *Creation*. Translated by John J. Scullion S.J. London: SPCK.

Wignaraja, Ponna. 1984. "Towards a Theory and Practice of Rural Development." In *Development* (1984:2), 3–11.

Wilber, Charles K., ed. 1984. *The Political Economy of Development and Underdevelopment*. Third edition. New York: Random House.

Wink, Walter. 1992. *Engaging the Powers: Discernment and Resistance in a World of Domination*. Mineapolis, Minn.: Fortress Press.

———. 1984. *Naming the Powers: The Language of Power in the New Testament*. Philadelphia: Fortress Press.

Wittenberg, Gunther. 1978. "The Message of the O.T. Prophets During the Eighth Century B.C. Concerning Affluence and Poverty." In Nurnberger 1978: 141–52.

Wogaman, Philip J. 1990. "Toward a Christian Definition of Justice." *Transformation* 7/2 (April/June), 18–23.

World Bank. 1990. *World Development Report 1990*. Oxford and New York: Oxford University Press.

World Bank. 1993. *Annual Report*.

Wright, Chris J. H. 1983. *Living as the People of God: The Relevance of Old Testament Ethics*. Leicester: InterVarsity Press.

Wrong, Dennis Hume. 1979/88. *Power: Its Forms, Bases and Uses*. Oxford, Basil Blackwell.

Yeager, Roger. 1989. "Democracy, Pluralism and Ecological Crisis in Botswana." In *The Journal of Developing Areas* (April), 385–404.

Yoder, John Howard. 1972. *The Politics of Jesus*. Grand Rapids, Mich.: Eerdmans.